Other books by Jerry Mack Johnson

COUNTRY WISDOM
THE CATFISH FARMING HANDBOOK
WHAT IT'S WORTH AND WHERE YOU CAN SELL IT: THE
COLLECTOR'S MARKETPLACE

Country

Scrapbook

Jerry Mack Johnson

SIMON AND SCHUSTER / NEW YORK

Copyright © 1977 by Jerry Mack Johnson
All rights reserved
including the right of reproduction
in whole or in part in any form
Published by Simon and Schuster
A Division of Gulf & Western Corporation
Simon & Schuster Building
Rockefeller Center
1230 Avenue of the Americas
New York, New York 10020
Designed by Edith Fowler
Manufactured in the United States of America
1 2 3 4 5 6 7 8 9 10

Library of Congress Cataloging in Publication Data

Johnson, Jerry Mack
  Country scrapbook.

  Includes index.
  SUMMARY: A collection of nature facts and
rural lore on such topics as the weather, plants, ani-
mals, farm foods, cleaning methods and pest purges
of the past, and country cures and pastimes.
  1. Folk-lore—United States. 2. Farm life—United
States. [1. Folklore—United States] I. Title.
GR105.M3   973   77-24912
ISBN 0-671-22848-X
ISBN 0-671-22895-1 pbk.

Dedication

This book is dedicated to the feelings, sights, smells, and sounds
that God gives us every day but that we sometimes miss in the
rush of life: such as,

   . . . a calf nursing
   . . . a bushy-tailed squirrel scolding the wind
   . . . the bobwhite's cheerio to sunrise
   . . . discovering a mustang grapevine on the creek bank
   . . . the creaking, groaning sound of a windmill lifting water
   . . . a locust song from the mulberry tree
   . . . the smell of sweat from a fresh-ridden unsaddled horse
   . . . red birds flitting among blackberry vines
   . . . the sound of an ax on cordwood in still, cold winter
   . . . sitting around the table talking after supper
   . . . a cow bawling to be milked
   . . . drawing cool, fresh water from a hand-dug well
   . . . watching birds eat crumbs you scattered
   . . . the booming of bullfrogs after a heavy spring rain
   . . . bullbats zooming in the twilight
   . . . your horse pointing his ears when you walk into his stall
   . . . geese honking south on an autumn evening
   . . . cows chewing their cud
   . . . a smart south wind running through the treetops
   . . . the squeaking of saddle leather
   . . . the silence of the country
   . . . a proud blue jay sassing at nothing
   . . . drinking sweet well water from a long-handled dipper

Contents

Foreword

Maple leaves stained gold and crimson, sent by friends from the Northeast, brightened our home. A visitor, unaccustomed to leaves of such vivid hues here in West Texas, remarked on their beauty—adding, however: "I don't know what kind they are, but as far as I'm concerned, leaves are just leaves." That commentary set me to recalling the varied roles leaves had played in my boyhood, valid evidence that leaves were more than "just leaves."

At the first signs of spring, shoes were kicked aside, and boys ran barefoot. By midsummer, quite a callused pad had built up on the bottoms of our feet. The roughest terrain of stones, stubble, or even nettles scarcely caused us to wince, so protected were we by our leathery soles. But feet at summer's start were tender, having been pampered through the winter months by such civilized gear as socks and boots or brogans. As a consequence, many a foot suffered from bruising. Grandfather had a sure-fire remedy for this. He gathered Madeira vine and bound the mashed leaves around each stone bruise. By next morning I'd be off and running, the cure complete.

We didn't have bottled air fresheners in those days; instead, they sprang from the ground. I remember Mother picking mint sprigs from around an old water spigot, drying them, and crumbling their brittle leaves into small china pots, placed strategically throughout the house.

I accepted as fact that Nature could satisfy almost any need, if we but had the knowledge of her secrets. My elders appeared to exhibit an unending supply of that vital knowledge with their ability to heal with herbs, to predict weather and animal behavior, and to locate underground water with a forked twig.

Such reminiscences of my country boyhood led to others: my string of pets. While city boys might cherish their pedigreed dogs, my pets came to me from the surrounding fields and range—without credentials as to genteel genealogy, but each winning my affection in its own unique way. I wondered how many folks had a firsthand acquaintance with possums, armadillos, and other small country creatures. (Not all animals are to be recommended as pets, however, as my interesting and odoriferous possum soon proved when he sank his needle-sharp teeth through my hand.)

Pets weren't our only diversion. Outings to medicine shows, tent circuses, Wild West shows and rodeos, horse races, brush-arbor camp-meeting preachings, and the simple but enjoyable games we indulged in after school were deeply satisfying forms of entertainment.

I can't forget the way our house gleamed, despite the lack of today's highly touted cleansers. Homemade soap and plenty of elbow grease kept both clothes and home sparkling.

Many an old recipe handed down from before Grandma's time was responsible for the tantalizing smells that permeated our kitchen.

My friend's observation that "leaves are just leaves" sparked the thought that perhaps we need to be reminded of the bounty of Nature's offerings. Her riches are all around us; yet so often they are taken for granted. With such feelings and memories in mind, I wrote *Country Scrapbook* as a means of sharing them with others. And so maple leaves, not the Muses, inspired this book.

JERRY MACK JOHNSON

San Angelo, Texas

Of this fair volume which we World do name
If we the sheets and leaves could turn with care,
Of Him who it corrects, and did it frame,
We clear might read the art and wisdom rare.

—W. Drummond
"The Lessons of Nature"

1
Weather Wisdom

A change in the weather is enough to renew the world and ourselves.
—Marcel Proust

Over the ages, country people developed an oral catalogue of weather wisdom through their observation of weather patterns, atmospheric conditions, and their consequences on living creatures and inanimate objects. Each generation handed down its accumulated knowledge to the next, new information being added with the years. Such knowledge, both inherited and gleaned from experience, was relied upon in daily life by farmers, cattlemen, sheepherders, and navigators. Gradually, oft-noted weather sequences and their effects became incorporated into sayings, frequently based on dependable lore but sometimes solely on superstition.

Wind

Sayings of the past concerning winds are in general borne out by today's findings. Winds are prognosticators of the weather. As Bacon put it, "Every wind has its weather."

East winds proverbially bring rain; west winds herald fair or clearing conditions. Winds from the northeast forewarn of violent storms of wind and moisture. Winds blowing from the southeast indicate storms of less severity. Both northwesterly and southwesterly winds are harbingers of fair weather, the chief difference between them being that those from the northwest are cold and those from the southwest, warm.

Three hundred years ago, Izaak Walton put his observations of wind behavior into rhyme:

> When the wind is in the north,
> The skillful fisher goes not forth;
> When the wind is in the east,
> 'Tis good for neither man nor beast;
> When the wind is in the south,
> It blows the flies in the fish's mouth;
> When the wind is in the west,
> There it is the very best.

Winds are created by variations in the temperature of the atmosphere over land masses and water surfaces. The following sayings are concerned with various types of weather generated by specific winds:

■ People in the Southwest foretell relief from drought when there is a sudden, strong shift of wind.

■ When a lively wind from the south and southwest blows for a day or more, folks prepare for a "norther."

■ In most parts of the country, a strong, steady southeast wind means rainfall within thirty-six hours.

■ When winds come from a northeasterly direction, look out for severe cold and heavy snow.

- When the wind is centered between north and west, and the temperature descends to 40 degrees or less, expect frost.
- A sudden wind shift in the midst of a storm is a sign that foul weather will soon turn to fair.

Clouds

The hooded clouds, like friars,
Tell their beads in drops of rain.
—Longfellow

Clouds are indicators of storm. Their formation is the first step in the production of rain or snow. When cirrus and cirro-stratus clouds (popularly called "mare's tails") appear, rain or snow will follow within eighteen to thirty-six hours. These clouds gradually change into stratus and nimbus, at which time precipitation commences. The lower clouds are not long-range prophets of rain, for they usually either accompany rainfall or precede it by very little time.

FOUL-WEATHER SIGNS

- A red morning sky signifies a day of bad weather.
- Cirro-cumulus clouds appearing in winter mean warm, wet weather.
- The sight of threadlike cirrus clouds brushed back from the west is an indication of rain and wind.
- The formation of cirrus clouds in good weather, with the barometer falling, means rain is certain.
- Cirrus clouds are forerunners of the east wind. If the cloud wisps streak upward, rain is indicated.
- Clouds that sail contrary to the wind foretoken rain.
- When a heavy cloud builds up in the west and then appears to settle back, be on the watch for a storm.
- Clouds moving in opposite directions at differing rates and heights foretell heavy rains.

- Masses of thick clouds of a greenish hue gathering in the southeast and remaining for a few hours indicate a series of heavy rains and gales.
- If cumulus clouds continue to increase in an evening sky, rain can be expected.
- Clouds over hills, when descending, portend rain; clouds that are rising over hills do not cause rain.

FAIR-WEATHER SIGNS

- The approach of clear weather is heralded by the appearance in the northwest of a patch of blue sky big enough to tailor a Scotsman's jacket.
- When cirrus clouds disappear, fine weather can be expected.
- When clouds that are driven by the wind at the same height slowly thin and descend, good weather can be anticipated.
- Upper clouds coming out of the northwest in the morning ensure a day of fair weather.
- When cumulus clouds begin to diminish at sunset, fine weather can be expected.

DRY-WEATHER SIGNS

- When wisps of cirrus clouds streak downward, expect dry weather with wind.
- The longer the duration of dry weather, the less is the likelihood that cirrus clouds will be followed by rain.

Atmospheric Pressure

The barometer measures the pressure of the atmosphere, which is useful in determining future weather. A low barometer is associated with stormy conditions and a high barometer with fair weather or clearing. The indications of the barom-

eter precede wind shifts. Rapid alterations in barometric readings are indicative of pronounced changes in weather.

BAROMETRIC WEATHER SIGNS

- Winds frequently are strongest just as the barometer, immediately after having been very low, starts to rise.
- If the barometer remains low although the sky is clear,
more precipitation can be expected within twenty-four hours.
- If the barometer slowly falls for a few days while the
weather is fair, much rain will probably fall. If the barometer
continues to rise during wet weather, fair weather will follow
within several days and last for some time.
- If the barometer and the thermometer both rise together,
  It is a very sure sign of coming fine weather.
- If the barometer does not rise again after a storm in sum-
mer, expect several days of unstable weather.
- A summer storm that fails to depress the barometer will
be local and not very severe.
- When weather is unchanged despite a falling barometer, a
storm is raging at some distance.
- In winter, descending atmospheric pressure coupled with
rising temperature foretokens heavy rain.
- Stormy winds depress a barometer more than heavy rains.
- When the glass falls low,
  Prepare for a blow;
  When it rises high,
  Let all your kites fly.

UNSEASONABLE WEATHER

Unseasonable weather accompanies abnormal atmospheric
pressure. Summers of unusually low temperature are associated
with below-normal barometric pressure and an excess of rainfall. Summers of extraordinarily high temperature are associated with above-normal barometric pressure and a marked lack
of rain. Extremely cold winters are associated with above-

normal barometric readings and scarce or no precipitation. Unusually high winter temperatures are associated with barometric pressure below the norm and with rain or snow.

EFFECTS OF ATMOSPHERIC PRESSURE

Atmospheric pressure exercises a definite influence on living creatures and their bodily functions. This is not difficult to imagine when we consider that the normal weight of the atmosphere is approximately 1 ton to each square foot of surface at sea level, and a variation of 1 inch in the barometer means a change in pressure of about 70 pounds to each square foot of surface. A barometric change of 1 inch in twenty-four hours is not unusual. Such a change is related to a change of one-half ton in the atmosphere's weight sustained by the human body. Instinctively man has come to associate sensations felt under various atmospheric pressures with the types of weather that they evidence.

Those in delicate health and many animals are especially susceptible to atmospheric variations. During the period of rapidly decreasing atmospheric pressure that precedes and accompanies storms, these effects are manifested by nervousness, aches, and pains in humans and by restlessness among animals, birds, and insects. The flight of birds is higher when the barometer is high and low when the barometer is low. A high barometer signifies heavier, denser air with more sustaining power. Consequently, birds are able to fly high with less exertion than is needed at those periods when the barometer is low and the air less concentrated.

- A coming storm your shooting corns presage,
  And aches will throb, your hollow tooth will rage.
- When rooks wing low, expect rain.
- When a storm is nigh, bees will not swarm.
- When bees make but short trips from the hive or stay within, rain is due.
- Prior to rainfall, smoke descends to the ground.

■ Wild geese fly high in fair weather and low in foul weather.

■ The sound of the cuckoo in low lands signifies rain; when it is heard on high ground, the weather will be pleasant.

■ Swallows flying high in the evening sky are a sign that fair weather follows. When they swoop low, rain will ensue.

■ A favorable time for business transactions exists when the wind blows from the west, for then the barometer is high, and man experiences a greater feeling of well-being.

Temperature

During the warm months the temperature usually rises prior to rain, with the barometer falling. After rain starts to fall, the temperature drops, with a rising barometer. In cold months the temperature rises before and during rain or snow, remaining above normal until the rain or snow ceases, at which time it falls, with the barometer rising. Rainy periods in summer are unseasonably cool; periods of precipitation or snow in winter are unseasonably warm.

In the hinterland, high temperature is identified with south and southwest winds and low temperature with west and northwest winds. On coastlines, however, summer's warmth and winter's chill are affected by water temperature when onshore winds blow.

Variations in temperature before, during, and after storms also exert an influence on plant and animal life. Many weather adages stem from observation of these influences. Since temperature changes result from wind directions, proverbs concerning temperature are generally linked with those dealing with winds:

■ The south wind's warmth is debilitating.
■ The cold of the north wind is invigorating.
■ The east wind's chill leads to aches and pains.
■ In summer, when the sun burns excessively, thunderstorms can be expected.

■ When the temperature rises between 9 P.M. and midnight and the sky is cloud free, watch out for rain.

■ If, during an extended period of low temperature in winter, the temperature rises between midnight and dawn, a thaw is indicated.

At some time in the past, people dwelling in the country observed a relationship between the number of calls of tree crickets and prevailing temperature. The chirps of the snowy tree cricket, for example, are so closely allied to air temperature that it has been called the "temperature cricket." Listen closely to the insect, and by counting the number of its chirps in fifteen seconds and adding 40, you can calculate the current temperature fairly accurately.

Humidity

The air's humidity and temperature increase before a rain. As the temperature rises, the air's moisture-holding capacity rises proportionately. Increase in humidity is not always a forerunner of rain. In coastal areas, it may be due to fog or wind temporarily blowing off the water. Generally, however, a rise in atmospheric moisture foreshadows rain by twelve to twenty-four hours.

The air's moisture probably shares with atmospheric pressure and temperature a role in affecting animals and plants for good or ill. A falling and low barometer is attended by warm, moist air which causes physical and mental lethargy. A rising and high barometer with attendant cool, dry winds is felt to be invigorating.

These sayings developed from observations of the effects of humidity preceding rain:

■ Prior to rain, tobacco becomes moist.

■ The stone in quarries exudes moisture before a coming rain.

■ The sweating of dishes and metal plates foretells foul weather.

- Salt increases in weight preceding rain.
- When humidity is high, doors and windows are difficult to close.
- A bunch of hemp that becomes damp forewarns of rain.
- Flies sting and are more annoying than is customary when humidity rises before rain.
- Rain is due when walls are unusually damp.
- Indians used to say rain was likely when the hair in the scalp house became damp.
- An increase of moisture in the atmosphere causes ropes to shorten. When ropes are difficult to straighten out, rain is due.
- Sailors are on the lookout for rain when the ship's rope-work tightens.
- When horses sweat in their stables, rain can be expected.
- With an increase of humidity, some plants contract their blossoms and leaves.
- If wounds, sores, and corns are more than ordinarily uncomfortable, there is the likelihood of rain.
- Three foggy mornings in succession foretell rain.
- When the scent of flowers is unusually noticeable, rain is in the offing.
- When pain of rheumatism is worse than usual, rain will probably fall.
- Hoarfrost is a sign of impending rain.
- Dry weather is indicated when floor matting shrinks, but when it expands, wet weather can be expected.
- Country wives say that when their cheese salt is soft, rain will come; when it tends to dry, they predict fair weather.
- The bigger the moon's halo, the closer the rain clouds, and the sooner rain will fall.
- Moss that is cushiony and moist indicates rain; dry and brittle moss means fair weather.
- When sunflowers raise their heads, expect rain.
- A lifting fog means fair weather; a settling fog, foul weather.
- When the aroma of a tobacco pipe is stronger and lasts

longer, a storm can be predicted.

- Prior to rain, guitar strings tighten.

- A morning rainbow signifies that a shower to westward will soon approach; an evening rainbow signifies that rain is falling to the east and will pass away.

- Oiled floor boards turn damp immediately before rain.

- When rain is imminent, snakes come forth.

- Candles burn faintly and lamp wicks crackle prior to rainfall.

- Halos around sun and moon and the abnormal elevation of distant images through refraction, especially when inverted, are foretellers of foul weather.

- Hair tends to curl when a storm is imminent.

- The odor of ditches, drains, and dung heaps becomes more offensive previous to rain.

- When dry creeks and springs show moisture, approaching rain is indicated.

Nature and the Weather

Mother Nature has instilled animals, birds, and insects with an unknown sense of approaching weather changes long before we humans are aware of them. By this means they are able to take precautions against coming adversity. Being sensitive to minute atmospheric changes, they become unusually restless, return to their lodgings, or eat with greater voracity than normally. Cats and dogs, in particular, have long been considered wise in the ways of weather. Folklore is replete with sayings regarding animals and their characteristic behavior when sensing subtle atmospheric changes prior to approaching weather.

ANIMALS

- Good weather is in the offing when a cat cleans herself. If she licks her fur contrary to the grain, washes her face over her ears, or settles down with her tail to the hearth, bad weather is due.

- If dogs shun meat, eat grass in the morning, and dig holes, rain can be expected.
- Rain will soon fall when hogs run uneasily about with hay in their mouths.
- When cattle out at pasture recline early in the day, rain is indicated.
- Shepherds have observed that sheep gambol about before a storm.
- When cattle extend their necks and sniff the air, rain will come.
- Bats seen flying late at night signify good weather. When they cry while flying, expect rain on the morrow.
- When cattle congregate at one end of a field, their tails toward the wind, rain or stronger wind can be expected.

BIRDS

- When bird song ceases, listen for thunder.
- Birds and fowl oil their plumage before a rain.
- If crows are noisy and agitated, rain is on the way.
- Chimney swallows that fly in circles, calling on the wing, tell of rain.
- A solitary crow in flight signifies bad weather; a pair of flying crows means good weather.
- If the cock goes crowing to bed
  He'll certainly rise with a watery head.
- When birds that are accustomed to flying long distances stay near home, a storm is nigh.
- A noisy crane
  Means rain.
- Wild geese honking south over water mean that the weather will turn colder. Geese flying north mean the weather will grow warmer.
- When birds take dust baths, rain is close.

■ When grouse are heard to drum in the night, a heavy snowfall can be predicted.

■ A whistling parrot foretells rain.

■ Gulls circling aloft and crying shrilly mean a storm is approaching.

■ When chickens pick up pebbles and are unusually noisy, rain is coming.

■ If roosters crow early and late, flapping their wings now and then, rain is due.

■ Rain is expected when herons appear indecisive about a place to roost.

■ Pigeons return home earlier than is customary when rain is close.

■ When the peacock loudly bawls,
  Soon we'll have both rain and squalls.

■ Robins alight high in treetops and sing loudly and long before a rain.

■ Sea birds seeking shelter on shore or in marshes mean a storm will ensue.

■ When blackbirds sing more than usually of a morning, rain will come.

■ A flock of stormy petrels assembling in a ship's wake is an omen of impending storm.

FISH

■ Fish swimming close to the surface and biting avidly mean rain.

■ Rain or wind is close when pike lie motionless in stream beds.

■ When blackfish congregate in schools, expect a gale.

■ Trout leap and herring form schools more quickly preceding rain.

■ Bubbles appearing over clam beds are a sign of rain.

INSECTS

■ Swarming flies foretell rain.

- If spiders are inactive, rain will soon fall. When they are busy during rain, it will not last long.
- Stormy weather will come when ants move in columns; when they disperse, the weather will turn fair.
- Flies assemble in the house just before precipitation begins
- When bees to distance wing their flight,
  Days are warm and skies are bright;
  But when their flight ends near at home,
  Stormy weather is sure to come.
- Crickets become energetic before a rain.
- When the ground is spread with spider webs sprinkled with dew, yet no dew is on the ground, rain will come before nightfall.
- Flies collect on horses immediately before a rain.

PLANTS

- The scent of flowers is more perceptible prior to a shower, the air being damp.
- Corn fodder is extremely sensitive to variations of moisture in the atmosphere. When dry and crisp, it indicates fine weather; when damp and limp, it indicates rain.
- Mushrooms and toadstools are abundant before rain.
- Clover tells us that rain is coming by turning up its leaves, showing their light undersurface.
- If milkweed closes at night, rain will follow.
- Before precipitation the leaves of the linden, plane, poplar, and sycamore trees expose more of their undersides when fluttering in the wind.
- Rain can be expected when the pink-eyed pimpernel closes during the day.
- Before a storm, trees turn dark.
- When the sugar maple turns its leaves upside down, watch for rain.
- Expect rain when tree leaves curl in a south wind.

Heavenly Bodies and the Weather

The sun, moon, and stars are indicators of future weather only as their appearance is altered by prevailing atmospheric conditions.

SUN

- When the sun sets bright and clear,
  An easterly wind you need not fear.
- If the sun draws water in the morning, rain will fall before evening.
- When the sun goes down after a pleasant day behind a bank of clouds, with the barometer falling, rain or snow is indicated (depending upon the season) either that night or the following morning.
- When the sun is a dazzling white before setting, its light diffuse, a storm will ensue.
- If the sun goes down amid heavy dark clouds, rain will fall on the morrow.
- When the sun sets in a purple-tinted sky, the zenith being vivid blue, fair weather can be expected.
- A halo around the sun means bad weather.
- When it is evening, ye say, It will be fair weather: for the sky is red.

  And in the morning, It will be foul weather to day: for the sky is red and lowering.

  —Matthew XVI: 2, 3

- Red evening skies are followed by fair tomorrows.
- Haziness about the sun is a sign of storm.
- When a burning morning sun breaks through clouds, expect thunderstorms in the afternoon.
- Evening red and morning gray,
  Two sure signs of one fine day.

MOON

- When the full moon is pale on rising, expect rain.
- A large lunar halo with low clouds means rain within twenty-four hours.
- It is a sign of rain when the moon is darkest close to the horizon.
- A small ring around the moon with high clouds means rain in a few days.
- When a large red moon rises, accompanied by clouds, rain will fall in twelve hours.
- A full moon rising clear indicates good weather.
- A halo about the moon is a sign of rain; the bigger the halo, the sooner will rain fall.

STARS

- When the stars appear to twinkle excessively, heavy dews, rain, snow, or storms can be anticipated in the near future.
- If stars seem to flicker in a dark sky, rain or snow is due.
- When the North Star seems nearer than usual and flickers oddly, look out for rain.
- A sky studded with very large, dull stars means rain is in the offing.
- When the sky appears crowded with stars, be prepared for rain, or frost in winter.

Long-range Weather Prediction

Centuries ago onions were used for long-range weather forecasting. Six onions were sliced in half, each half being heavily salted and designated as a particular month of the year. On the following day the wetness of future months could be determined from the condition of the salt on each half.

In very early times people were receptive to the pronouncements of those held to be wise men and sages. Much stock was put in their predictions of future events and of future weather as well.

The following are sayings embodying long-range forecasts.

SUN

Sun spots were thought to exert an influence on the earth's weather:

▪ When sun spots are most numerous, rainfall will be greatest.

▪ Solar changes are related to excessive heat waves, prolonged droughts, and great floods.

MOON

The belief that the moon has a controlling influence on the weather has been handed down through centuries of time in the form of sayings or proverbs:

▪ If three days old her face be bright and clear,
   No rain or stormy gale the sailors fear;
   But if she rise with bright and blushing cheek,
   The blustering winds the bending mast will shake.
                              —J. Lamb's "Aratus"

▪ If a dry moon appears, a crescent with tips pointing upward, a dry month will ensue; if the tips are turned down, it is a wet moon and the month will have rain.

The Indian reasoned that if he could hang his powder horn on the crescent, the woods would be too dry for still-hunting. If he could not hang it on the crescent, he prepared to hunt, carrying his powder horn with him, knowing this was a sign that the woods would be wet for silent stalking of prey.

The Welsh, too, say, "It is sure to be a dry moon if it lies on its back, so that you can hang your hat on its horns." Sailors, however, often believed the opposite concerning the crescent moon.

It has been said that the moon's rays cause specific chemical effects, spoiling fish and certain kinds of meat. This is probably the source of the belief that hogs should be slaughtered in the dark of the moon. Though this cannot be classified as a weather saying, it does show a correlation between weather and activity, a dark-of-the-moon time or a cloudy and rainy night being favorable to certain pursuits.

STARS

Long before the calendar was devised, putting in order the time periods for the months and seasons, country people depended upon the rising and setting of constellations to plan their farming operations, including the breeding of animals. A Greek poet once wrote that the harvest begins when the Pleiades, that group of stars representing the seven daughters of Atlas, rise. Sayings of this nature often came to be interpreted as pointing out either a beneficent or a harmful influence of stars, whereas originally such weather lore had only signified a need of the observer to note an approaching season and its attendant weather.

ANIMALS, BIRDS, ETC.

A persistent belief among rural people of the past was that animals are endowed with an ability to determine in advance weather conditions for an entire season. In fact, such a faculty is limited to an instinctive interpretation of prevailing atmospheric conditions which indicate weather changes in the near future, from one to twelve hours away. Migrating birds commence their southern migration when autumn first chills the air and return north at the first hint of temperature modification in their wintering grounds. Oftentimes their flights are premature. The physical state of animals—for example, the thickness of their coats—depends upon past weather and its effect on their food supply and health in general, instead of upon future weather. This thinking applies also to plants that are the subject of sayings predicting the weather of a coming season.

The following are old weather sayings concerning the habits

of birds and animals and the appearance of plants as signs of long-range weather conditions:

- When bears store food in autumn, a cold winter will follow.

- The chattering of flying squirrels in midwinter indicates an early spring.

- When the winter is expected to be early and long, beavers ready their lodges and stock their larders sooner than before mild, late winters.

- You can anticipate the direction of future storms and winds by observing which of its two holes the hedgehog plugs up.

- When the ground squirrel frisks about in winter, it means that snow is almost over.

- Severe weather can be expected when migrating birds wing south early.

- If the first snowfall is patterned with bear tracks, a mild winter is ahead.

- If the cat basks in a February sun, it will warm itself by the stove in March.

- The mole stores his food supply of worms in abundance in a winter that is expected to be severe. When less food is stocked, the coming winter will be mild.

- The early arrival of cranes in the fall signifies a cold winter.

- When squirrels are seldom seen in the fall, a cold winter can be anticipated.

- When summer birds fly away, summer goes too.

- An early arrival of the woodcock means a hard winter is due.

- When woodpeckers depart, expect a severe winter. When they peck low on tree trunks, it is a sign of future warm weather.

- The swan makes its nest low when the coming season will not be rainy; the nest is built high when a season of rain and high water is expected.

- Intense cold can be predicted when field larks are seen to assemble in flocks.
- If crows wing south, a cold winter will follow; if they fly north, the opposite is true.
- The first robins betoken the coming of spring.
- When wrens are about in winter, snow can be expected.
- The whiteness of a goose's breastbone is believed to show the amount of snow that will fall during the coming winter: If the breastbone has red spots, a cold, stormy winter will ensue; if but few spots are evident, a mild winter is due.
- After martins appear there will be no killing frost.

Days, Months, Seasons, and Years

Rural folk paid special attention to weather during winter and spring because of its effects on the seasons of planting and harvesting. Saints' days were believed to have particular influence on the weather.

DAYS

- If St. Vincent's [January 22] has sunshine,
  One hopes much rye and wine.
  If St. Paul's [January 25] is bright and clear,
  One does hope a good year.
  Candlemas Day [February 2]! Candlemas Day!
  Half our fire and half our hay.
(The last line means that we are halfway through winter and should have half our fuel and hay supply remaining.)
- If Candlemas Day be fair and bright,
  Winter will have another flight.
  But if Candlemas Day bring clouds and rain,
  Winter is gone and won't come again.
- Badger, bear, and woodchuck come forth at noon on Candlemas Day to look for their shadow. If they fail to see it, they remain out. If their shadow is visible, they return to their

dens for another six weeks, and cold weather will last for six weeks more.

- If the ground hog is seen basking in the sun on February 2, he will go back to his winter lodging for four to six weeks.
- If February 2 is a stormy day, spring is close at hand; if the day is fair, spring will arrive late.
- The warm side of a stone turns up on St. Patrick's Day [March 17]
  And the broadback goose begins to lay.
- Is't on St. Joseph's Day [March 19] clear,
  So follows a fertile year.
  Is't on St. Mary's [March 25] bright and clear,
  Fertile is said to be the year.
- If it thunders on All Fools' Day [April 1]
  It brings good crops of corn and hay.
- Hoarfrost on May 1 means a good harvest.
- Rainfall on St. Barnabas' Day (June 11) is favorable to grapes.
- We pray for rain before St. John's Day [June 24];
  After that it comes anyway.
- A rainy St. John's Day means harm to the nut harvest.
- However dog days [July 3 to August 11] begin, in such a way do they end.
- Dog days bright and clear
  Indicate a good year;
  But when accompanied by rain,
  We hope for better times in vain.
- In this month is St. Swithin's Day [July 15]
  On which, if that it rain, they say
  Full forty days after it will
  Or more or less some rain distill.
  —*Poor Robin's Almanack*, 1697
- St. Barthelemy's [August 24] mantle wipes dry
  All the tears that St. Swithin can cry.
  If the 24th of August be fair and clear,
  Then hope for a prosperous autumn that year.
- September 15 is said to be fair six years in seven.

■ If acorns are abundant on St. Michael's Day (September 29), the fields will be white with snow at Christmas.

■ On the 1st of November [All Saints' Day], if the weather hold clear,
An end of wheat sowing do make for the year.

■ If the beechnut is dry on All Saints' Day, winter will be severe; if the nut is wet, a wet winter will follow.

■ If All Saints' Day brings out the winter, St. Martin's Day [November 11] will bring Indian Summer.

■ If Martinmas is fair and cold, winter's cold will not long endure.

■ If tree and grapevine leaves do not fall before St. Martin's Day, a cold winter is due.

■ A green Christmas means a heavy harvest.

■ If on Friday it rain,
'Twill on Sunday again;
If Friday be clear,
Have for Sunday no fear.

■ When the first Sunday in the month is stormy, every Sunday of that month will be stormy.

MONTHS

■ The month that starts with fair weather will end with foul.

■ If no snow falls before January, more will fall in March and April.

■ A favorable January means a good year.

■ A thaw can always be expected in January.

■ A mild January, a chilly May.

■ If February gives much snow,
A fine summer it doth foreshow.

■ The rain of February is good only for filling ditches.

■ Thunder in February or March indicates a poor maple-sugar year.

■ A dusty March means foliage and grass.

■ Snow in March harms fruit tree and grapevine.

■ March flowers make no summer bowers.

- March damp and warm will do the farmer much harm.
- When March has April weather, April will have March weather.
- However much rain falls in March, the same amount will fall in June.
- March comes in like a lion and goes out like a lamb.
  March comes in like a lamb and goes out like a lion.
- March winds and April showers
  Bring forth May flowers.
- The winds of March and rains of April make for a bounteous May.
- Rainy April, fair June.
- A damp, cool May fills the barns and wine barrels.
- Rainy May,
  Dry July.
- Calm weather in June sets corn in tune.
- A damp, warm June does not impoverish the farmer.
- When June is cold and wet, the rest of the year will be unpleasant.
- July, God send thee calm and fayre,
  That happy harvest we may see.
- As is July, so will next January be.
- Don't trust the sky in the month of July.
- Whatever July and August do boil, September can not fry.
- As is August, so will the following February be.
- August's rain is honey and wine.
- Dry August and warm
  Doth harvest no harm.
- As September is, so will the next March be.
- Heavy rainfall in September brings drought.
- Much rain in October, much wind in December.
- Warm October, cold February.
- Heavy frost and winds in October mean that January and February will be mild.
- Whatever the weather in October, the same will occur in March.

- As the weather is in November, so will it be the next March.
- A cold, snowy December is favorable to rye.

SEASONS

- Early thunder means early spring.
- A great blessing is a late spring.
- Better late spring and bear than early blossom and blast.
- A late spring never misleads.
- A late spring is favorable to corn but unfavorable to cattle.
- When spring is dry, a rainy summer follows.
- If wet and chilly the spring, then cold and dry will be the fall.
- Rain in midsummer spoils grain, stock, and wine.
- A wet fall with a mild winter means a cold, dry spring that retards plant growth.
- A mild winter means a poor wheat crop.
- A mild winter and a cold summer mean a poor harvest.
- After a wet winter comes a fruitful spring.

YEARS

- A cold year follows a rainy one.
- Rainy and dry years come in threes.
- Wet year,
  fruit dear.
- Snow year, good year. Frost year, good year.
- Years of radishes, years of health.

Warm and Cold Fronts

The following tables show the usual succession of weather conditions before, during, and after a warm front and a cold front. The more rapidly the front travels, the faster such weather conditions form and dissipate. The changes and their duration also depend upon the hour of the day or night, the season, and the general weather picture. The following se-

quences of weather variations attending the movement of a
warm front and a cold front are, therefore, generalized ones.

WARM FRONT

	PRIOR TO THE WARM FRONT	AT THE TIME OF ARRIVAL	AFTER THE WARM FRONT
WIND	increases in velocity; direction frequently easterly	alters direction to south-east	changes direction to south-west
BAROMETER	descends; the more rapid the fall, the faster the arrival of the front	falls to its lowest reading	frequently rises but slightly
TEMPERATURE	minimal rise	gradual rise	rise; amount depending on discrepancy of temperature between cold air prior to front and warm air after it
HUMIDITY	augments slowly	increases rapidly to almost 100 per cent	possible minimal increase
VISIBILITY	steadily worsening	poor, sometimes fog or mist	slight betterment possible
CLOUDS	cirrus overhead, followed by cirro-stratus or alto-cumulus, then stratus or nimbo-stratus	nimbostratus or sometimes cumulo-nimbus	usually significant clearing of bad weather with scattered nimbo-stratus, stratus, or strato-cumulus

	PRIOR TO THE WARM FRONT	AT THE TIME OF ARRIVAL	AFTER THE WARM FRONT
WEATHER	light rain from alto-stratus, followed by heavy rain or snow from nimbo-stratus	drizzle, rain showers, or snow	possibility of occasional rain or snow, but usually clear or clearing conditions

COLD FRONT

	PRIOR TO THE COLD FRONT	AT THE TIME OF ARRIVAL	AFTER THE COLD FRONT
WIND	velocity increases; direction frequently easterly	quick change of direction to the west, with gusting	strong and steady from the west to northwest
BAROMETER	rapid, steady falling; the quicker the fall, the earlier the front arrives	descends to lowest reading	fast rise
TEMPERATURE	constant rise	slight change	abrupt fall, amount depending on difference of temperature between warm air prior to front and cold air after it
HUMIDITY	constant	decreases	marked fall, except during rain
VISIBILITY	poor, possibly fog or mist (low wind velocity)	poor to good, according to intensity of precipitation	fine

	PRIOR TO THE COLD FRONT	AT THE TIME OF ARRIVAL	AFTER THE COLD FRONT
CLOUDS	alto-cumulus or alto-stratus, followed by stratus, strato-cumulus and cumulo-nimbus or (sometimes) nimbo-stratus	cumulo-nimbus with low stratus; sometimes nimbo-stratus	alto-cumulus and cumulus or strato-cumulus; speedy decline in amount of clouds; pro-nounced in-crease in the height of their bases
WEATHER	fog, rain, snow, or thunder-showers de-veloping in strength	heavy rain or snow	sometimes in-termittent showers; in general, clear-ing conditions

Comparison of Fahrenheit and Celsius (Centigrade) Scales

FREEZING: 32 degrees Fahrenheit (F.)   o degrees Celsius (C.)
BOILING: 212 degrees F.   100 degrees C.
To change F. to C., subtract 32 and multiple by 5/9.
Thus 212 degrees F. = (212 − 32) × 5/9 = 100 degrees C.
    176 degrees F. = (176 − 32) × 5/9 = 80 degrees C.
To change C. to F., multiple by 9/5 and add 32.
Thus o degrees C. = (o × 9/5) + 32 = 32 degrees F.
    80 degrees C. = (80 × 9/5) + 32 = 176 de-grees F.

2
Water
Witching

You never miss the water till the well
runs dry.
    —Rowland Howard
    "You Never Miss the Water"
    1876

Dowsing

Anyone who has witnessed dowsing in action is already familiar with its procedure and fascination. For the uninitiated, the gift of dowsing is the ability of a person to locate underground sources of water or minerals while carrying in his hands a Y-shaped stick called a dowsing rod or divining rod. Other terms synonymous with dowsing are doodlebugging, striking, water witching, radiesthesia, and rhabdomancy.

Most dowsers, sometimes referred to as water witches, are men in their middle years and older. However, there are also women dowsers. And children up to the age of fifteen or sixteen are especially sensitive to the dowsing reaction. I have seen very young boys with the power, their wand forcefully turning down over water veins.

Because the ability to dowse sometimes runs in families, some persons believe that dowsing is a learned art, passed along from one family member or generation to another. Others contend that the familial pursuit of dowsing means it is an inherited gift. People seem to have this ability in varying degrees: in some the skill is immediately obvious; others achieve success only through patient practice.

Dowsing is practiced in England, continental Europe, Africa, North and South America, Australia, New Zealand, and parts of Asia. It is continental Europeans more than any other peoples who have used dowsing rods.

Over the ages the most popular rods have been made from peach or hazel trees, though maple, persimmon, willow, witch hazel, poison oak, and plum have also served. Divining rods have been fashioned from materials other than wood, such as oxhorn, ivory, gold, silver, and whalebone. Dowsers seem to have had equal success with bent coat hangers, watch springs, scissors, pliers, specially cast metal rods, and rods of wood with metal coils attached, with compasslike pointing devices, or with battery-powered lights.

The dowsing rod is generally a forked twig, one branch of which is held in each hand, the juncture usually pointing upward. The two most common holds are with the palms up and with the palms down. When the rod is carried over a spot where underground water or minerals lie hidden, the pointed end will be attracted downward; it has been known to whirl around. Straight twigs are sometimes used. The smaller end is held, while the opposite end bobs up and down when indicating water or ore, the number of bobs signifying the depth in some unit of measure.

Dowsers often experience one or more kinds of distress, to a greater or lesser degree, while working: convulsive pains, pounding heart, racing pulse, muscle spasms, a stinging sensation on the skin, and dizziness and nausea. Some develop a feeling of nausea immediately prior to the stick's downward thrust. All agree that their work is physically exhausting, leaving them with the feeling of being drained of energy. For this reason, finding three to four wells per day is the limit.

The original dowser could have been a magician, discovering his gift accidentally while using his wand. Early manifestations of dowsing were related to magic and sorcery. The ancients used it to predict future events, to warn of the presence of ghosts, and even to forecast the weather. Long ago, wizards accompanied their use of the forked rod with incantations. Righteous men, spurning incantations, nonetheless retained the practice of dowsing.

The birthplace of modern-day dowsing was in the Harz Mountains of Germany, where the most advanced mining practices were developed. Miners believed that metallic ores attracted certain trees, causing them to lean over the spot where the ore lay underground. A branch of such a tree would be cut so that it might be observed where else it drooped. Later, a branch was cut for each hand, their extremities being tied together. Finally, as a matter of convenience, a forked branch was cut, an end grasped in each hand with the palms upward. A common practice in those times was to bury money for safekeeping. So the rod functioned as a detector of buried treasure as well as of metallic lodes.

The churches held that the power of dowsing meant an affiliation with the Devil. Those persons found engaged in mysterious practices risked being burned at the stake for sorcery. In Germany, dowsing was therefore enveloped with religious ceremonies and prayers as a shield against persecution. In an attempt to prove that both operator and rod were not under demoniac influence but were recipients of a divine gift, elaborate rituals were observed: 1. The dowser must purify himself through fasts, novenas, and sexual abstention. 2. Rods must be cut only on holy days. 3. The rod, wrapped in swaddling clothes, should be carried to church for baptism and laid in the bed of a newly baptized infant, by whose name it was thereafter to be addressed.

Early dowsing reflected the credence that the rod was the source of power; therefore, its manufacture, as to both ritual and material, was of utmost importance. Hazel twigs were considered most efficacious in searching for silver, ash twigs for copper, pitch pine for lead and especially tin, rods of iron and steel being best for finding gold.

German dowsers achieved excellent results in locating deposits of metals. The French tried to vie with them by training their own miners. The English, following the more expedient path, wisely imported German dowsers.

A favorite Cornish toast is "fish, tin, and copper," for Cornwall's wealth lies chiefly underground and in the surrounding seas, mining and fishing being her primary industries. The mining industry endured periods of depression, as it did shortly before Queen Elizabeth I came to power. During her reign German miners were imported to revive the industry. Thus the dowsing rod was introduced to England. Tradition among Cornwall's miners has it that fairies, custodians of the earth's mineral treasure, guide the rod to ore deposits.

The dowsing rod was used in Europe as much in the quest for water as for metals. Water was an important factor in mining; if its taste was metallic, the dowser could be confident that metal deposits were nearby. Those lacking interest in mining but desirous of a water supply would ask the dowser to stop once water was found. Early water dowsers called themselves "water switchers," referring to their work as "switching for water." By this time dowsers were able to determine not only the location of water but its width and depth as well, estimation of its volume remaining yet unsolved.

Prior to the end of the seventeenth century, use of the rod spread throughout Europe and was transported to Asia, Africa, and the New World by colonists.

Early Spanish explorers employed dowsing instruments in mining operations in the Southwest and Mexico. During the days of colonization, there was an urgent need for water. Settlers developed numberless wells through the aid of dowsers, wells that continued to furnish water until at least the end of the last century. The Indians were ignorant of dowsing until it was introduced into North America by European settlers and their descendants.

By the late 1700's, dowsing power had become associated in America with witchcraft, which is why the practice became known here as water witching. The term is not used in any other English-speaking country.

Despite the preaching of churchmen that dowsing was anti-religious, people in every walk of life experimented with it. Innumerable theories were proposed to explain the operation of dowsing. In the fifteenth century the view was held that the failure of a twig to turn downward over a metal deposit indicated that some peculiarity in the user impeded the power of the vein to attract. Five conditions for successful dowsing were set forth: 1. The twig should be of proper size: the vein of ore is unable to turn too large a stick. 2. It should be of a forked shape. 3. The power of the vein to turn the stick must be present. 4. The stick must be properly held. 5. Impeding peculiarities in the operator must be absent.

Others concluded, in the 1600's, that because the rod did not work in all hands, its movement was due to some specific favorable quality within the dowser. Since the rod was only the instrument through which the dowser's gift worked, its shape and material were of less consequence than the power controlling it.

Some men explained the power of dowsing by the principle of attraction and repulsion, influenced, no doubt, by the evident phenomena of gravity and magnetism. They believed that the rod received magnetic vibrations from underground ore and water.

In the late 1700's the study of electricity was making great strides. The theory was proposed that water witching was an electrical phenomenon, the explanation being that the rod depended on electrical currents transmitted from the ground through the body, forming a magnetic field between the rod and the ground.

At the beginning of the twentieth century, French dowsers

called themselves practitioners of radiesthesia—believing that unseen currents emanating from the rod were affected by the presence of water or minerals, causing the rod to move. Currents of physical force, perhaps similar to electricity, were thought to travel from underground water up through both dowser and rod, moving spirally up one branch of the stick, through the man, and down the other fork, returning to the water's source in the earth, thus making a complete cycle. Some dowsers, wearing leather gloves and rubber boots, were hampered by what they considered the insulating effect of these clothing articles; other dowsers, similarly attired, experienced no hindrance to their dowsing performance. Electrical and magnetic theories have been used in support of the radiesthesia reasoning.

In the late 1930's, German dowsers purported the existence of rays rising from the earth's center which continually pierce the earth's crust, traveling into space. Underground water, oil, or minerals soak up these rays so that the surface over them is lacking in rays. Such places are referred to as "shadow" areas. Devoid of rays, they act on the sympathetic nervous system of the dowser. This idea was widely entertained in Europe, even outside the circle of dowsers. Adolph Hitler, in an effort to locate a restful "shade" area, requested that his sleeping quarters be dowsed so that he might sleep undisturbed by rays. In Mexico the ray, not the shadow, is believed to affect the nervous system.

More recent theories are modifications of the principle of the radiesthesiasts. Some physical force, it is believed, is responsible for dowsing, but its effect is not so much on the rod as on the muscles of the operator's forearms, inciting the dowsing reflex—an imperceptible movement but made obvious by the action of the rod. One school of thought is that the rod senses currents of radiation from water molecules underground. Some people believe that a physical power from underground water acts directly on the nerves of the dowser's hands, stimulating unconscious muscle movement made manifest by the rod or other dowsing device.

There are those who look on dowsing as a natural gift. The water-witching talent is considered an enlargement of normal perception through which the dowser accepts information, subconsciously sending it to the rod by indiscernible muscular movement of fingers and palms. Telekinesis, the ability to move objects by mental power, has been suggested, as has the idea that dowsing is a seventh sense, physical rather than psychic. Long-distance dowsing by use of a rod over a map of the area in question borders on the parapsychological stand.

What dowsing has detected makes up a varied and fascinating list: water, petroleum, potash, diamonds, gold, graves, and buried treasure. Over the ages the dowsing rod has been used to ensure immunity against misfortune when preserved as a fetish; to analyze human character; to locate lost landmarks and redefine property boundaries; to determine the direction of the cardinal points, measure heights of trees, detect criminals, find archeological sites; to trace lost domestic animals, pinpoint malfunctions in appliances, cure diseases, trace underground streams; to ascertain the amount and depth of water present at a specific underground spot; and to analyze ore and water. Dowsing has revealed that ancient stone monuments were invariably constructed over underground water sources. The military has used dowsing to detect buried land and underwater mines, underground bunkers, and enemy caches of food, ammunition, and fuel. Some unusual experiments to which dowsing has been put are revealing human blood types, answering questions, tracing escaped prisoners, finding lost disaster victims by use of the rod over a map of the disaster area, and distinguishing the paintings of one artist from those of another.

Should you be prompted to try your hand at dowsing, make your initial step that of locating a good Y-shaped branch with a 45 to 60-degree angle between the forks. The stick should be no more than 2 feet in length. One from a young tree is most likely to have the required supple, resilient quality. The most common hold is with the branches in upturned palms, the fingers encircling the wood, thumbs held firmly against the ends. Some dowsers have the branch passing inside the little and third fingers, grasping the branch by the middle and index fingers and allowing it to protrude beyond the palms. Others prefer the rod to lie loosely in the palms with the ends extending beyond the hands. Dowsers believe that anyone can achieve success through patient practice, perseverance, and concentration. Concentration on the material sought is considered very important.

A good many dowsers, after much practice, have been able to dispose of the divining device, depending solely upon concentration and their bare hands, believing that the true dowsing instrument is the dowser's body. There are dowsers who feel that the rod can be unfavorably influenced by metallic objects on the operator's person—objects such as rings, coins, and eyeglasses. Some find that they have "active" and "inactive" fingers on each hand, those which are sensitive to the dowsing reaction and those which are not. Skillful dowsers are able to identify different underground metals and to distinguish water and petroleum from metal. Some dowsers are so sensitive as to detect the very grade of the ore deposit. I personally have never witnessed the use of the divining rod in locating metal deposits or buried treasure but have seen it used in finding water. Roy Baker of Tennyson, Texas, witched for water on our little farm and discovered a pretty good well in what was otherwise thought to be a dry area. While watching others successfully dowse for water, I've seen the rod turn downward with such power that the bark on the branch was skinned off or broken in the hands of the operator.

In the southern United States, a twig of the accepted shape is used, but one considerably longer and more flexible. In this area, branches from fruit trees are preferred. Elsewhere in the country, more complex man-made rods have become popular—the swing rod, the magnetic mineral rod, the gold-digging compass, the Spanish needle, and the pendulum fork, to name a few.

Those accepting dowsing as a mysterious but important potential for the future perceive it as one day functioning for the general good. Dowsers in Mexico find the rod sensitive to rock variations, such as faults. Should this prove consistently true, dowsing could be valuable for mapping possible earthquake areas. Claims have been made for its use in detecting certain organic diseases when it is passed over a person's photograph, just as land areas have been dowsed first by map. Further inquiry into this aspect could lead to diagnosis and healing. Opportunities for the employment of dowsing are limitless.

Dowsing has proved successful an outstanding number of times. To reject it solely because its secret defies scientific explanation would be to preclude us from a realm fraught with untold possibilities for the betterment of mankind.

Testing Water

In days gone by people devised simple methods of testing water which, though not completely scientific, were generally effective. Here are two methods that were used to determine the color, odor, taste, and purity of water.

- Fill a clear glass bottle with water. View some black object through the water to judge its clarity. The object's outline should appear well defined. Then empty half of the water, cork the bottle, and set it in a warm place to stand for several hours. Now shake the bottle, uncork it, and smell the air inside. If there is any odor, the water is not fit for domestic purposes. If there is no odor, see if one develops when the water is warmed. After it has been warmed, the water should be tasteless as well as odorless for home use.

- Put water in a gallon jug, and add a good amount of sugar. Let the jug stand for a week. If, at the end of that time, the sugar is not discolored, the water is safe for drinking. If it has become discolored, boiling the water will be necessary for safe consumption.

3
Hunter's Bag

The hare, the partridge, and the fox
must be preserved first, in order that
they may be killed afterwards.
—John Lubbock
The Pleasures of Life
1887

Hunting Hints

Here are some helpful hints for better hunting that I've
gleaned over the years from various parts of the country.

■ Sam Odin of New York State suggests that you start to
grow a beard before hunting season. He claims that a beard
cuts down the glare from your skin and you'll bag more game.

■ Break in your hunting boots with rubbing alcohol instead
of water. It penetrates the leather faster, dries more quickly,
and will make them fit your feet better.

■ If you plan to wear heavy woolen socks, your hunting

boots should be two sizes larger than your normal shoe size; for light socks, boots should be one size longer and wider.

■ Old-timers say that excellent bootlaces can be made from the inner tube of an automobile tire. Cut narrow strips of the same thickness and length as leather laces from a tube that has not become dry and brittle. Thread them through the eyelets of your boots. You'll find them nonslip and comfortable. Being flexible, they'll give with the movement of your feet.

■ If the noise of gunshot makes your horse bolt, tie 20 feet of stout rope to its halter with a large steel hook on the other end. Before shooting, throw the anchor into the brush.

■ Because rifle-cleaning rods are too bulky in your pocket, carry a stiff leather lace. You can easily push it through the bore, pulling a patch fastened to it.

■ Never place wet leather shoes or hunting boots by a fire for quick drying. Heat a handful of pebbles in a skillet. Pour them into the shoes and shake them about. The shoes will not become stiff, as with fast-drying methods; you will find them warm, dry, and comfortable.

■ If you're hunting with a shotgun and become separated from companions, you can use it for sounding a distress call. Remove all the shells from your gun, leaving the breech open. Put the muzzle to your lips and blow hard. The first note will be high, gradually tapering to a lower note as your pressure declines. The sound will carry a surprising distance. Don't forget to clean the moisture from the gun's bore afterward. This was a method used long ago to call coon or fox hounds when the hunter lacked a proper horn.

■ You might enjoy the satisfaction of fabricating your own hunting horn. One can be made from cow horns or steer horns. A short cow horn emits a high sharp note; a long steer horn gives a deep sound.

Saw off the first two inches of the pointed end. Heat a piece of strong wire until red hot, and bore through the horn. Carve a mouthpiece at the blowing end similar to that of a bugle. To make the sound carry farther, carefully scrape it down with a piece of glass. You can give your horn a high polish by rubbing it with oil and pumice.

Hunting Game in General

Cloudy, windless days are best for hunting, although a wet day is sometimes good. Early morning or late afternoon proves the most favorable time for hunting every kind of game. Try to avoid periods of temperature extremes. Check the direction of the wind; make sure it is blowing from the quarry toward the hunter.

Game Birds

The ideal country for locating all species of game birds is well-watered land that affords a variety of terrain: hills, level ground, woods, meadows, and marshes.

When birds rise on the wing, they fly against the wind. Shoot at the moment when the bird is turning or steadying itself in the air. As birds are descending to alight on the ground, your aim should be underneath. Allow a bird that is flying head on in your direction to pass by without firing at it; otherwise, you will be shooting against the dense breast feathers instead of under the feathers.

BAY SNIPE

In summer and fall, bay snipe are most effectively taken when a southwest wind is blowing steadily. Birds traveling out of the north and against the wind fly low, winging along the edges of bars and meadows. They spot decoys more clearly than when they are flying with the wind in the clouds. Wet summers are especially favorable for bay snipe shooting, for then the meadows furnish an abundance of feed.

DOVES

Though not waterfowl, doves must have water and won't stay in an area where water is not within easy flight. The best spot for successful dove shooting is over a water hole, where such holes are at some distance from one another. You can surprise the birds in pea patches, wheat stubble, or standing cornstalks.

DUCKS

On windy days ducks will fly low, close to the water. Without the aid of the wind, ducks fly at the rate of about 90 miles an hour. When heading against the wind, they wing low in dense formation.

Don't shoot ducks when they are traveling "dead on"; the shot will be kept from entering their bodies by the thick breast feathers. Shoot when they have passed by or are on a line with you. Since all waterfowl have an acute sense of smell, approach ducks on the water against the wind.

LOONS

Loons habitually plunge forward into water. So when hunting these birds, aim in front of them.

PHEASANTS

The pheasant is a wily bird. If a brook is in the vicinity, the bird will hop back and forth across it to confuse the trail. You'll need a sense of humor when hunting pheasants!

PRAIRIE CHICKENS

Look for prairie chickens, or pinnated grouse, in fields of stubble during the morning and evening; at midday expect to find them in cornfields or near bottom-land creeks.

QUAIL

Early in the morning quail are running about in pea or wheat fields in search of food, providing poor targets. By the time the dew has evaporated, they will have finished eating and be resting in some sheltered spot in their feeding grounds or close by. They are not nearly so prone to take wing at this time, but if they do, their flight will be short and sluggish.

RUFFED GROUSE

To tree a ruffed grouse, you should be familiar with its habitat and habits.

Exclusively a bird of the woods, the ruffed grouse is skilled at flying through brush and timber without slowing its speed. It can slip through any cover.

The favorite haunts of the ruffed grouse are hillsides dense with cedar, hemlock, and an undergrowth of laurel. In flat territory it seeks patches of scrub oak and swampy areas with briery, tangled coverts.

When disturbed, the ruffed grouse squats close to the ground or alights in a tree, concealing itself under branches close to the trunk. If flushed on a hillside, it will usually fly uphill and can be discovered just over the crest. When flushed on flat ground, the ruffed grouse will fly low and once again land on the ground. If it ascends gradually and suddenly shoots upward, the bird can probably be seen on the evergreen closest to the one where you last spotted it. When it rises immediately to a treetop and then darts off, it will fly some distance. If the grouse flies up a steep incline, it will alight on the ground. Should it fly from a hill down toward a level area, the bird will alight in a tall spruce or hemlock and remain completely still on a limb close to the body of the tree. If it wings from one hill over a ravine to another rise, it will land on the ground. The shorter the ruffed grouse's flight, the more quickly it again takes to the air.

SNIPE

Snipe can be found in low willow bottoms and marshy thickets. To hunt them to advantage, set out on a warm, sunny day with gentle winds. Make sure the wind is behind you, for snipe rise in a zigzag pattern against the wind.

WILD TURKEYS

The hearing of turkeys is considerably better than that of deer, and their eyesight is as good as that of antelope and sheep. By nature they are as wary as all other game combined. Remember that one suspicious sight or sound is sufficient to cause their disappearance.

In the northern area of the wild turkey's range, hunting is frequently successful shortly after the first snowfall. You can judge the freshness of the turkeys' tracks and be alert while following them. In most of the range, however, careful preliminary planning is required. It's vital to learn where the turkeys run, what they're feeding on, the size of the bands, and, most important, where they are watering.

To find out where birds are running, look for shed feathers, for tracks, for spots where birds have scratched in search of bugs, or for acorns and pine nuts. Try to discover their preference in food; what they're eating will determine where to look for them. When autumn remains mild, plenty of insects are still available. With the early arrival of frost and snow, turkeys seek acorns and tiny pine seeds.

Try to locate their watering place. Turkeys are creatures of habit: unless disturbed, they will go to the same spring or the same spot on a stream bank and at about the same time each day. Look for or build a natural-looking blind close by.

Keep an eye out for flocks in sunny spots during the morning; watch for them in shady places by afternoon.

Calls

Old-timers didn't set out to hunt equipped with fancy "store-bought" bird calls; they generally made their own. Practice and experience in using them brought favorable results.

DUCK CALL

A squawker, or duck call, was made from a tube of wood, preferably bamboo, about 8 inches long and ¾ inch in diameter inside. To one end fit a 3-inch-long plug. Split it in two, and groove one half to within ¼ inch of its smaller end. The groove should be ¼ inch wide and deep. Pound a thin piece of metal about 2½ inches long and ½ inch wide to use as the tongue. One end should be thinner than the other, with rounded corners. Place this over the grooved half, the rounded end almost covering the groove. Shorten the other half of the plug 1½ inches from its smaller end. Place it on the grooved half. Holding the metal tongue in place, push both pieces of the plug into the tube. Blowing into the opposite end of the tube will produce the duck call. You can vary it by moving the shortened end of the plug in or out.

SNIPE CALL

Use a curlew's leg to make a snipe whistle. Thoroughly dry it. With a red-hot knitting needle, push out the marrow. Plug up one end, and start practicing.

TURKEY CALLS

▪ Maple or dogwood makes the best turkey calls. Take a piece some 6 inches long and 1½ inches in diameter, and bore a hole through it lengthwise with a small-sized bit. With a tapering bit ream out the interior to 1¼ inches. Insert a piece of wood or cane at the opposite end to serve as a mouthpiece. The size of the mouthpiece will control the tone of the call.

Some hunters put the caller in the middle of their mouth; others call from the side of the mouth. You'll want to vary the sound according to the game you're pursuing. If you're after an old hen, the note should imitate a young turkey; if a young one is your prey, mimic the hen.

- Run a cedar stick (roughly the size of a pencil) through a corncob that is only a little longer than half the length of the stick. The cob is the handle, with the centered stick protruding from either end. Take a piece of slate, three inches square, and round the edges. With the slate held in one hand, scratch it with the tip of the cedar stick, holding the cob loosely.
- Some old-timers prefer the wing bone of a turkey, sucking on it to make the appropriate noise.

Calling can be overdone. One false note will cause a bird to vanish. Limit your calls to four.

Fowlers' Terms

- a *badelynge* of ducks
- a *bevy* or *covey* of grouse
- a *bevy* of quail
- a *brood* of hens
- a *building* of rooks
- a *charm* of goldfinches
- a *colony* of gulls
- a *congregation* of plovers
- a *covert* of coots
- a *covey* of partridge
- a *depping* of sheldrakes
- an *exultation* of larks
- a *fall* of woodcocks
- a *flight* of swallows
- a *gaggle* of geese
- a *herd* of swans, cranes, or curlews
- a *host* of sparrows
- a *murmuration* of starlings
- a *muster* of peacocks
- a *sege* of herons or bitterns
- a *spring* of teals
- a *sword* or *sute* of mallards
- a *walk* of snipe
- a *watch* of nightingales

Bird Flight

- duck   80 to 100 m.p.h.
- pheasant   25 m.p.h.
- quail   50 m.p.h.
- ruffed grouse   40 m.p.h.
- woodcock   30 m.p.h.

Preserving Dead Birds

The following methods of preserving dead game birds were used by hunters in the past and are just as effective today:

■ Draw the birds and stuff them with green grass. Cover the bottom of a box with coffee grounds that are absolutely dry. Place a layer of birds on top. Alternate layers of grounds and birds until all are packed in the box.

■ Draw the birds. Suspend them by the head to allow them to drip thoroughly. When their natural body heat has dissipated, stuff them with fresh leaves. Put the birds head first into paper bags. Tie the bags tightly closed to keep out air. Place them in a shady cool spot until they are to be moved. Birds preserved in this way are said to keep for more than forty-eight hours and to be fresh and palatable when eaten.

Small Game Animals

RABBITS

After a night of meandering, cottontails will bed down by day, sleeping or sunning themselves in a small round nest in some sheltered spot. Look for them in bramble patches, cornfields with nearby cover, small copses, marshes, overgrown fields, and scrub pasture land.

In early autumn on a warm sunshiny day, cottontails can be found over the entire countryside. By midwinter with snow on the ground, rabbits seek shelter from the open country in the woods. Tracks in the snow will indicate the areas that rabbits are frequenting and how good the hunting will be. The dark gray fur of the rabbit will be a more obvious target against the snow, which also makes tracking a wounded animal easier.

A midwinter day just after a cold spell that ended in a sudden thaw is advantageous to the rabbit hunter. Rabbits will emerge to frisk in the mild air. You can make quiet progress toward your target in the soft snow. If it disappears into its hole, persevere. Rabbit holes are not very deep. Close to the entrance there is a crook, after which the passageway continues at an angle for a short way. A hunter can usually work his hand in to grasp the ears or hind legs of the fugitive. Failing this, cut a fairly long, supple stick with a strong fork at the end. Work it around the crook in the tunnel, inserting it as far as it will go. If you find bits of rabbit fur on the fork, push the stick in again, twisting it. You can twist the fur up so tightly that the rabbit can't move, and you can pull the animal from the hole as if he were part of the stick. If you can't reach the cottontail with the twister, and the den has more than one entrance, tie a piece of weasel fur to the stick. The sound of the switch working down the passageway, plus the scent of the weasel, will usually send your quarry into the open.

SQUIRRELS

The best time to still-hunt squirrels is at break of day, when they frisk about, chattering noisily. At other hours they are silent.

In bygone days veteran hunters used to say that the only palatable squirrel was one shot squarely in the left eye. The most skilled of huntsmen didn't shoot squirrels at all. They favored "barking them off," which required a great degree of accuracy. The target wasn't the squirrel but the bark immediately beneath its feet. The resulting concussion, not the bullet, killed the animal.

These are the requirements for a good squirrel call: a sharp knife; a piece of stiff paper; a forked stick roughly ⅜ inch in diameter and 5 inches in length. First peel the bark from the twig. Carefully split the twig down the middle with your knife; the fork will prevent the cut from splitting the twig completely. Insert the paper in the split. Holding the end tightly, trim the paper as close to the twig as possible. Blow against the paper, slightly squeezing the end opposite the fork to adjust tension. With a little practice you'll soon have an inquisitive squirrel peeking around a tree trunk to satisfy its curiosity.

Deer

Learn where deer are feeding and bedding, what trails they're using, and where these trails intersect. The presence of deer is revealed by their hoofprints and droppings, by saplings with bark rubbed away when bucks polish their antlers, and by the nipped-off tips of plants which form their diet.

In autumn, deer head for the woods to feast on acorns. When scouting for feeding grounds, check woods where oak trees are plentiful. In descending order of preference in the deer's diet are corn, buckbrush, sumac (including poison ivy!), grasses, and sedges. In northern forest regions, whitetails favor white cedar, yew, apple, mountain maple, striped maple, dogwood, and red maple. If these are unavailable, they browse on elderberry, high-bush cranberry, hemlock, mountain ash, arbutus, honeysuckle, blueberry, and willow. During the hunting season mule deer prefer mountain mahogany, sagebrush, oaks, and evergreens, such as bearberry and myrtle. Blacktails feed on willow buds, evergreens, ferns, manzanitas, and acorns.

Deer in secluded areas will browse almost as much by day, when the moon is up, as by night. If the moon has shone throughout the night, they will bed down all the following day. If the moon has been up during the day, they will bed down for the night.

Dress the deer carcass as quickly as possible with a very sharp knife, emptying the body cavity. Remaining blood will drain out. Wipe the cavity with a cloth, except in blowfly country; there, allow dried blood to glaze the meat, forming a hard crust which flies won't be able to penetrate for laying eggs. You can also protect your freshly killed game from insects by sprinkling the carcass with pepper and covering it with cheesecloth. Another effective way to keep insects from game is to rub the meat, after hanging it, with cooking oil. Make a smoldering fire in a place where the smoke will reach the game. The meat will be kept moist by the oil, and the smoke imparts a delicate smokehouse flavor.

Trapping

Place the bait in a steel trap in such a way that when the animal sniffs the food its foot will be on the pan. Try suspending the bait from a stick over the trap, or put it in an enclosure, causing the animal to step over the trap in order to get it. After game has been caught, traps should be smoked or cleaned.

Bow Hunting

Long ago the bows of Indians in the Ozark wilderness area were noted for their durability and strength. They were far superior to those of other tribes and of the French explorers, who recognized that these qualities were due to the wood of which they were made. They called this wood *bois d'arc,* meaning "wood of the bow." The name was corrupted into "bodock" by English settlers.

The bodock tree is easily identified by its large, inedible fruit which resembles an orange, so that the tree is also called Osage orange. For generations country people have made their fence posts from bodock wood, many being serviceable for more than fifty years.

Bodock trees were so highly valued by the Indians that wars were often fought for possession of land where they grew in abundance, for the bodock bows were held in high regard by the Indians themselves, as well as by explorers and traders. Such a bow was a chief item of barter; a fair young squaw wasn't considered too high a price for a well-balanced bow.

Look for the bodock tree with its fruit the size, shape, and color of oranges. It sends up several stems rather than one trunk. You'll find making your own bow a genuine challenge and satisfying accomplishment. Make your arrow shafts from the straight branches of older bushes of the wild rose or from wild currant wood.

SMALL-GAME BLUNTS

Small-game blunts are used for hunting rabbits, gophers, etc. You can make them easily by tipping ordinary arrows with old-fashioned erasers that slip over the end of pencils. These rubber tips won't stick in tree trunks or bury themselves in the ground as deeply as regular arrows.

Falconry

Falconry is more an art than a sport, requiring long hours not only for the initial training period but for daily practice to keep yourself and your bird in top form.

The choice of bird depends upon the area available for hunting. If the country is limited, broken by small fields and woods, choose a short-winged bird, like the sparrow hawk or goshawk. In open country, a long-winged falcon, such as the peregrine or merlin, is best. To capture their hawks, the Plains Indians would conceal themselves in the carcass of a large animal and pounce upon the bird as it devoured the carrion.

The bells carried by the hawk on its legs are an interesting feature of falconry. One bell should be a half tone higher than the other. The resulting discord carries for very long distances.

Acquire a handbook on falconry to guide you in its intricacies. In order for your bird to attain and maintain peak physical condition and skill, she (the female in the hawk family is larger and more powerful than the male) must be flown every possible day throughout the season.

Blackfly Remedy

Hunters are often plagued by biting blackflies. Old-timers had an effective remedy: Combine equal parts of rubbing alcohol and household ammonia. Apply the mixture to the bites on a piece of cotton. It will reduce both itching and swelling.

Witch Hazel

While hunting, you may spot a shrub with yellow flowers, somewhat resembling forsythia. It is witch hazel, a shrub that blooms in late fall and winter. Note its location. In spring gather its leaves, soak them in water, and add alcohol, one part alcohol to five parts of the witch hazel infusion. You'll have an excellent liniment for tired, aching muscles after a long day of hunting.

Firewood

In gathering wood for a fire, pass up any that is on the ground. It is usually beginning to rot and may be damp or even water-logged. Choose deadwood that is standing or hanging in bushes or low trees.

For kindling select the bark of white birches. It ignites quickly and is easily removed from trees. Dead twigs from the tops of small evergreens also make good kindling.

Select hardwoods for a long-burning fire. Hickory is excellent because it burns well whether seasoned or green. Oak makes good firewood, particularly white oak. White ash and yellow birch burn better when green. White birch and northern alder burn well when somewhat green.

Softwoods, when dry, serve only as kindling or for quick-cooking fires.

To maintain a campfire, occasionally add resin-filled pine and balsam knots.

To start a campfire quickly when the woods are damp, cut an inch off a candle. Place it next to a good-sized stone. Lean twigs against the stone above the wick. Light the candle. In no time it will dry the wood enough for it to ignite.

Camp Cookery

BANNOCK

4 cups flour
6 tablespoons sugar
4 teaspoons baking soda

1 teaspoon salt
⅓ cup cold bacon fat
milk or water

Combine the dry ingredients. Cut in the fat with a fork, gradually adding a little water or milk until the dough becomes a ball without dry places. Press this into a 1-inch-thick pancake, dusting top and bottom with flour. Heat a heavy cast-iron pan. Grease it. Brown the bannock on both sides. Cook it for approximately 15 minutes or until done.

COOKING SMALL BIRDS

Dress the birds. Remove the head and legs. Bake each in a hollowed-out potato.

WOODCOCK RECIPE

Cook the woodcock over burning coals for about 10 minutes. Meanwhile make a sauce of the following:

½ cup currant jelly
1 tablespoon butter

1 tablespoon prepared mustard
3 tablespoons red wine

Melt the jelly; stir it to prevent scorching. Add butter and mustard. Allow the mixture to boil for 1 minute. Stir in the wine.

When the skin is brown with the flesh pink and juicy, remove the bird from the fire and serve with sauce.

SQUIRREL WITH RICE

If the squirrels you've bagged are too tough for frying, try preparing them this way:

Cut 2 squirrels into serving pieces. Rub them with salt and pepper and brown in a deep kettle with a chunk of salt pork. Add 2 quarts of water and simmer until tender, adding water when necessary. Put in 1 cup of rice, ¼ cup of ketchup, ½ sliced onion, and 1 teaspoonful of salt. Cook until the rice is done.

BROILED VENISON STEAK

Cut steaks approximately 1½ inches thick. Carefully wipe them with a damp cloth to ensure removal of any stray hairs. Rub the steaks on both sides with cooking oil. Place them on a grill over the coals of your campfire. For the first 2 minutes turn them every 30 seconds. After that, turn them every 2 minutes until done to your liking: 10 minutes for rare steaks; longer if you prefer them well done.

Combine the following for an excellent venison-steak sauce:

¼ *cup melted butter*
2 *tablespoons lemon juice*
½ *teaspoon salt*

1 *tablespoon finely chopped parsley*

PAN-COOKED VENISON

Cut venison into 1-inch-square pieces. Wrap bacon around each piece, securing it with a toothpick. Put them in a cast-iron skillet. Add the following:

2 *cups water*
½ *cup Worcestershire sauce*

salt
black pepper

Boil rapidly until most of the water has evaporated. When the fire dies down somewhat, cover the pan and continue cooking until the meat is brown.

4
Hook, Line, and Sinker

You will find angling to be like the virtue of humility, which has a calmness of spirit and a world of other blessings attending upon it.
—Izaak Walton
The Compleat Angler

When to Fish

There are many theories, some of them conflicting, as to the most favorable times for fishing. The following are recommendations of rural folk from different parts of the country:

The best time to fish is . . .

- when the barometer is high or rising
- when a storm is imminent
- after a brief storm at any time of the year
- during a steady light rain
- when rain has just stopped
- when the wind is from the south or west, or while any

offshore breeze is blowing (A slight breeze breaks up the surface of calm water, hindering the fish from spotting you.)

- when the moon is between the new and the full
- when water is clear
- when water is murky
- on an overcast day
- when water is rising
- when a lake starts to drop
- when oak leaves are the size of squirrel ears
- when the dogwood blossoms
- when ants build high mounds
- when spider webs are taut
- when cattle are up and grazing (Old-timers say that if they're resting, you can bet that's what the fish are doing.)
- when the water temperature is between 55 and 74 degrees (A good fishing thermometer should be used.)
- at the crack of dawn during hot, dry months (Large fish, in particular, are active during darkness and into the dawn.)
- one hour before and after high tide; one hour before and after low tide
- on a calm evening for bass and trout
- on stormy days, especially during warm months, for pike, pickerel, and walleyes
- after the first thunderstorm of spring for catfish (Since catfish usually don't bite until the weather is warm enough for a thunderstorm, this claim has some validity.)

What to Wear

When wading and fly fishing, wear clothes of brown, green, or gray. They will be least discernible to the fish's keen eye, for these colors of low intensity blend in with the background along stream banks. For fishing from a boat, clothing of light color is less visible against the sky and clouds.

Bait

These days most folks are turning to natural foods for wholesome nutrition; fish, too, favor a variety of natural foods. To stir the fish's appetite, you might first chum the water (where it's legal) with diced pieces of the following tempting morsels, in addition to using them for bait:

- Bass: pork chunks (what country people call "sowbelly"); small eels
- Black bass: live black chub minnows; small carp, not more than 4 inches in length (It makes a lively, long-lasting bait.)
- Carp:

RECIPE I

1 cup boiling water   ⅓ cup cottonseed meal
1 cup oats   ⅓ cup flour
1 teaspoon vanilla

Cook 1 cup of oats in 1 cup of boiling water. Add the other ingredients, working them into the oatmeal one at a time. Form small balls of this doughy mixture to bait your hook for carp.

RECIPE II

Make a dough ball of equal parts of corn meal and white flour by mixing in a bit of molasses or honey and enough water to make the mixture adhere. Heat the dough over a low fire for 5 minutes. Remove it from the heat, and knead it for 10 minutes or until it is a good-sized, firm ball. Use chunks about the size of a walnut as bait for carp.

- Catfish: muskrat liver, chicken liver; striped frogs; pieces of unscented soap; fish or meat scraps in a burlap sack weighted down with stones; cooked macaroni (It is delicate when impaled on the hook, so cast with care.)

RECIPE I

Mix 2 parts of beef brains and 1 part Limburger cheese with a small amount of water. Put the mixture in a jug and bury it in the ground for 2 weeks. Then keep it refrigerated until needed for fishing. Dip small pieces of sponge into this odoriferous mess as bait for luring catfish from afar.

RECIPE II

Mix 1 pound of Limburger cheese with a 1-pound can of wallpaper cleaner. Add 1 tablespoon of vanilla. Blend the mixture thoroughly by kneading it. Keep it in a tightly sealed container.

- Flounder: clam bait (Put clam bait in a jar, adding sufficient water to cover it. Add enough red or yellow food dye to color the water. After 8 hours, drain off the water. Cut the dyed bait into slender 1-inch-long strips. The fussiest flounder will go for it.)
- Sunfish: cockroaches
- Trout: crayfish; worms; salmon eggs; cicadas; dry fish meal; minnows (To restore vitality to listless minnows, add six drops of iodine to their water.)
- Walleyes: leeches (Try to catch leeches in a screen trap, attracting them with a bait such as raw liver, which contains a lot of blood.)

More Bait Lore

- Country people will tell you that bait is quickly seized when mixed with the juice of lovage. Several drops of rhodium oil also bring good results.
- Catfish, carp, buffalo, and suckers (especially catfish) like cheese baits. Swiss cheese and cream cheese are very effective.
- Don't use a sinker with a grasshopper bait; allow it to float

on the water's surface. Use it for catching trout in very still areas of streams. Before worms can be dug in the spring, raw beef makes good trout bait.

▪ Earthworms can be used to catch any kind of fresh-water fish. In salt water, eels and white perch are attracted to them. Place the worms in moss overnight to clean them. They will keep fresh and active for several days if you wrap them in earth inside a strong cloth.

▪ One old-time fisherman recommends a piece of mackerel as a trolling bait for pike. Cut a piece 1½ inches long and ¼ inch wide, tapering it at one end. Insert the hook as close to the edge of the broad end as possible.

▪ When using bait for bottom fish, fasten the sinker loosely above the hook. Run the line through the hole in the sinker, and tie something (a small stick or button) between hook and sinker to keep them apart. In this way the fish can carry the bait without the sinker and will more likely mouth the hook.

CATCHING AND KEEPING BAIT

▪ In spring and summer, suspend a light over a pond to attract insects for the fish. Hang it close to the water so that the bedazzled insects will hit the surface. You'll need to use this light lure for only the first few hours of evening.

▪ Wherever cattails grow, frogs and minnows seek shelter. They make excellent bait for catching bass and pike.

▪ Small creatures, like caddis worms, water beetles, and helgrammites, make fine fresh-water bait. You can collect them by holding a piece of screening downstream while rocks are overturned upstream. The bait will be carried into the screen wire by the stream's current.

▪ Crickets are good bait for catching panfish. Here's an easy way to capture them: Slice a loaf of bread in two. Remove the soft inside. Make a hole in one end about the size of a fifty-cent piece. Using rubber bands, fasten the two halves together again. Place the loaf in tall grass where crickets are most numerous. The following morning, put the end with the hole over a quart jar and shake out the crickets.

To maintain lively crickets for bait fishing, keep them in a clean garbage can. Polish and wax it inside for the first 10 inches down from the top; this will prevent the crickets from climbing out. Put about 5 inches of fine, moist sand in the bottom. Place a glass-jar drinking fountain (the kind used for chicks) on the sand. So that the crickets won't tumble in and drown, put cotton in the dish; they'll take needed moisture from the cotton. Give them a small container of poultry mash for food. The can will accommodate fifteen males and an equal number of females. Keep it in a spot where the temperature can be maintained at roughly 80 degrees. You'll be able to raise about four hundred crickets per month.

- Cicadas make excellent fishing bait. During the early morning search for them on tree bases, fence posts, and rocks. Keep them in a ventilated tin can. Big trout and smallmouth bass can be quickly caught on cicada bait.

- When you go fishing in the spring, take along a butterfly net to catch some dragonflies. They make excellent fly-fishing bait. Any surplus can be sprayed with plastic and preserved until the next fishing trip.

- Salmon eggs for trout fishing can be kept unspoiled with sugar or salt. Spread out the roe to let it dry slightly. Put it into a container that can be closed tight, alternating layers of salmon eggs with the salt or sugar. Sugar, which is more generally used, will form a syrup, keeping the eggs for considerable time, provided that the jar is well sealed against air. With salt, the roe is preserved in brine.

- Search for sandworms beside the sea at low tide. Look under large rocks for a red, fringed worm some 14 inches long. Beware of its pinching beak! To preserve sandworms for days, keep them in a box with a small quantity of sand. Place a little seaweed over them. A whole worm is needed for striped bass; a half portion is sufficient for other fish.

- Wherever you see a large round hole in the sand at ebb tide, dig there for a soft-shelled clam. Toss the shells and soft portions of the clams overboard to lure fish. Use the firm parts for bait. Snapping mackerel and blackfish are particularly partial to soft-shelled clams, and other kinds of fish that do not frequent the bottom will feed on them.

▪ Look for the best bait for salt-water fishing, the soft-shelled crab, among rocks or half-submerged logs at the margins of low water. Under its shell you'll find a thin but strong skin. Put the hook into it in such a way as to expose as much as possible of the white flesh. One crab should provide about five baits, including the claws. Blackfish, bluefish, eels, flounders, porgies, and weakfish accept it readily.

Pack soft-shelled crabs, claws up, close together in a box. Place fresh grass or seaweed over them; keep them cool.

▪ All salt-water fishes favor shrimp. You can catch them in still-water areas of salt-water creeks or rivers by using a hand net among the reeds close to shore. Keep them in a box of moist sawdust or in a container of salt water to preserve them all day. Impale them on the end of the hook for lively mobility, or run the hook through from end to end, tail first, concealing the hook.

▪ To keep minnows fresh, add 1 tablespoon of common salt to each 3 gallons of water. In chilly weather, several hundred minnows can be transported long distances in a 3-gallon container with a tight cover. Fill the container two-thirds with water and one-third with handfuls of clean wheat straw or rye. Some fishermen say that you can keep two minnows alive for more than a week by sealing them in an airtight jar two-thirds full of water.

▪ Pack crayfish and frogs in wet moss to keep them alive for some days.

Fly Facts

▪ When you're fabricating artificial flies, make some that imitate the insects most frequently seen in the area to be fished.

▪ On sunny days and in clear or shallow water, use small,

plain-colored flies. On gray days, in the evenings, and in deep or murky waters, use large, brightly colored flies.

■ In areas where the soil doesn't get too dry, you can find the bright yellow flowers of the wild plant celandine. The orange-colored juice in the roots and stems provides a yellow-orange dye for coloring fur and feathers for jig flies and streamers. This shade is unusually attractive to trout.

■ Learn to recognize bedstraw, a trailing weed that is easily uprooted. It can be identified by six to eight leaves sprouting in a whorl around the square stem. You can use the roots to dye streamer flies red.

Fish Poles

Before fishing rods were made of steel or fiber glass, traditional materials were Osage orange, hickory, straight-grained white ash, and split bamboo.

If you'd like to try your hand at making your own rod, Osage orange (the bodock tree) is the best when you can find straight-grained billets. Hickory has great strength, but its tendency to be slow in action makes it less than desirable for a casting rod. However, it's excellent as a big-game trolling rod, having greater shock resistance than other woods. White ash can be used for an acceptable rod, but since it is a softer wood, a larger diameter—especially in the tip—is required, which makes it rather clumsy.

Bamboo is actually a kind of grass. It's never perfect enough to furnish a top-notch fishing pole. In order to make a proper rod, it must be seasoned, split, and then glued. It will last indefinitely if kept well sealed by a coat of varnish to prevent moisture from seeping in, rotting the wood, and softening the glue.

The notion of splitting bamboo into strips and then gluing them together to eliminate the hollow center, thus obtaining the complete strength of the cane, probably originated in

China. The technique was used in that country almost three thousand years ago. The first split-bamboo rods were made in America in the 1860's.

For your fishhook, try using the hooked thorn of barrel cactus. You'll catch many a fish with it.

Where to Fish

In ponds and lakes, fish frequent places where bottom springs or streams supply cold water to the larger body of water.

Fish prefer those spots in brooks where the water current carries the surface food. You'll find that the bigger fish dwell in such select areas.

Fish downstream when bait-fishing. When fly-fishing, fish either up or downstream, just so the sun is in front of you.

Preserving Your Catch

To preserve freshly caught fish and their excellent flavor, here are some suggestions from veteran anglers.

- Kill a fish as soon as it comes from the water. If it is permitted to thrash about, the bruising of its flesh causes quicker deterioration. To kill a fish quickly, rap it smartly on the back just behind the head, using a knife handle or stick; or you can insert your thumb in the gill and break the neck. When killed as soon as caught, fish will keep for a longer period of time and the flesh will be better.

- As soon as it's feasible, clean the fish, washing the body cavity thoroughly.

- To preserve trout, clean them and wipe them dry. Sprinkle the insides with corn meal. Pack the fish in meal in a snug box.

- Trout can be kept fresh and sweet for several days, without salt or ice, in the following way: Dress the fish and wrap them in the long white moss often found in marshy areas near trout streams. Keep them in a cool, shady place, such as a hole in the ground covered with at least a foot of earth.

- Pack the body cavity of bass or trout with the large, broad leaves of the plantain, a common weed growing in fields or sunny spots in woods. This will keep the body from drying out and in addition lend a delicious flavor to the meat.

- Cool your catch by evaporation: keep it in a wet burlap sack. Don't pack fish snugly; layer them, placing them on pine boughs or grass. Keep the bag moist and away from direct sunlight. If the sack is exposed to a breeze, evaporation will be increased and the temperature lowered even more. Following these pointers, you should be able to cool your catch some 30 degrees below air temperature with good results.

- On fishing trips, stuff cleaned fish with mint. It helps to repel flies and serves as a deodorizer for the fishy smell. Place mint in the bottom of your creel, too.

Fish-fin Wounds

- There is a quick and simple remedy for the sting of a catfish barb. Mose Barlow of Missouri says that rubbing the sore place against the fish's belly will bring immediate relief.

- Make a paste of the white of an egg and 1 spoonful each of common salt and gunpowder. Apply it to a fish-fin wound, and bandage it. Use a fresh application as the mixture dries. To keep the paste moist, cover it with a damp cloth.

Swimming Speeds of Fish

- Swordfish   70 m.p.h.
- Blue marlin   50 m.p.h.
- Bluefin tuna   45 m.p.h.
- Tarpon   35 m.p.h.
- Blue shark   35 m.p.h.
- Atlantic salmon   25 m.p.h.
- Brown trout   25 m.p.h.
- Pike   20 m.p.h.
- Striped bass   15 m.p.h.
- Pacific salmon   10 m.p.h.
- Perch   10 m.p.h.
- Mullet   10 m.p.h.
- Carp   8 m.p.h.
- Eel   8 m.p.h.

Kinds of Fishing

Over the ages men have devised many means of catching fish.

Where waters teemed with big southern catfish, Indians would dive in holding anything red for bait. While the fish were trying to swallow the bright object, they were seized and lugged ashore.

SPEAR FISHING

Fish were often speared with cane, which wasn't sturdy enough to pull a fish out at first stab. Once the cane was driven in, the fish was permitted to run. Each time the spear reappeared on the surface, it was thrust in anew. Finally the fish tired and could be taken easily.

BOW FISHING

The Indians shot fish in the water with arrows. Though not as popular as pole fishing, this means is sometimes used today. Fishermen with bow and arrow shoot large carp when they are on the spawning beds.

The biggest difficulty in getting your fish by this method is the distortion in distance caused by seeing an object from one medium, air, in another, water. Because of this problem of refraction, the target is really closer than it seems, except from a vertical angle. So aim low to be on target. The deeper the water, the lower should be your aim.

ICE FISHING

During the bitter winters of early North America, the Indians maintained their supply of fish by ice fishing. They built huts over holes in the ice, enabling them to see to a depth of some 50 feet, because they were peering from darkness into water which at that time was transparent. They could spear large muskellunge, bass, lake trout, pike, and pickerel with 40-foot poles.

If you enjoy ice fishing, you may find helpful these tips, contributed by experienced ice anglers.

■ The best line for ice fishing is one of your old, stiff fly-casting lines. It will run freely and won't freeze, tangle, or collect snow out of water.

■ To prevent your fishing hole from freezing up, pour glycerine or cooking oil into the hole. This will create a thin film, keeping ice from forming for some time.

■ A small, lightweight rod is best for ice fishing. The fish, being more sluggish in winter, bite more delicately. A light rod responds more easily to this gentle nibbling, so that you can quickly detect a potential catch.

■ Use a small hook and small bait in winter.

ICE-FISHING BAIT

The following are baits for ice fishing, guaranteed to win you a winter feast of fish:

■ Meal worms: They are brownish beetle larvae an inch in length. You'll find them in stored grain that has become damp.

■ Mud daubers: Collect the larvae from the nests of mud dauber wasps.

■ June bugs: Look for the white larvae of the June bug in piles of decaying sawdust.

■ Goldenrod galls: Goldenrod galls are the knobs found on dry stalks, actually being a type of cocoon. Choose one without holes; cut it open, and you'll find tempting white grubs for fish.

■ Corn borers: These are small white worms that can be found in cornstalks left in fields during the winter.

Taking Turtles

You'll find turtles in almost all waters, including streams and man-made lakes. Use a sturdy fishing rod and raw meat for bait to capture them. Cautiously walk along the water's margin until you spot a turtle floating or sunning itself. Flip the bait just in front of the turtle, and leave it undisturbed for a while before another try.

For extra-good eating, try to catch soft-shelled fresh-water turtles or snapping turtles. Be on your guard when handling all turtles, but especially the snappers.

Protection While Fishing

To prevent pesky insects from spoiling your fishing trip, here are some old-time remedies that have proved successful over the years.

■ Mix 3 ounces of sweet oil and 1 ounce of carbolic acid. Apply the mixture to all exposed parts, being careful to avoid the eyes. Use it every half hour when flies are irksome or for the first two or three days. From then on it will be needed only occasionally, as the skin will be filled with it.

■ A good preparation for repelling insects consists of 1 part creosote, 1 part pennyroyal, and 6 parts sweet oil.

■ Simmer 3 ounces of pine tar, 2 ounces of castor oil, and 1 ounce of pennyroyal over a low flame. Bottle it for use.

■ To make a good mosquito smudge, evaporate a piece of gum camphor (about one-third the size of a hen's egg) in a tin vessel over a flame.

■ Cut 6-foot strips of bark from a dry fallen cedar log to make a bundle a bit larger than two hands can encompass. Using strips of the white inner bark of a live cedar, bind the dead bark together at intervals of about 9 inches. Put it in your tent, and light one end. It will smudge in the tent with fragrant, pleasing smoke. Mosquitoes will leave, and none will return if you leave the smudge at the tent opening through the night.

■ When attacked by a squadron of mosquitoes, you may find that Nature has afforded you an antidote in the very vicinity of your fishing. Learn to recognize the wild geranium. You'll find it from April through summer in woods and thickets and along shady roadsides. Crush its leaves between your fingers; its unpleasant odor, similar to that of a he-goat, repels mosquitoes. (You may find yourself followed by a line of bleating nanny goats, but mosquitoes—never!)

Cooking Fire

Use clean, dry hemlock bark to kindle your cooking fire. When the flame is bright and steady, keep it so with sweet woods, such as black birch, hickory, sugar maple, yellow birch, and red beech. Split wood is best. Sticks should be short and not over 2 inches in diameter.

Camp Cookery

Be sure to take salt along on your fishing trip. You'll find it has uses other than seasoning.

■ Put a dash of salt in your coffee pot; it will enhance the flavor of the coffee.

■ You can remove the odor of fish from your hands by washing them in salt water.

■ Sprinkle a little salt in the frying pan before frying fish, and they won't stick to the bottom.

BROOK TROUT RECIPE

2 pounds small trout, dressed   2 tablespoons lemon juice
1 pound sliced bacon

Clean the trout as if for frying. Brush them inside with lemon juice and sprinkle with salt, pepper, and preferred seasonings. Wrap each fish in slices of bacon. In a large skillet cook them for 5 minutes or until crisp. Turn them over, and crisp the other side.

FIDDLEHEAD FERN SOUP

The perfect appetizer before a trout dinner is fiddlehead fern soup:

Pick a bunch of these ferns, equaling about 1 quart. Boil them for 15 minutes, drain, and reserve the liquid. Chop the ferns fine. Add 1 cup of evaporated milk, ½ cup of regular milk, and 2 chicken bouillon cubes, dissolved. Add 2 tablespoons of butter, a pinch of basil, and salt and pepper. Mix with the liquid and simmer.

POT-BAKED FISH

Put a slice of bacon or salt pork in a heavy pot. Place 4 pounds of cleaned fish, cut into pieces of serving size, on top. Sprinkle with salt. Cook about 20 minutes over a low fire. Meanwhile, fry sliced onions, adding tomato paste, pepper, and 6 tablespoons of vinegar. Serve the fish with this sauce.

PLANKED FISH

Heat a slab of wood (avoid pine) until very hot. Clean the fish. Split it to open flat, and tack it to the wood, skin side down. Prop the slab vertically before the fire, periodically turning it end for end to ensure even cooking. Every half minute baste it with a chunk of salt pork dipped in vinegar.

CATFISH SOUP

2 or 3 pounds catfish	salt and pepper
2 quarts cold water	bay leaf, parsley, thyme
1 onion, sliced	1 cup milk
1 celery stalk, chopped	2 tablespoons butter

Cut the fish. Put all the ingredients in a pot over a low fire. Stir now and then. When the fish flakes easily, the soup is ready to serve.

TURTLE SOUP

2 cups turtle meat, cut into bite-sized pieces
1 onion, diced
1 carrot, diced
1 large potato, diced
1 cup peas, tomatoes, or other vegetables
salt and pepper
2 cups water

Combine all ingredients and simmer until tender. Thicken with flour.

CHICKEN-FRIED FROG LEGS

Salt and pepper the legs to taste. Beat 2 eggs with ¼ cup of milk. Dip the legs into this mixture, then coat them with corn meal or dry bread crumbs. Fry in a skillet of hot vegetable oil, rolling them to ensure even browning, for no longer than 5 minutes.

NATURE'S LARDER

If you discover you've forgotten to pack the seasonings, Nature will provide substitutes:

- Wild onions: They can be used fresh, cooked, or dried and in salads or soups.
- Cow parsnip: Burn its dried leaves and the lower part of the stalks. Use the ashes as a salt substitute. The lower stalks, after being dried, can be chopped and added to other foods for salt flavoring.
- Coltsfoot: The dried, burned leaves provide a good replacement for salt.
- Yarrow: This plant is often called "old man's pepper." Chop the fresh or dried leaves fine and use them as an alternative to pepper.

WATER CRESS

Water cress, a member of the mustard family, can be found along stream beds. Some old-time anglers gather this nutritious plant, pour hot grease over it, and sprinkle it with salt. They also use it to keep their catch cool and fresh.

Anglers' Adages

- The harder you fish, the luckier you get.
- A boat is a hole in the water into which you throw money.
- The two best days in a fisherman's life are the day he buys a boat and the day he sells it.

5
Creatures
of the
Countryside

God made all the creatures and gave
them our love and our fear,
To give sign, we and they are His
children, one family here.
—Robert Browning
Saul, VI

Armadillo: Living Xerox Machine

Long of snout, with naked, mulelike ears, the armadillo ambles
about on stubby legs covered with hardened scales. Its body is
encased in an armor of bony plates (mottled brown to yellowish white in color), interspersed with flexible transverse bands.
A flat plate covers the head from nose tip to crown; the tail is
safeguarded by a series of hard rings. This mail-clad, piglike
animal is about 30 inches long, 7 inches in height, and weighs
from 12 to 17 pounds.

Picture, if you can, a creature similar in all respects, but
having the proportions of a modern-day rhinoceros. This was

the ancestor of the armadillo that roved the plains of South America eons ago. A smaller version of the original armadillo is now found from Patagonia to Texas and Louisiana. It is the nine-banded armadillo, one of the larger members of the present-day family and the only species living in the United States.

The front of its mouth is devoid of teeth. The existing molars are rootless pegs, lacking in enamel, which continue to grow as they are worn down. A relative of sloths and ant-eaters, it too is equipped with a long, sticky tongue for capturing its favorite food, insects. Ants, including fire ants, and their eggs; roaches; cane borers; termites; scarab beetles and their larvae; wireworms; centipedes; grasshoppers; and other destructive insects make up 90 per cent of its diet. The armadillo's hunger for ants, which assail freshly hatched chicks, has been to the advantage of quail and other bird populations. Scorpions, tarantulas, snake eggs, and occasionally an unwary salamander add variety to its nutritional intake. Fungi (especially puffballs), blackberries, mulberries, and wild plums are also part of the armadillo's fare. In searching for insects it moves erratically, sometimes walking, sometimes trotting, pushing its long, pointed snout into loose soil and plowing a furrow about 4 inches deep. After locating an insect beneath the soil through its sense of smell, it quickly digs a hole with its front feet, grunting softly as it labors. At times it sits up on its hind legs, propping itself with its tail, to inspect plants for insects and berries. It also assumes this position when sniffing the air for danger.

Despite its armor, the armadillo is a good swimmer. Should it estimate that the width of a waterway is not sufficient to warrant the effort of swimming, it will nonchalantly stroll across the bottom to the farther side. If it finds that one deep breath is not providing enough oxygen for the crossing, it feverishly paddles its short legs until, reaching the surface, it can gulp in air. When it has taken in enough, the buoyed body relaxes, and the armadillo swims vigorously toward its destination.

As far as land locomotion is concerned, the armadillo can

most times outrun a man by weaving through underbrush. And fortunate this is, for the nine-banded armadillo, when threatened, is not sufficiently armored to find protection by rolling up tightly, as can its South American cousins. The armadillo is not adequately forewarned of menace through the senses of hearing and eyesight, for both are poor. Therefore, speed is its only recourse. Once in the safe refuge of tangled brush, it digs frantically, the two large middle claws on its front feet gouging the earth. Upon disappearing into this emergency tunnel, the armadillo arches its body, and the plates become embedded in the soil. So tenaciously does it maintain a hold that extricating the animal is almost impossible. If the creature is cornered, with no opportunity for rapid digging, lacerating claws and offensive odor from a pair of anal glands are its only means of defense.

Though the armadillo favors the protection of tall grasses and thickets, it appreciates limestone formations where ready-made burrows have been created by seeping water. If such a prefabricated dwelling is not handy, the armadillo sets to work excavating one himself. The earth is first loosened with its pointed snout and forefeet. After a small heap of soil has accumulated under its belly, it balances on its forefeet and tail and, with arched back, brings its hind feet over the pile and with a quick backward kick scatters the dirt to a distance of several feet. Digging a few more inches at a time, it continues the same routine. The completed tunnel is about 8 inches in diameter and can be as long as 25 feet, though it is usually shorter. At the enlarged end, roughly 1½ feet in diameter, the nest is made. The armadillo gathers nest material—grass, mesquite leaves, or weeds—composing it into small bundles with its forefeet. Pushing these back into the area between the raised body and hind legs, it lowers its shell, clamping the material securely. Slowly working its way backward into the tunnel, picking up any fallen litter with mouth and forefeet, it deposits the bedding at the nest site. The nest is actually no more than a heap into which the armadillo wriggles.

With few exceptions, a mother armadillo consistently bears

four babies. The offspring are all of the same sex, identical down to the smallest detail—the size, shape, and number of scales, the number of hairs sprinkled on their tiny bellies, etc. Armadillo young enter the world with wide-open eyes and are otherwise well developed, though their shell is as pliable at first as soft leather. Since they do not change their shells periodically through life, as do lobsters or crabs, the armor does not harden completely until they are fully grown. Within several hours after birth, these miniature replicas of their parents are able to toddle after the mother to explore for insects. Equipped with exactly the appropriate number of breasts, four, the mother nurses her "quadruplicates" for the first two months.

The armadillo usually has several dens, sometimes as many as ten. Those with very shallow tunnels are used to lure insects, whereas the larger ones serve as emergency refuges. The armadillo is gregarious and generous of nature and often shares its home with other animals—opossums, rabbits, and rats. Abandoned armadillo tunnels provide shelter for skunks, rabbits, burrowing owls, opossums, and minks.

Prolonged periods of severe cold can prove fatal to the armadillo. It does not hibernate and must seek sustenance. Those armadillos which do not freeze to death in their dens find digging in frozen soil for food a futile effort: most of the surface-dwelling insects that would suffice as nourishment have perished from the cold. Therefore, the armadillo either starves to death or expires from defenselessness against the elements. It is better able to tolerate extreme heat by remaining in underground shelter and confining its search for food to the cooler hours of evening. Its eyes are well suited for nocturnal hunting.

The armadillo is a sociable animal. When captured, it is easily tamed and makes an unusual, interesting, and clean pet, uncommonly exempt from parasites, such as fleas, lice, or ticks.

After the Civil War, armadillos were not a familiar sight in Texas outside of the Rio Grande Valley. With the spread of civilization, however, and resulting decrease in their natural enemies, the animals ranged farther and farther northeast. Shortly before the turn of the century they had reached the Brazos River, and by the first quarter of the twentieth century they had entered Oklahoma, Louisiana, and Arkansas. Even prior to the construction of bridges spanning the Mississippi River, they began to appear on the east bank. The animal has been gradually increasing its range and is now found as far east as Florida.

All armadillos look and act alike; at maturity their size and weight are the same. So to see one armadillo is truly to have seen them all. Though their physical selves and habits seem to be Xeroxed copies of one another, perhaps each individual's personality is unique—at least to its mate!

The shells of armadillos have long been turned into ornamental baskets by craftsmen. The value of their meat also should not be overlooked. It is a favorite food with dogs, cayotes, peccaries, and other carnivores. Country folk often find its porklike flavor delicious. One old-timer in Texas insists that the only way to serve the white, tender meat of the armadillo is to barbecue it over an open campfire and then flavor each juicy morsel with hot chili sauce.

Badger: Grave Robber?

When you see dirt flying through the air for yards, propelled by the short legs of a flattened-appearing animal with retroussé nose, you are witnessing the now-you-see-me, now-you-don't vanishing act of the badger. This large, grayish animal is ideally adapted to digging, using all four feet and its mouth to burrow beneath the ground in a matter of seconds. When completely buried, it clogs up the hole behind a disappearing tail. If cornered, it slashes with long, powerful claws and knife-like teeth set in strong jaws. Because of this ferocity and the ability to disappear into the earth almost in the wink of an eye, few animals willingly assault it. However, in England dogs were deliberately set against badgers, the sport being known as badger-baiting, or badger-drawing. By the mid-1800's this unfortunate pastime was prohibited. From it comes the expression "to badger," meaning to tease or worry a weaker opponent. An attacker has difficulty in grasping the badger firmly with its teeth, because of the heavy fur and loose skin. Thick neck and shoulder muscles on the sturdy, low-slung body protect nerves and arteries. When angered the badger hisses a warning to the world.

A body 30 inches long and weighing 15 pounds, supported on bowed legs with pigeon-toed feet, does not exactly evoke the picture of a fastidious dandy. Nonetheless, when it comes to nails, the badger is fastidious indeed. It gives itself frequent manicures and pedicures, leaving not a trace of dirt beneath the nails or between the toes. The blackish face is distinguished by a white stripe over the forehead and a white crescent behind and encircling each eyes. These facial markings led our ancestors to call the animal "bageard," meaning one who wears a badge.

The badger's long claws are used not only for defense but as a means of securing food. By digging faster than its prey, underground inhabitants such as marmots and moles, it overtakes and devours them. In the northern and eastern parts of the United States, the badger feeds on ground squirrels, field mice, deer mice, rabbits, insects, and ground-nesting birds and their eggs; in the Southwest, prairie dogs, pocket gophers, kangaroo rats, wood rats, mice, insects, and lizards make up the diet. In the open country of the West, horn sheaths shed by the antelope and made soft by rain or snow find favor with hungry badgers.

During the mating season, in autumn or early winter, the male badger—in skunklike fashion—raises his short tail and discharges an odoriferous secretion when courting the object of his affection. One litter per year is produced, averaging three in number. At four to six weeks of age, the babies' eyes open in their nest of dried grasses in a chamber 2 to 6 feet beneath the ground, located at the end of a long tunnel. When half grown they are weaned, after which the mother supplies solid food until they are two-thirds grown. From then on they are capable of accompanying her on foraging trips. Since the father undertakes no responsibility for the young, the mother must, perforce, be an even fiercer, more competent fighter. By the following autumn, young badgers are almost fully grown and can hunt for themselves. The family then breaks up. Their substantial appetites require a more extensive food range for them to survive.

The badger goes into winter well padded with fat. Actually it does not hibernate but retires underground below the frost line, shoving dirt back up the tunnel to prevent drafts. Nature helps the animal to survive the winter by curtailing the desire for food and keeping it drowsy. From time to time, nudged from napping by appetite, the badger emerges for food. If fortunate enough to find an abundance, it buries the surplus, digging some up when necessary. A rather unsocial creature, the badger leaves its burrow after sundown, a lonely hunter in the night.

Not only is the badger a facile swimmer, but on land it can travel backward almost as swiftly and easily as forward.

It is an affectionate pet when caught while small. Perhaps because it is relieved of self-responsibility, in captivity it is carefree to the point of prancing and skipping about.

Among some country folk the badger has been indicted as a grave robber. The animal favors sandy hillocks, where digging is less difficult and rodents tend to abide. Coincidentally, sites of this sort were chosen by early American settlers for burial places. During the badger's energetic excavating for food, skulls and bones would often fly about with the loosened dirt. However, I feel sure that satisfying its hunger, not robbing graves, was the badger's sole aim.

Because badger hairs maintain a fine point, they are used for shaving brushes, for good-quality artist's brushes, and for pointing up lower grades of fox fur. Besides serving man with its usable hair, the badger is influential in reducing the rodent population that consumes grain and other crops. It is one of Nature's best natural exterminators.

Beaver: Environmentalist

Eons ago a gigantic rodent, 8 feet in height and weighing 700 pounds, lumbered over the earth. The sole descendant of this immense creature is our present-day beaver.

Indians regarded the animal with profound respect. Cherokee legend has it that the Great Spirit enlisted the help of giant beavers to create the world.

The beaver is North America's largest, cleanest, cleverest rodent. It can grow to 4 feet in length, the tail being one-third of this dimension, and weigh as much as 60 pounds. In captivity a beaver survives approximately nineteen years; in the wild it seldom exceeds twelve years of age. An oddity in the world of mammals, the beaver, like reptiles, continues to grow until death.

The heavy body, supported on short legs, is covered with fur composed of two types of hair: one, silky, gray, and close set, the guard hairs; the other, coarser, longer, and reddish brown in color, the woolly undercoat.

For years old-time woodsmen and trappers said that the teeth of beavers were orange. Folks who fancied themselves knowledgeable about such matters labeled this a myth. However, improbable as it sounds, the beaver's teeth *are* orange; the four front incisors are covered with bright-orange enamel, their backs being of softer dentine. Since the dentine wears away faster than the enameled sides, constant gnawing hones the incisors to chisellike sharpness. The lower incisors, grinding against the upper teeth, also help to keep them keen edged. With such admirable equipment the beaver is capable of felling a tree 10 feet in circumference. Because the teeth grow continuously, they are never eroded away. Between the four incisors in front and the remainder of the teeth lies a considerable gap. Enough space is afforded so that two folds of skin can converge behind the incisors, sealing off the rest of the mouth. For this reason the beaver can gnaw down a tree without risking a mouthful of splinters and can chew under water without danger of drowning. Early pioneers believed that powdered beavers' teeth served in soup would cure almost any ailment.

Both nose and ears are valvular, closing as the beaver submerges. By being positioned on the sides of the nose, the nostrils are spared direct water pressure when the animal dives. The transparent lids of the eyes furnish the beaver with a pair of underwater goggles.

The other end of the animal is as functionally designed as are the eyes, ears, and teeth. The broad, flat, scaly tail, 12 inches long, 6 inches wide, and almost an inch thick, serves three main purposes: when the beaver is swimming, it is used as a rudder and, sometimes, a diving plane; it provides a convenient prop to lean back on when the beaver is gnawing a tree; in times of danger it works as an alarm signal, being slapped loudly against the water's surface.

The back feet have five fully webbed toes. The claw of the second hind toe is split and serves as a comb. Upon emerging from the water, the beaver preens his fur with this double nail, using oil from its castor glands as a grooming aid.

This oil, castoreum, is a creamy, bitter orange-brown substance. It is a secretion of many uses, for both beaver and man.

In addition to being used for grooming, castoreum helps the animal to communicate with other beavers by sign heaps. These are small mud patties which the beaver forms and places in strategic spots in the shallows or along the shore, moistening them with castoreum. They mark the boundaries of beaver territory or announce the beaver's presence to the opposite sex. This musky substance also plays an important role in mating. The beavers' love-making takes place in an intoxicating cloud of musk.

Beaver musk, so stimulating during coupling, possesses such tantalizing properties that for generations trappers have employed it as a bait to catch a variety of animals, for almost all animals are attracted to its scent. Early American settlers used castoreum as a remedy for a long list of afflictions, including hiccups, apoplexy, deafness, poor eyesight, colic, and sciatica. Man has long used castoreum as a base for expensive perfume. It possesses the quality of retaining a fragrance until warmth of the body releases it.

The industrious and gregarious beaver is one of the few animals able to alter their environment. To make a pond a suitable habitat, the beaver constructs a dam in the stream feeding it, both upstream and down. The dam may be crooked or straight, from several to 100 yards long, and from 1 to 12 feet high. Its purpose is to maintain a constant water level in the pool and prevent its freezing to the bottom. The beaver is then assured of reaching its underwater larder of wood and bark throughout the winter months.

To start the dam, the beaver cuts willow and alder limbs, transporting them to the stream's bottom and arranging them with the stub ends pointing upstream. To this are added mud, gravel, and stones, followed by another layer of saplings plus more mud and stones, until the desired height is reached. The beaver sometimes constructs canals to float its cuttings to the pond. These canals are more common in the western part of the country than in the East; they may be as long as 750 feet, having two or three water levels. When it comes to repairing the dam, the male takes the initiative, though all family members share in the work. Leaks are repaired on the upstream side.

The beaver's lodge is built of the same materials as the dam, and both are constructed in the autumn. The animal seems to prefer working at night. Before starting its noisy labor of felling trees, the beaver—according to the Indians—posts a sentinel. When a menace nears, the heavy tail is slapped loudly on the water as a warning, and the beavers dive to safety. To fell a tree, the beaver first notches the trunk and then removes a piece of wood about three inches below the notch. Saplings are cut through from one side; larger trees, from two sides; very large trees are brought down by cutting around the entire circumference of the trunk. Louis Viccinelli of Mississippi says that, contrary to popular belief, the beaver is not able to control the direction of the tree's fall and must scurry to safety at the final gnaw.

Limbs are chewed from the trunks and stacked in mounds under water. These reach from 6 to 7 feet in height and more than 30 feet in diameter. The one large room within is lined with grass; the outside is plastered with mud, which freezes as hard as stone, protecting the inhabitants from enemies, such as wolves. The spacious room is left both floorless and roofless until the dam is completed, raising the water level. The lodge is built to accommodate the beaver couple and its last two litters. At the age of two, being on the brink of maturity, the young are driven from the family to prevent overpopulation. Passageways leading to the lodge are dug downward through a bank into the water. Not all beavers dwell in lodges; some, at least temporarily, may inhabit burrows that open under water, which they dig in the banks of streams.

When lodge and dam are completed, the beaver sets to work building up his winter food supply. In the pond's muddy bottom near the lodge, it infixes branches and tree trunks of poplar, aspen, cottonwood, and willow, using the bark as food through the long, cold months. They are submerged deeply enough to prevent their being frozen in ice. Each beaver requires from 20 to 30 ounces of bark per day for food.

The beaver's extra-large lungs and liver permit it to stay under water for periods of fifteen minutes or to swim submerged to a distance of one-half mile or more. Upon returning to the surface for air, the animal renews 75 per cent of its lungs' content, in contrast to the renewal of the 15 to 20 per cent in man's lungs. During swimming, nine-tenths of the body is beneath water. The front legs, unused for locomotion in water, are folded back under the chest. The hind legs alone, moving simultaneously, drive the animal forward. By employing only its tail, it can paddle along at slow speed.

When the ice thaws, beavers leave their lodge for a rambling existence, feeding on berries and aquatic plants. Roots of water lilies are real gourmet fare to the beaver. The father beaver usually stays away from his family in summer, rejoining it in autumn.

European hatters, long before America's pelts were available, used the fur of beavers on their own continent, finding that it was easily incorporated with felt because of its infinitesimal barbs. In England all hats had to be fashioned from beaver fur by royal decree. The pelts were much sought after and highly valued by European noblemen.

The widespread demand for this product in Europe made it imperative that new sources be found. Because beavers were far more plentiful in North America than abroad, much of the exploration of this continent was due to the search for their pelts. Thus the beaver played a major role in opening up the North American continent.

The French, seeking pelts, explored along the St. Lawrence and westward through Canada. The Dutch combed the Hudson River Valley. The English chartered the Hudson's Bay Company, whose men scoured the Far West for beavers long before gold was discovered there. The beaver pelt soon became a unit of barter: 1 pelt equaled 1 pound of tobacco, 2 axes, or a kettle; 6 pelts equaled a fancy lace coat; 12 pelts, a long rifle. The Hudson's Bay Company became famed not only for its success in trapping beavers, but also for its manufacture of fine blankets. Black bars woven into their edges represented the number of pelts at which each was valued.

Until the early 1800's, beavers were trapped by deadfalls and snares. Then the steel trap was invented, increasing catches. The quest for beavers continued for three centuries until beaver hats were no longer fashionable. By this time the beaver population was heavily depleted. In 1900 protective measures were advocated by conservationists, and since that time the population has increased.

The beaver was not valued for its fur alone. Many found its flesh very palatable. The front part of this semiaquatic animal was considered meat; the nether parts, usually submerged, were looked upon as fish and, therefore, could be eaten on fast days as Lenten food. Beaver meat is said to have a porklike flavor.

The red man too enjoyed the beaver's flesh, especially its large, flat tail. The Indians held that the manner in which one treated the dead animal's bones would determine later success or failure in hunting it. The souls of defunct beavers visited the men who had killed them to ascertain the fate of their bones. If they discovered dogs chewing on them, the offense was indignantly reported to other beavers. They would then make themselves less available to their hunters in the future. It was the consensus among Indians that the beaver was satisfied to have his bones thrown into either fire or a river.

The Indians utilized beaver pelts for warm clothing, stitching the skins together for robes. Traders soon discovered that used Indian beaver robes were superior to new skins, because they were saturated with the oils which the red men rubbed on their bodies. Indians were much amused by the exorbitant prices willingly paid for their used clothing.

The beaver has donated more to the world than its pelt. Its dams, by stopping the outflow of silt, create areas of richly fertile, arable land. For this reason such silted areas were highly valued by North America's pioneers, who termed them "beaver meadows." The beaver acts as a conscientious environmentalist by reclaiming land along streams in wasteland areas. Had the beaver been properly protected during the past three hundred years, the value of its flood-control work would have outweighed the total worth of all pelts seized.

Fox Facts

A group of foxes is known as a skulk. In North America there are the red fox, the gray, the Arctic fox, and the kit fox—cross foxes, black foxes, and silver being color phases of the red fox.

Have you ever wondered whether foxes climb trees? Red do not, but gray foxes are able to climb as easily as a cat and can go up a perfectly straight tree trunk.

Fox fare consists of field mice, wood rats, rabbits, wild grapes, various berries, some game birds, insects, frogs, and shellfish.

If someone labels you foxy, accept it as a compliment! The fox is a clever creature who has learned to outwit man on numerous occasions. When being pursued by hunters and hounds he has devised many cunning means to break the line of scent left on the soil by his paws, even to jumping upon the backs of sheep.

Pet owners might well wish that their dogs would adopt the following custom developed by the fox to rid himself of fleas. Holding a tuft of fur or piece of wood between his teeth, he will slowly submerge himself in a pond, tail first, gradually driving the frantic fleas to seek refuge on the only thing remaining above water—the wool or wood. The fox then allows the parasite-ridden object to float away from him and, well groomed, swims to the nearest bank.

In Pennsylvania, Matt Sikes says folks have a sure-fire scheme for foiling a fox. Across a field plow a furrow. Set No. 2 traps along it, and cover them with soil. He'll trot into one of them every time, as he can't pass up the opportunity to walk on newly plowed ground. Since foxes don't hibernate, they are as active in the winter months as in summer. So you can trap one at any season—if you can outwit him!

The Prancing Porcupine

If some morning you wake up to find your ax, hoe, or shovel missing its handle, there's no need for assistance from the sheriff to solve the mystery: the culprit is probably the porcupine. Its strong desire for salt drives it to consume anything bearing a trace of it, even a trace so slight as that left by human perspiration. With its powerful incisor teeth, the porcupine will devour sweat-stained saddles and harness or barrels in which salted meat had once been stored, though but a hint of salt be found there.

The porcupine is a squat, heavy-bodied animal with stiff quills scattered through its fur. The quills are actually hairs modified into sharp spines; like hair, they can be replaced when lost. Erect only in fear or anger, the quills normally lie passively along the back and sides, protected by coarse guard hairs. They are loosely fastened to the skin by a slender base. When threatened, the porcupine thrashes its tail wildly, sending loosened quills flying. From this action developed the myth that the porcupine could truly eject, or "shoot," its quills at will. Under attack it assumes this typical defensive posture: drawing its feet together, it hunches down close to the ground and, by a contraction of the skin, erects all of its 25,000 to 30,000 quills, thus appearing twice its size. As the porcupine flails its tail, ever moving backward into its attacker, the quills become embedded in the assailant's flesh. The structure of the quill is such that it can move by itself into the victim's body. From one-half to 5 inches in length, the quills are equipped with thousands of diamond-shaped scales on their black tips which induce them to progress deeper into the flesh, furthered by the victim's muscle movement. Many a large animal has been found dead with internal organs punctured by porcupine quills.

One old-timer vows that you can safely pick up a disturbed porcupine, in spite of its quills, if you proceed in the right way. When the tail has stopped moving, grasp the long hairs that extend past the tail quills and tug hard. This action, according to Paul English of Texas, causes the animal to try to pull out of your grip, neither backing nor biting. Because the possibility exists that the porcupine may not be aware of the behavior expected of him, I don't really recommend that you try this method of capture. A porcupine's powerful incisor teeth can nip off a finger at one bite.

To the nearsighted porcupine, anything more than 6 feet away appears as a shadow. But the animal does not rely on eyes alone to encounter the fairer sex. Using its nose, it snuffs along the ground and up tree trunks for that very particular porcupine odor—much like that of a fruit salad, with the aroma of pineapple predominating.

Porcupine babies are referred to as porcupettes. While they are yet in the womb, their quills, overlaid with silky hairs, are soft and moist. At birth, when helped from the fetal sac by the mother, the porcupette erects its quills several times to encourage drying. They become dry and harden after a period of fifteen minutes in the air. The baby porcupine makes its appearance in the world in a very well-developed state, weighing more than a pound. Within two days it is able to make its way up tree trunks and feast on leaves and tender shoots. A porcupette is easily tamed and soon learns to respond to its owner.

What the porcupine lacks in eyesight is compensated for by its acute hearing. In spite of other sounds in its vicinity, it can detect a whisper at 30 feet.

Slow and awkward, the porcupine ambles along at a sluggish rate, its jauntiest pace only equaling a human's leisurely sauntering. When under attack, a porcupine tucks in its nose as much as possible, for the nose is so sensitive that its being struck by a stick could cause the death of the animal. These two characteristics of the porcupine, slowness of movement and sensitivity of nose, are a boon to a lost camper or hiker, ill from hunger. The porcupine is easily overtaken, and a blow on the nose from stick or stone will quickly dispatch it.

In winter should you come upon trees with trunks bare of bark to a great height, you may be in the feeding areas of porcupines. During that season their diet consists solely of the inner bark of hardwoods and evergreens. In spring they favor the sap-filled cambium (a soft layer of formative tissue under the bark) of maples, especially of the sugar maple. Tree-dwelling porcupines almost never descend to the ground to quench their thirst; they obtain moisture from dew and the juice of leaves.

Few animals care to contend with the porcupine, with the exception of the fisher, a large marten known also as the North

American sable, or black fox. It is about 20 inches in length and weighs approximately 20 pounds. The fisher successfully flips the porcupine over on its back and attacks the soft belly. Any quills it may swallow somehow pass through its digestive tract without piercing the stomach lining. Quills that become embedded in its hide do not penetrate far, because an underlying layer of skin and muscle forces them to work their way back out.

The fisher's name is misleading, since the animal rarely fishes. If, however, you enjoy fishing frequently, a porcupine can be responsible for increasing your catch. For still-fishing, the very lightest bobber available should be used; a porcupine's quill, being hollow, has the required buoyancy. To the back tip, the pointed end of the quill, fasten a loop of fine wire— either copper or brass. Turn the loop, using an inch of the wire to fasten it securely to the quill. Run the line through the loop. Blacky Adams says that the quill bobber responds so sensitively to the most delicate touch that at least fifty per cent more fish are caught by its use.

The porcupine has an odd, rather appealing custom rarely witnessed by humans. An adult animal, despite its bulky 10 to 25 pounds of weight, stands on hind legs and tail, rhythmically swaying from side to side, while lifting and stamping the hind feet. In an attempt to explain this baffling behavior, naturalists conjectured that it is done to burn up excess energy. Some country folks who have witnessed this prancing think that the porcupine is simply dancing to music that humans can't hear.

Possum: Unintelligent and Unique

When the word *marsupial* is mentioned, people tend to think of a female animal with a pouch. Features that characterize all members of this order are particular bones—marsupial bones— attached to the female's pelvis, a lower jaw that curves inward at the posterior end, and a very primitive brain.

For hundreds and millions of years marsupials inhabited all

land areas. Today they exist in only a few places, among them the United States. Our only native North American marsupial is that unique but rather stupid animal, the opossum. It was the first pouch-bearer that Western civilization encountered. From 1500 onward it was a subject of amazement and growing surmise, inspiring poetry, fables, folklore, and legends. Zoologists of the time regarded the opossum as simply another peculiar beast, failing to realize that it was a different type of animal life.

Captain John Smith of the Jamestown colony in Virginia was responsible for the name by which it is known. *Opossum* is a rendering of the Algonquian Indian word *apasum*, meaning "white animal," for the opossum has a pointed face covered with soft, short white hair. In most parts of the country it is commonly known as the possum.

In striking contrast to the white face are the prominent jet-black shiny eyeballs surrounded by a dusky area. Because the iris is visible only in very bright light, which the opossum avoids, the eye is all pupil, suited to the animal's twilight and nocturnal habits. It does not have good eyesight and is thought to be lacking in color vision.

Well-developed whiskers help animals to avoid bumping into objects. The opossum has two groups of long, stiff whiskers located on either side of the face, one group sprouting on the cheeks, the other near the snout. At the base of these bristles is a highly sensitive nerve complex; the slightest touch triggers a defensive reaction.

The long, sharp-pointed snout is provided with an adequate sense of smell. It is of major importance in foraging for food.

The thin black ears, rounded and hairless, have been likened to those of a bat and are sometimes, as in the Virginia opossum, banded on the tips with white. The outer ear serves not only for hearing but also for shutting the ear canal against the intrusion of insects while the animal slumbers.

A coat of gray to yellowish white covers the thick, rounded body, 2½ to 3 feet in length and weighing from 8 to 15 pounds. Oiliness renders the soft, dense underfur impermeable to rain, so that the skin beneath remains moisture free. Protective overhairs, long and coarse, reduce wearing of this underfur, which keeps the opossum both warm and dry.

Though clumsy when walking—waddling along in a ponderous, shuffling gait on short legs—the opossum is adept at climbing, because of its well-developed dark paws and gripping tail. The five toes of the front feet are provided with white claws as sharp as those of a squirrel. The big toe on the hind feet, nailless and flexible, serves as a thumb, enabling the opossum to grasp branches firmly. This opposable first digit is a feature the opossum shares with man and apes. Except for the hairy base, the tail is covered with small scales—the first half being black, the remainder, white. Loosely wrapped around a bough, the tail is of great value when the animal is traversing a tree limb. Should the branch be shaken and the opossum slip, the tail immediately tightens, safely anchoring the animal. Young possums, weighing little, suspend themselves more easily than do adults.

The tail is borne in a downward, curled-under position. People find the tail a convenience when picking up the animal, using it as a handle. When being transported by it, the opossum is perfectly capable of climbing up its own tail and will bite the hand holding it. One should carry the animal by the tail with one hand and firmly seize the nape of the neck with the other.

To satisfy its chief needs—water, food, and shelter—the opossum chooses to live along wooded stream beds where hunting and fishing are good. In seeking a den for safe drowsing during daylight hours, it selects a cavity in a hollow tree, a secluded nook under a wood pile, a rock crevice, or a vacated squirrel nest. If these are not available, it may move in underground with an armadillo or skunk or take over an abandoned den, not being itself a dexterous digger.

The possum always lines its lodgings with grass and dead leaves. In the Deep South where trees bearded with Spanish moss abound, it filches these festoons for its nest. The bedding material is transported in a unique manner. After gathering mouthfuls of dry grass and leaves, the opossum shoves them under its body, where the prehensile tail is readied in a loop to receive them. Roughly seven mouthfuls make a good loopful. The possum then makes its way home, dragging the load of bedding along behind in the curled tail. Among country people of the South, a legend has survived concerning the nest material of this unusual little animal. It is said that the female possum, shortly before giving birth, gathers suitable bedding with her mate. She then lies upon her back while the male piles the grass and leaves between her paws. He drags her home by the tail, her body serving as a sort of sled.

Pregnancy for the possum is a scant twelve days and eighteen hours. The babies, extremely premature at birth, urgently seek the haven of the mother's pouch, which acts as a kind of incubator while they are continuing to develop.

Prior to giving birth (January or February in the South, later in the North) the mother becomes restless, and sitting on her haunches, the tail extending forward between her legs, she commences to ready her pouch for the young. From time to time, inserting her muzzle, she cleans it with her tongue. The babies do not travel the length of the two vaginal canals but take a short cut directly down the middle, a new birth passage being forced through the tissue connecting them. Each baby makes its appearance capsulated in a membrane filled with fluid, from which it is freed by the mother's tongue. The female opossum does not actively aid her young in their 3-inch-long journey to the pouch, but by moistening the furry route over which they struggle, she facilitates their progress. The babies are extremely underdeveloped—so tiny that the entire litter can nest in a teaspoon, and their transparent bodies weigh a total of about one-fifteenth of an ounce. The internal organs are visible through the skin, and eyes and ears are not yet completely formed. Though blind, they instinctively work their way upward toward the pouch, depending totally on the well-developed front legs, armed with strong claws, for locomotion. The immature hind legs are still nothing more than stubs.

The pouch is small, with a strong muscle at the rim, enabling the mother to close it at will. Within are thirteen teats no bigger than the heads of straight pins. Since the usual litter consists of eighteen to twenty young, some are destined to perish from starvation. Once safely in the confines of the pouch, the young explore for a nipple, and the luckier ones quickly attach themselves to it with the aid of their powerful tongues. Sucking starts immediately, and within an hour the nipple's length is doubled. Little by little it becomes elongated, acting not only as a conduit for nourishment but also as a tether for wider mobility. For weeks the baby possums cling constantly to the teats. At this stage they have no functioning mechanism to control their body temperature, so they must depend upon their mother's body heat for warmth. The sharp deciduous claws, so essential for the hazardous climb to the pouch, are now unneeded and drop off. At one month the babies peep from the pouch, their first view being the grass-lined interior of their den. By two months they are approximately the size of mice.

During hunting trips the mother closes her pouch to prevent the babies from toppling out. She searches the treetops for birds and their eggs. Possums are good swimmers, and should the mother navigate a watercourse, the young will be safe and dry in their watertight compartment, the closed pouch. Before long the babes are mature enough to leave the sheltering pouch and view the world from their mother's back, clinging to her coarse fur. During the days following weaning, they are most vulnerable as prey for meat-eaters: hawks, owls, coyotes, bobcats, foxes, and wolves. At three months the little possums are capable of fending for themselves.

Opossums passively accept the intrusion of others of their kind on their home territory or hunting range. Though meat is preferred, they eat a varied menu of insects, small mammals (such as moles and mice), snakes, lizards, frogs, crayfish, snails, fish, birds and their eggs, mushrooms, berries, grapes, apples, persimmons, pawpaws, greenbrier, field corn, and even carrion.

When cornered, the opossum bares its many teeth, set in

powerful jaws. While confronting an antagonist, it coils and uncoils its tail, which serves as a sort of defense mechanism because of its resemblance to a snake. The customary means of protection is feigning death, or "playing possum." The opossum falls on its side, inert, pulse and heartbeat lowered. Closed eyes and lolling tongue complete the deceptive picture of death. When the enemy leaves the scene, the opossum returns to its normal state. This action has sometimes been attributed to cleverness and cunning on the part of the opossum. Jack Denton Scott of Connecticut, however, believes that "the possum isn't playing"—it is out cold with fright.

The animal does not truly hibernate but roams about during the cooler months until a cold spell strikes. Then, insulated by its considerable fat, it rolls up in leaves in some hole and there remains torpid for a few weeks.

Because possums have spurred the imagination of man over a period of four centuries, a great deal of folklore exists concerning this common yet extraordinary little animal. The forked penis of the possum is doubtless responsible for the long-held belief that copulation took place through the female's nostrils, those openings being the only obviously visible dual orifices. Since the mother was frequently seen pushing her snout into the pouch shortly before delivery, country people believed she was blowing the babies out of her nose into it. This belief was strengthened when soon thereafter babies were discovered in the pouch. The American Indian supposed that the young were not only bred in the pouch but conceived there, and not inside the female's body. Early American settlers and explorers, perplexed by the external pouch, presumed that young were born in it, somehow growing from the female's nipples and then breaking off.

Generations ago, medicinal properties were ascribed to the possum's tail. A woman suffering unduly prolonged labor was given a broth of the tail to bring about immediate delivery. The broth was also considered a remedy for constipation, a severe cough, and distress of the kidneys. For the easy removal of a thorn, a piece of the possum's tail was thoroughly chewed and then held on the spot where the spine was embedded.

The possum's white flesh has long been considered palatable but fat by country people. As a first step in preparing the possum for cooking, they recommend the removal of all the fat around the kidneys, which is presumed to be the source of the animal's offensive odor.

Lacking intelligence, possums are easily caught in traps. Those caught this way are not nearly as savory as the ones hauled down from a tree. The trauma of injury produces changes in the body which influence the flavor of the meat. Anyone who cooks possum seems to have his own idea as to how this should be done, but all cooks agree that sweet potatoes are essential to a possum feast.

The possum is not an animal one would recommend as a pet. Being nocturnal, it is sluggish and unresponsive by day. The animal is dirty in its personal habits and has a repellent odor. In spite of not indulging in self-grooming, it is surprisingly free of ticks and fleas. Because of its small brain, the opossum exhibits a rather dull personality.

Despite the animal's defense of "playing possum" and its remarkable ability to recover from injury, its life expectancy is short. Yet the breed has continued to expand its range, possibly because it eats anything—animal or vegetable—and reproduces prolifically.

Raccoon or Screech Owl?

The raccoon, better known most places as coon, exists nowhere in the world but in North America. Though it is found through the northern United States and Canada, it is not a cold-climate creature; it is most widely spread throughout the southern states and more temperate parts of the West Coast.

Since much of the raccoon's diet comes from the water, it generally makes its nest in forest areas less than a mile from a stream or lake. It prefers to reside high in a hollow tree. Though a nocturnal meanderer and hunter, by day it enjoys draping itself in the crotch of a tree to sun-bathe. Sure-footed in trees, it uses them not only as lodgings but as a haven when threatened.

An excellent tree-climber, the raccoon is not a swift runner. When hunted, it relies upon clever tactics invented spontaneously to fit the circumstances, intelligence compensating for its lack of speed. An old, wise coon has been known to draw a pursuing dog into water, climb on its head, and drown it. Often as cunning as a fox, the raccoon may destroy its trail by wading along the edge of a stream or crossing fallen logs. It will even, as a last recourse, dive into water. When cornered, it defends itself by cutting and slashing at its attacker.

If a hollow tree is not available for living quarters, the raccoon uses the abandoned dens of other animals. Trees being scarce on the plains of Central Texas, here the coon lives in large rock crevices or the burrows of skunks and badgers. In New Mexico and Arizona it finds water and shelter in canyon cliffs.

A relative of the giant panda, the raccoon is a bushy-haired animal some 30 to 36 inches long, weighing from 10 to 25 pounds. Its pointed face is marked with a black band across the cheeks and eyes and a streak running from forehead to nose. The black mask serves as protective coloration, making the black eyes more difficult to detect in a fight. The fur coloring ranges from gray to brown and blackish. Six or seven black bands ring the yellow-gray tail.

The raccoon tends toward gluttony but is redeemed from uncouthness by its dainty manner of eating, facilitated by delicate front paws equipped with long, marvelously dexterous fingers. Its diet varies from fresh-water foods to nuts and fruits, vegetables, and birds and their eggs. Full-sized mussels usually prove too great a challenge to the raccoon, which finds smaller mollusks easier to crush and eat. It customarily washes muddy frogs, turtles, crayfish, and clams prior to consuming them. Science has given the coon the Latin name of *lotor*, meaning "the washer," and its name in German is *Waschbär*. Several theories to explain the habit have been put forth. Some naturalists believe that the raccoon is not so much washing its food as dipping it for the sensory satisfaction of feeling the food under water with its sensitive fingers. Another, and perhaps more valid theory, is offered by John Brazier of California. He believes that the raccoon softens and dampens its food whenever possible to help swallowing. It is reported, however, that where water wasn't available, raccoons have been observed "washing" their food in dust.

In April the raccoon's undercoat becomes less heavy and the outer guard hairs thinner. The first signs of the developing winter coat become evident in late August.

Since food is scarce in northern winters, several coon families, for both warmth and sociability, will snuggle down to sleep in a den. From time to time, during less severe spells, they are stirred from slumber by quickening appetites and venture forth to catch mice, rabbits, and other prey.

The urge to mate also rouses the raccoon from slumber. Mating takes place in December in the South, during February in the North. Nine weeks later, four to five blind young are born, complete with masks and furry coats. At three weeks their eyes are open, and at two months they are able to sally forth on short hunting trips with their mother.

At sunset mother and young, with flat-footed gait, make their way to the margin of a stream to explore shallow pools for their favorite food, crayfish. Their tapering, agile fingers flip over rocks to reveal insects, mussels, and snails. Coon babies are instructed in the delicate art of catching frogs and slower-swimming fish. Slippery earthworms that emerge after a summer shower are easily picked up with their long black fingers. Crumbling rotten logs are investigated for grubs; crickets are pounced upon in the grass; fragile-shelled turtle eggs are dug from nests; and the eggs of ground-nesting birds are discovered. Periodically a raccoon family will raid cornfields. Pokeweed berries, cherries, blackberries, raspberries, grapes, plums, persimmons, and pecans are all relished by these animals. In short, they will consume anything edible and when favorite foods are not available, will adapt to whatever circumstances provide.

The mother keeps the cubs by her side for nearly a year, and it is not unheard of for her to adopt an orphan. They travel long distances while foraging for food, the mother continually guiding and instructing them. At night they wander considerable distances from the den, from one-half mile to a mile, sometimes covering as much as 5 miles. Footprints left by the roving raccoons resemble those of little children. When danger strikes, the mother will lead her young up a tree and then dash away, luring the dogs after her. The polygamous father assumes no responsibility for his offspring and lives alone.

When sensing trouble, the raccoon makes a noise somewhere between a hiss and a snort. It can also purr like a cat, though its usual talk is a churring birdlike sound. Some dark night when your ears are assailed by the eerie call of a screech owl, coming not from a tree but from the ground, its source may not be an owl. The raccoon makes a sound strongly resembling the fluttering reiterations of the screech owl's tremolo.

Trappers have discovered that coons are attracted by bright, shiny objects. They take advantage of this trait by affixing tin foil to their traps. The pelts of northern raccoons are considerably heavier than those of the South.

Country people value raccoon oil as an aid to keeping leather in prime condition. Pioneers used it in both farm and home. Though light, it was a good lubricant for machinery. During those times the skins served as a unit of barter. Raccoon flesh, roasted, is very palatable.

Cubs thrive in captivity and quickly adapt to human ways. They make affectionate and intelligent pets, although decidedly mischievous ones. With age, coons tend to become surly.

It is true that raccoons have been known to invade chicken

coops to dine on poultry; however, they are mainly beneficial because of their great consumption of harmful insects.

The Short-lived Shrew

When on a walk in the country, should you spy a tiny mouse-like creature scampering over the surface of a pond or stream, your eyes are not deceiving you. What you are watching is the shrew, not only adept at swimming, diving, and walking along the bottom of a stream, but actually able to run on the water itself. The long hairs on its delicate feet prevent it from submerging.

The shrew, smallest of all mammals, weighs when fully grown approximately one-fourteenth of an ounce—less than the weight of a dime. At quick glance it resembles a mouse, but its long, narrow muzzle, extending far beyond the lower lip, betrays its relation to the mole. Minute bright eyes, always on the alert for food, peer from a densely furry face topped by wide ears with deep folds inside, which are used to close off the openings when necessary. Its soft, thick fur is brown above and gray below. The tail, in section, is four sided.

The tiny shrew possesses courage and savagery considerably out of proportion to its size. Ferocious and bloodthirsty, it will attack and eat quarry of twice its own dimensions, even cannibalizing on another shrew if no other food is at hand. The animal lives at a frenzied pace, necessitating a large food intake. Every twenty-four hours it eats the equivalent of its own body weight. Even a few hours without sustenance can result in its death. Chiefly an insect-eater, the shrew feeds on tent caterpillars, cutworms, moths, slugs, grasshoppers, crickets, flies, bees, and centipedes and their larvae. In its incessant search for food, it will invade a nest of rats, slaughtering and devouring the young. Snails also form part of the shrew's diet, and in an emergency it will eat vegetation. When food abounds, the shrew burrows in soft soil and buries the surplus, caching reserves of pieces of small animals, large beetles, and mollusks.

Primarily nocturnal, the shrew is frequently about by day as well. It sleeps for periods of one to two hours, alternating them with periods of activity of the same length.

When pursuing a female with amorous intent, the male makes a series of unmelodious clicking sounds. Though shrews generally live in damp moss and earth, for raising a family the female fashions a nest of dry grass and leaves in a stump hole or under a rock. Two to ten fast-growing young are born. When the mother shrew and her offspring move about, they travel in caravan formation: the mother leads, with the first baby grasping her skin near the base of the tail with its teeth and the rest following in single file, each holding to the one in front in the same manner. They are so strongly linked that when the mother is picked up, the whole family is lifted.

So tense and delicately balanced is the nervous system of this little animal that when caught in the human hand, it often dies instantly from shock. Nervous and high strung, it can die from hearing a loud noise, such as a clap of thunder. In a state of fear, its heart beats 1,200 times per minute, and it breathes 800 times in the same period. A shrew's life span seldom exceeds one year; should it survive longer, at sixteen months it dies of old age.

For generations country people, trappers, and woodsmen asserted that the bite of the shrew was venomous. Learned men dismissed the claim as a piece of traditional superstition. Investigation has since proved that the shrew does indeed have a toxic bite. Its saliva is poisonous, and the venom, drop for drop, is as potent as the cobra's. A small amount is sufficient to kill mice and other prey, but not enough to harm humans. That the shrew's bite is venomous is no longer considered a myth; folklore has been vindicated and the claim incorporated in our store of animal knowledge.

Life Spans (Years)

bat	3–5	goat	15–20
mouse	3–5	deer	18–25
snail	8	pig	20
fox	8–10	bear	20–30
rabbit	8–10	horse	20–35
squirrel	8–10	newt and lizard	25
wolf	10–15	large snake	25
beaver	12	toad	30
dog	15	crocodile	40–50 plus
cat	15–20		

6
About Birds

A light broke in upon my brain,—
It was the carol of a bird;
It ceased, and then it came again,
    The sweetest song ear ever heard.
            —Byron
            The Prisoner of Chillon
            1816

Bird Migration

Migration, the movement of birds between their summer and winter homes, has attracted attention and speculation over the ages. Mention of it is made in the Bible and other writings of long ago.

The phenomenon of bird migration was graphically evident to early colonists because of the sheer multitudes of birds at that time. So numerous were passenger pigeons, for example, that when they roosted for the night their combined weight broke the limbs from trees. Shooting them was a needless effort; because of their dense swarming, catching them in nets was easier.

As an aid to understanding migration, isolated attempts were made over the years to mark individual birds by various means for later identification. John James Audubon, by banding several phoebes with silver thread tied around the leg, discovered that these birds return year after year to the identical nesting site. Not until 1899, however, was the banding method (metal bands took the place of Audubon's thread) used scientifically in Denmark, whence it spread to Europe and the United States.

In addition to bird banding, other studies have revealed many interesting facts about bird migration. The ruby-throated hummingbird, though less than 3 inches in length and weighing only slightly more than one-tenth of an ounce, defies 500 miles of open water when crossing the Gulf of Mexico on its migratory journey.

A means to observe bird migration, used by men since the days of Galileo, can be practiced by anyone having a telescope. Simply point it at the moon, preferably between 8 P.M. and 12 midnight, to note the passage of birds silhouetted against its illumination and estimate their number on a given night. Though the bulk of birds fly during those hours, from 4 to 6 A.M. is also a favorite period.

Smaller birds, such as mixed warblers, flycatchers, orioles, and small perching birds, generally fly by night. Being accustomed to the shelter of wooded areas, they seem to prefer the protective cover of darkness for their flight. Then, too, they are less conspicuous as prey for destructive enemies during the dark hours. Feeding is probably the most important factor governing the choice of nocturnal flight among the smaller birds. It enables them to arrive by day to find food according to their diurnal habits. Some birds, such as swallows, swifts, and nighthawks, feed on the wing. Night navigation is thought to be guided by an innate sense of direction and superior eyesight, with the visual orientation of moon and stars as a compass bearing.

Because of certain distinct characteristics peculiar to their families, some birds fly segregated from other groups; for example, nighthawks, by reason of their erratic flight, do not fly in mixed company. Other migrating flocks are composed of a variety of birds drawn together by similarity of size, form, and methods of searching for food.

Flight patterns, too, differ. Some birds—blackbirds, waxwings, snow buntings, shore birds—move in close formation; others, such as vultures, blue jays, warblers, larks, and bluebirds, fly in loose order. Still others travel separately—owls, wrens, shrikes, grebes, kingfishers—flocking occasionally where food is abundant along the way.

In certain species males migrate first, reaching their breeding grounds to stake out territory a week or more before the arrival of the females. Robins, rose-breasted grosbeaks, sparrows, and black-capped vireos are some birds of this practice. Among others, such as shore birds, male and female arrive simultaneously. Large birds of some species, such as the Canada goose, mate for life.

The urge to migrate, even in the absence of whatever original motives, has become hereditary. Birds don't wait until their food supply is depleted and cold weather sets in before commencing migration. Exemplifying the hereditary urge are young birds which find their way to the specific winter quarters of their species, despite their parents' having migrated earlier, and cowbirds which, though reared by a different species, still reach their appropriate wintering grounds.

The four chief factors prompting the start of migration are day length, temperature, amount of available food, and changes within the bird's body.

Increasing light of lengthening days stimulates activity in birds' reproductive organs. (An interesting fact to note is that almost every species has but one functioning ovary, the left, which is active only during breeding season.) In addition, there is a fat accumulation—flight fuel—equaling one-third of the body weight. These changes trigger urges to return north to breeding grounds. At this period birds experience *Zugun-ruhe*, or nocturnal restlessness, most migrations taking place at night.

The benefit of migration is that it permits birds to live in each area when it is at its most favorable season. Both summer and winter quarters provide a milder climate and more abundant food supply; northern summers afford extra-long days for hunting food for nestlings.

The bobolinks travel farther than any other members of their family—5,000 miles from their wintering grounds in Brazil and northern Argentina to their summer quarters in the northern United States and southern Canada. New Englanders in colonial times found them nesting in coastal marshes and grassy river valleys. Over the years bobolinks gradually followed the spread of grain fields westward and now breed as far as California. Bobolinks that have nested in the West, prompted by their original hereditary instinct, return east to follow ancestral migratory routes. They head south along a flyway that in the nineteenth century took them over the extensive rice fields of South Carolina.

The following list gives you the approximate speed at which birds fly during migration:

- small perching birds   20 to 37 m.p.h.
  (larks, pipits, buntings)
- members of the crow family   31 to 45 m.p.h.
  (jays, magpies, ravens)
- starlings   38 to 49 m.p.h.
- falcons   40 to 48 m.p.h.
  (A peregrine falcon, diving after its prey, speeds at the rate of 180 miles per hour!)
- geese   42 to 55 m.p.h.
- grouse   43 to 47 m.p.h.
- ducks   44 to 59 m.p.h.
- swifts   70 m.p.h.

In their daily search for food, songbirds fly at an altitude of less than 150 feet. Hawks and vultures, scanning vast distances for food, may fly as high as a mile. When migrating, birds usually fly below 3,000 feet, although ducks and occasionally smaller birds have been observed above 20,000 feet.

Here is a list of migratory birds, the months of their migrations, and their summer and winter quarters:

BIRD	ARRIVES IN SUMMER QUARTERS		DEPARTS FOR WINTER QUARTERS	
Purple martin	Jan.	North America	Sept.	South America

Some southern Indian tribes stationed old squaws near newly planted fields outside the village to protect crops from hungry birds. Being isolated, the women often lost their lives and scalps to hostile Indians of other tribes. The Choctaws and Chickasaws capitalized on their knowledge of the purple martin's preference for breeding in colonies, thus sparing the scalps of their old women. They lured martins to appropriate spots by hanging up groups of hollowed-out gourds for nesting. The martins fearlessly drove away marauding crows and hawks from both crops and poultry.

BIRD	ARRIVES IN SUMMER QUARTERS		DEPARTS FOR WINTER QUARTERS	
Purple grackle	late Feb. and March	east of Rockies to Texas and Florida	Oct.	southern states, South America

| Belted kingfisher | March | North America | Dec. | southern states, South America |

At the end of a tunnel, sometimes 15 feet long, the belted kingfisher lays its eggs on a pile of regurgitated fish bones. Since the female is too short-legged to stand over the hatchlings, the newborn naked babies are obliged to cling together in a mass for warmth.

| Yellow-shafted flicker | March | North America, east of Rockies | Oct. | southern Texas, Gulf Coast, Arizona, California |

Alabama adopted the yellow-shafted flicker as its state bird, dubbing it the "yellowhammer." Civil War soldiers went off to battle with "yellowhammer" feathers decorating their hats.

| Eastern phoebe | March | North America, east of Rockies | Oct. | south of Carolinas to Gulf states, southern Mexico |

BIRD	ARRIVES IN SUMMER QUARTERS		DEPARTS FOR WINTER QUARTERS	
Scissor-tailed flycatcher	March	central and south-western states	Oct.	southern Mexico, Panama
Robin	March	North America	Oct., Nov.	south as far as Guatemala (some remain north in winter)

Have you ever wondered why the robin is obliged to tug repeatedly to free a worm from the earth? Each body segment of the worm, except for the first and last, is equipped with hooklike bristles with which it grips the soil around it. A robin nestling requires at least 14 feet of earthworms each day!

Wood thrush	March	eastern United States	Oct.	Mexico, Central America
Bluebird	March	North America	Oct.	middle states to Bermuda, West Indies (some remain north in winter)
Field sparrow	March	eastern United States	Oct.	Missouri and New Jersey to Gulf Coast (some remain north in winter)
Red-winged blackbird	March	North America east of the Plains	Oct.	southern United States
Purple finch	March	northern United States	Nov.	south of Pennsylvania to southern Arizona, Texas, Florida
Cowbird	March	throughout North America	Nov.	southern states, Mexico

BIRD	ARRIVES IN SUMMER QUARTERS		DEPARTS FOR WINTER QUARTERS	

The cowbird is well named: it alights on the backs of cattle, where it picks off ticks. In the 1860's the cowbird was known as the buffalo bird when it performed the same service for herds of buffalo.

Eastern meadow-lark	March, April	North America, westward to the Plains	Oct.	southward, to South America (some remain north in winter)
Canada goose	March, April	northern United States, Canada	Nov., Dec.	southward, to Mexico

Canada geese fly in V formation because this flight pattern maintains each bird in a position to see ahead and at the same time avoid air disturbances from the wing beats of birds in front. The leader may fly in any position in the wedge, guiding the flight by calling to the rest.

White-breasted nuthatch	April	eastern United States	Oct.	southward
Brown creeper	April	northern United States	Oct.	Gulf Coast
House wren	April	northern United States	Oct.	below the Carolinas

Indians, hearing prodigious bird song and noting its small brown source, gave the wren a long Indian name meaning "a big noise for its small size."

Ruby-crowned kinglet	April	northern United States	Oct.	southern United States, Mexico, Central America
Red-eyed vireo	April	northern United States, west to Rockies	Oct.	South America
Black-and-white warbler	April	eastern United States, west to the Plains	late Sept.	Baja California, central Florida, northern South America

BIRD	ARRIVES IN SUMMER QUARTERS		DEPARTS FOR WINTER QUARTERS	
Summer tanager	April	southern and eastern states	Oct.	Central Mexico to Bolivia

The summer tanager breaks the stingers from wasps in order to feed undisturbed on their larvae.

BIRD	ARRIVES IN SUMMER QUARTERS		DEPARTS FOR WINTER QUARTERS	
Rufous-sided towhee	April	northern United States	Sept.	southern United States, Central America
Vesper sparrow	April	northern United States	Oct.	Baja California, Gulf Coast
Junco	April	northern United States	Sept.	south to Gulf (some remain north in winter)
Rusty blackbird	April	northern United States	Nov.	Gulf Coast, Colorado
Short-eared owl	April	northern United States	Nov.	southern United States
Rail	April	Atlantic Coast salt marshes	Oct.	south of New Jersey
Spotted sandpiper	April	northern United States to Gulf	Sept.	southern states to Brazil
Chimney swift	April	east of Plains from Canada to Gulf	Sept.	south of United States
Barn swallow	late April	throughout United States	Sept.	Central and South America
Brown thrasher	late April	northern states east of Rockies	Oct.	south of Virginia
Bobolink	early May	northern United States west to the prairies	July to Oct.	Central and South America

BIRD	ARRIVES IN SUMMER QUARTERS			DEPARTS FOR WINTER QUARTERS	
Rose-breasted grosbeak	early May	southern Canada south to Kansas, Georgia	Sept.		southern Mexico to Ecuador
Baltimore oriole	early May	United States east of Rockies	Sept.		southern Mexico to Central America
Indigo bunting	middle May	Canada to Gulf	Sept.		Mexico, Central America
Ruby-throated humming-bird	May	eastern North America to Gulf	Oct.		Central America

The hummingbird was first observed in Canada and New England about 1600. Jesuit fathers, unable to detect the act of feeding, believed it lived solely upon the fragrance of flowers.

Catbird	May	northern United States to Rockies, south to Arizona, Georgia	Nov.		southern states, Central America, Cuba
Logger-head shrike	May	eastern United States west to the Plains	Oct.		Southern states
Scarlet tanager	May	Canada south to Oklahoma, South Carolina	Oct.		northern South America
Goldfinch	May	northern United States	Oct.		Gulf Coast, Mexico (some remain north in winter)

The goldfinch's nest is so tightly woven that it holds water, and hatchlings left unprotected by their parents have been known to drown during a rain.

Bittern	May	north of Virginia	Oct.		Virginia, south-ward

Were we to witness the arrival of migrating birds at their wintering grounds, birds so familiar to us in the North might prove difficult of identification. At the close of the nesting season, most birds begin to molt, a few feathers being lost at a time while others grow in. The resulting plumage differs in color from that of spring. Some birds change color without molting: feather tips break off, exposing already existent plumage of a different hue beneath.

Indian legends sometimes offered explanations for plumage of various colors. The Alaskan Indians, to account for the yellow crown patch of the northern three-toed woodpecker, claimed that famine forced this bird to consume its mate. After eating, he cleaned his claws on top of his head, and the fat he wiped there left a yellow mark.

There is vertical as well as horizontal migration. Some birds travel hundreds of miles to reach summer or winter quarters; others accomplish this by moving altitudinally up or down the sides of mountains. A few hundred feet of altitude are the equivalent of hundreds of miles of latitude. Birds that nest in the higher zones of mountains winter at their base.

Some birds are year-round northern residents. Those which, in spite of cold and lack of flying insects, can find food, such as weed seeds, dry berries, and hibernating insects and their eggs or can feed on other winter residents, as does the snowy owl, risk less by remaining in a severe climate than by hazarding migration. However, even among resident birds, like the blue-jays, woodpeckers, nuthatches, and chickadees, there is migratory movement, though on a smaller scale. They often wander widely in flocks according to the degree of food shortage or overcrowding.

A list of year-round resident birds follows:

BIRD	RANGE
■ Red-headed woodpecker	eastern United States, except New England

The red-headed woodpecker pecks out his home in trees and utility poles. Its ability to endure the shock of such drilling is due to these factors: the bones of the skull are unusually thick and extremely hard; the bony roots of the tongue, in most birds attached to the bottom of the skull, in woodpeckers are wrapped around the cranium and fastened at the base of the bill so that part of its tongue is actually on top of its head!

■ Blue jay	Canada to Gulf states, east of Rockies

The blue jay and his mate gather twigs, dragging them along with them until a proper nesting site is discovered. Southerners say that the jaybird is carrying sticks to the Devil.

■ Black-billed magpie	northern United States, south to California, New Mexico, Kansas

The black-billed magpie, besides being scavenger and mimic, is a thief. Magpies were reported to have rushed into tents of the Lewis and Clark expedition, seizing food from the dishes.

■ Common crow	throughout North America to Gulf

■ Tufted titmouse	Nebraska to Connecticut, south to Texas and Florida

A fearless pilferer, the tufted titmouse has been known to take hair for nesting purposes from living animals—including humans!

■ Mockingbird	California to South Dakota, southeastern States

A great mimic, the mockingbird was called "four hundred tongues" by the Indians.

■ Cedar waxwing	Canada to Kansas and North Carolina

The tips of wings, and sometimes tail feathers, of the cedar waxwing bear red splotches resembling sealing-wax drippings, hence its name.

■ Starling	throughout the United States

■ Cardinal	Connecticut to South Dakota, from Florida to Gulf Coast

The arrival and departure of birds have long been thought of as heralding seasonal changes. When the call of the phoebe bird is heard, one can expect to see the first traces of green across the land in early spring. In spite of the fact that swallows don't appear in their northern breeding grounds until late April, people are accustomed to dubbing them "harbingers of spring." New England folks are on the lookout for the gold of tasseled pussy willows and the red glow of swamp maple blooms at the first song burst from the brown thrasher. Naturalist John Burroughs noted that sap rises in the sugar maple simultaneously with the arrival of the bluebird. Residents of northern states have no need to consult their calendars to know that the first week in May has come when they hear the notes of the ovenbird. It appears on the same date every year at given points along its flyways.

Besides being thought of as vanguards of the seasons, birds have often been considered omens. The magpie, in English folklore, is such a bird. The appearance of one means sorrow; three magpies mean a wedding is in the offing. Over the centuries the raven has been viewed as a foretoken of evil. If its shadow crossed in front of a bird, she was doomed to disaster. Supernatural powers have been attributed to ravens. They have been kept for centuries, one wing clipped, at the Tower of London; Charles II firmly believed that if they departed, England would collapse.

Among the Indians of colonial America, fascinating superstitions about certain birds were many. Cherokee Indians thought of the wren as an eavesdropper who reported everyone's business. A wren brought the news of a newborn baby. If it was a boy, the birds appeared downcast, knowing the papoose would one day hunt them; if a girl, they were joyful, for she would do them no harm.

Early settlers of the North American continent believed the woodcock responsible for malaria, because where woodcocks were prevalent, so was malaria. Woodcocks favor swampy areas, where mosquitoes breed. The supposition was based on the wrong connection.

There were superstitions not only about the birds themselves, but about their migratory habits as well. In olden times people thought that small birds hitchhiked on the backs of larger birds. The view was even expressed that migratory birds wintered on the moon! Centuries ago certain birds were alleged to hibernate as an explanation for their disappearance during the cold months. They were believed to remain in a torpid state hidden in recesses or embedded in the mud of ponds and marshes. Such claims were made concerning swallows, kites, storks, ouzels, turtledoves, larks, and others.

Actually, some birds become torpid by slowing down their bodily processes to adapt to adverse circumstances, such as food shortage. When European swifts are unable to procure food for their brood, the nestlings become temporarily dormant, remaining motionless for days, their temperature below normal. With resumption of food intake, they revive immediately. Such torpor is the equivalent of small-scale hibernation. Though the theory that birds hibernate had long been considered superstition, recent observations have proved that whippoorwills do indeed sometimes hibernate, lying torpid in some sheltered retreat with respiration and temperature well below normal. Interestingly enough, the Indians named the whippoorwill "sleeper."

The movements of nomadic peoples have been governed by the migration of birds. Perhaps one of the most propitious effects of bird migration on the human race occurred in October, the month of mass migration. Mariners on three small ships bobbing in the Atlantic, despairing of ever sighting land, felt their hearts burst with excitement at the spectacle of feathered multitudes winging south. Where there are birds, land must be! Columbus changed his direction in pursuit, eventually finding safe harbor in San Salvador. Thus migrating birds determined the course of Columbus and of history as well.

Life Span of Birds (Years)

■ Wren	3	■ Nightingale	18
■ Thrush	10	■ Linnet	23
■ Blackbird	10	■ Crane	24
■ Robin	10	■ Crow	25–30
■ Pheasant	15	■ Skylark	30
■ Partridge	15	■ Sparrow hawk	40
■ Goldfinch	15	■ Pelican	50
■ Blackcap	15	■ Canada goose	70
■ Lark	18	■ Heron	80

Merrythought

If someone asked you, with regard to a bird, what a merrythought was, would you reply that it was probably what prompted his outburst of song?

The merrythought is the furcula—that forked bone between the neck and breast of a bird commonly called the wishbone. The name "merrythought" has reference to the long-time custom of two people's pulling a fowl's furcula to see who holds the longer piece when it breaks, the idea being that the one with the longer piece will be married first or be granted whatever happy wish was made at the moment. This expressive word was coined in England about 1600.

If the clavicles forming the merrythought are broken, the bird is unable to fly. In running birds they are absent or rudimentary, and in certain birds that do not fly much, such as some parrots, they are small.

This Thanksgiving, share a merrythought with a friend!

7
Bugs and Such

It makes all the difference whether you hear an insect in the bedroom or in the garden.

—Robert Lynd

Cicada: Denizen of Two Worlds

Perhaps there is no more typical sound of the summer countryside than that made by the cicada. As soon as the sun heats the earth, the insect rasps the air incessantly with a harsh whir that rises in a crescendo and slowly tapers off. Only the male produces this unmelodious sound, thought to be a sexual call to attract a mate. Ironically, the female lacks auditory organs as well as those for generating noise. A more appropriate arrangement might have been for the female to possess a hearing faculty in order to appreciate her suitor's overtures, and for the male to lack hearing in order to be spared his own din!

When cicadas emit their call in concert, they can be heard more than one-quarter mile distant.

With her spearlike egg-laying tube, the female penetrates twigs, depositing eggs, which often cause the death of the wood. Little more than a week later they hatch, and the ant-like nymphs drop to the ground, where they bury themselves. Life is sustained by their sucking juices from tree roots. With the passage of time, they burrow ever deeper into the earth, as much as 6 feet below the surface, remaining close to their food source, the roots. After more than a decade and a half in the dark, silent underground, Nature prompts them to move upward toward the surface. By now their brown bodies are a bit more than 1 inch long and equipped with enlarged, spined front legs, well adapted for digging.

During the dark of night, the cicada makes its debut into the upper world and clumsily inches its way up a tree trunk. Here it patiently awaits the final change to adulthood. A split begins down the back, ever widening until the mature cicada is revealed. At first nothing more than fluid-filled sacs, the two pairs of wings, large and membranous, gradually expand. Now, after its long internment beneath the earth, the insect is free to fly. One of the heaviest bodies of the insect world to be supported in air is that of the cicada.

On hot summer days innumerable cicadas can be found clinging to trees, their folded wings resembling peaked roofs. The cicada is a lover of heat and sunshine, perhaps as a result of having spent more than 95 per cent of its life as an underground lodger in darkness. During the daylight hours of its short adult life, it endlessly repeats its shrill call, reminding us that summers too are short.

Cicada Killer Wasp

One of North America's largest wasps, exceeding an inch in length, is the cicada killer, belonging to a group called digger wasps. Endowed with well-developed nervous systems, they are versatile and inventive, adapting ingeniously to prevailing circumstances.

The cicada killer, sometimes referred to as the king hornet, is most active during the heat of midsummer, when cicadas numerously stud the trees, for these insects alone are its prey. They are not eaten by the wasp but stored underground, providing nourishment for the young. Just after the middle of July, the female wasp selects a site for digging her burrow, preferably in dry clayey soil. Damp places, where buried cicadas would become moldy, are avoided. A tunnel is energetically dug to a depth of several feet. The wasp carries loose earth in her front legs and beneath her "chin," backing to the tunnel's opening on four of her six legs. At first she pushes the dirt sideways from the entrance, using her back legs. At length, accumulated dirt reaches such a height that her body, continually passing through it with new loads, creates a furrow. The rear end of the body shoves soft earth along in front of it as she repeatedly backs out. At the bottom of the tunnel, a few caverns of sufficient dimensions to accommodate one or two cicadas are excavated. These underground cavities not only will serve as safe hiding places for the young, but will provide good insulation against heat and cold. With burrowing completed, the wasp tours the neighborhood to establish landmarks in her mind for quick location of the shelter. Now she is ready to set forth on a hunting expedition.

The glossy black body, banded in yellow, hovers over branches, supported on rapidly beating wings. Its large compound eyes seek out victims. Abruptly the cicada's buzzing terminates in an anguished shriek as the one-quarter-inch-long stinger of the wasp stabs the underside of the prey, striking the vital nerve center. The paralyzed cicada continues to live, but remains in an unconscious state to the end.

In the attack both hunter and prey are likely to fall to the ground. If her subterranean chamber is close at hand, the wasp flips the cicada on its back and, straddling the body, drags it along head first. The resourceful wasp inverts the cicada so that the feet will be upraised and not retard progress by catching on obstacles, such as twigs, matted grass, and stones. Should the burrow be some distance away, hauling a burden six times her own weight over rough terrain would prove too difficult, so the wasp resorts to aerial tactics. Unable to raise the cicada from the ground into the air, she laboriously ascends a tree trunk, lugging the inert prey. From the vantage point of a tree limb, grasping her heavy cargo, she projects herself into the air, wings throbbing rapidly. Sometimes she is able to reach her destination with but one such launching. If the victim is particularly weighty, she may have to repeat the maneuver several times, for the wings are able to support the cicada's body only on a descending flight course.

The immobilized cicada is dragged down the tunnel and placed in the circular cavern at the bottom. Occasionally another cicada is deposited, but no more than one egg is laid in each tiny chamber. The single egg is fastened to the underside of the cicada, close to the front legs. Two to three days later, the larva hatches from the egg and immediately takes sustenance from the paralyzed insect. The fluid injected by the wasp's sting not only insensitizes and immobilizes the cicada without killing it so that the food supply remains fresh, but acts as a preservative should the insect die. After a week or so of continual feeding, the larva has devoured most of the food and attains full growth as an immature wasp. For the next two days, it busies itself in forming a cocoon of silk and soil. In this snug capsule it lies dormant through the chill of autumn and winter, changing into a pupa with the advent of spring.

When the earth is softened by summer showers and warmed by the sun's rays, the would-be wasp frees itself from the pupal shell and chews through the encasing cocoon. Now it must scratch its way upward through several feet of earth to freedom in the open air, emerging a fully developed wasp.

Though the female's short life is one of feverish activity, the male's existence is leisurely. With the exception of his one duty, to fertilize the female's eggs, he is free to explore whatever arouses his curiosity.

Only the larva of the cicada killer is carnivorous. Both male and female adults feed on nectar, varying this diet with sap. Trailing the flight of sapsuckers, they cluster at the holes made by these birds to sip the tree's oozing juice. They are especially fond of fermented sap and have been known to become inebriated from overindulgence.

With the first autumnal frost, wasps' tissues freeze, and death overtakes them. Beneath the cold soil, the next generation, silent in its cocoons, awaits the prod of summer's warmth to begin the cycle once more.

Cricket: Gladiator and Musician

Along about dusk in country homes, a reassuring chirping sounds from the vicinity of the hearth. The source is the brownish house cricket, which, being fond of warmth, seeks fireplaces. Its music is a symbol of peace and contentment to rural folk.

Throughout the world there are 22,500 species of crickets; the most common of these is the black field cricket. This ubiquitous little musician, when heard in English homes, was said to bring good luck. In both China and Japan, valued for its music, it was often kept as a pet in cages. During the years of the Chinese Empire, crickets were carefully tended in the royal palace. Their cages were veritable works of art, many being preserved in today's museums. They were made of porcelain or ivory with covers of carved jade. In humbler abodes crickets were confined in delicate bamboo cages or coconut shells. Even today they are sometimes kept as pets in Japan, Italy, Spain, and Portugal.

Cricket is a word formed in imitation of the creature's call. The insect should be termed an instrumentalist, not a singer, for it produces its sound by rubbing parts of its body together, not by forcing air between vocal cords. The wings of the two sexes differ in that the male's alone are characterized by the file and scraper for sound-making. A heavy vein at the front of each forewing has a rasplike surface of numerous ridges on the underside; a smooth rib on the upper side of the wings serves as a scraper. The cricket raises its forewings to a forty-five-degree angle and moves one across the other, like a bow and fiddle, to make music. The taut wing membranes act as a sounding board so that the chirping can be heard at surprising distances.

There is a direct relationship between temperature and call rate. During cool weather it is slower; when the mercury rises the tempo increases. Though most of the cricket's sounds are for communication, to announce its dominion or to attract a mate, some are thought to be for the sheer joy of living. The sounds are of varying quality: with the approach of a rival, the chirping is shriller, more defiant; when the cricket is attracting and courting a female, it is more musical.

Sometimes two crickets will engage in combat over a female. Their kicking and biting can be so fierce as to terminate in the death of one of the males. After attracting a female with his melodious serenade, the suitor caresses her with his antennae. Just prior to the first frost of autumn, the female deposits eggs in the ground for protection against the cold to come. With a needlelike appendage, sometimes as long as her body, she inserts tiny cream-colored eggs, as many as three hundred, under the soil. The eggs resemble diminutive peeled bananas, no more than one-twelfth of an inch in length. They remain underground through the winter, dormancy and cold being essential for successful hatching.

When the sun's rays sufficiently warm the soil in late May or early June, the eggs hatch, and cricket babies, lacking wings and egg-laying apparatus, make their way to the surface. Omnivorous like their parents, they eat dead insects and plants. Each day brings conspicuous growth until at last their horny garb no longer fits. The skin splits down the back, and out they crawl in new attire. This will be the first molt of many before they reach adulthood. With each molt their size increases. Wing pads appear at the next-to-last molt. Roughly twelve weeks after birth, the cricket reaches maturity, sporting fully developed wings at the final molt.

Some crickets carry the right wing higher; others, the left. During the first hour following the last molt, the wings are yet soft. However the cricket has lapped its wings, once they have hardened the arrangement is maintained for life. If the natural position is forcibly changed, the uncomfortable insect moves about until the wings are restored to their original placement.

The cricket seldom flies, but projects itself through the air in great leaps by the aid of its powerfully muscled hind legs. They are equipped with spikes that dig into the ground for traction, enabling it to jump remarkable distances for its size. Other spikes on the legs, pointing backward, help the cricket to maintain a firm hold as it climbs and runs about amid grass blades and leafy plants. The little creature is as capable of propelling itself through water as it is of leaping about on land.

The front legs hold the food while the strong jaws are at work. There is great variety in a cricket menu—vegetables, seeds, grain, meat, rubber, and clothing, particularly when stained with food or perspiration. Meat is an essential in the diet, and if it is unavailable the cricket will not hesitate to cannibalize.

The body of the adult cricket is about 1 inch in length. The antennae are half again as long as the body. Though only the male has the file-and-scraper feature on its wings, both male and female have dual spines projecting from the rear. Minute hairs on them detect vibrations on land and in the air. They act as auxiliary hearing aids, the major auditory organs being small elongated apertures on the front legs. So the insect truly listens with its legs!

The cricket often sits at the entrance of its home, a small, cavelike hole scooped out beneath a stone or dirt clod. When possible it chooses a homesite where the sun's rays are sure to strike the doorway. Here the little instrumentalist grooms itself, passing the many-jointed antennae through its jaws, thoroughly washing them. By bringing the wings forward, it is able to clean them. The body's personal hygiene the insect attends to by rubbing it on the ground. To complete its toilet, the cricket puts its foot in its mouth to nip off any bits of dirt.

An interesting species of cricket is the ant-loving cricket that dwells underground in ant nests. It is tolerated as a kind of house pet by the ants, corresponding in height to a point about midway on an ant's leg. This tiny cricket survives by licking oily secretions from the bodies and legs of its ant hosts.

The carnivorous leaf-rolling cricket hunts aphids by night. Its long, responsive antennae, twice the length of its body, are typical of nocturnal insects. During the day it must have safe lodging, so it creates its own by constructing a tent from a leaf. Using its jaws, it makes slits along the leaf's edge. Then, positioning itself on the leaf, it gathers the severed portions around it with its feet. As the margins begin to meet, the cricket commences attaching them together with fine silk thread from its mouth. This creature's capability of producing silk is unique among crickets. The head moves back and forth, fastening silk on one side and then the other. Gradually the thread hardens, contracting and drawing the leaf edges closer and closer together. In this leaf-tube shelter the cricket settles down to pass the daylight hours in safety, the long antennae wrapped lengthwise about its body. Each evening a new structure is built.

Crickets have long been esteemed for more than just their music. As early as the latter half of the tenth century, the cricket was valued in China for its fighting abilities. Cricket combat became a national diversion. Records of individual accomplishments were preserved much as records of athletes are kept today. A fighting cricket was given a special diet consisting of rice and boiled chestnuts. It was believed that female mosquitoes should be included in its nutrition to augment the cricket's fighting skills, but only those which had fed on the trainer's blood. The combatants were meticulously weighed on tiny scales for proper classification as to heavyweight, middleweight, or lightweight. Before the contest the crickets were stirred to belligerency by being antagonized and tickled with small brushes of rabbit or rat whiskers. The struggle ended only with the death of the defeated. Considerable sums of money were wagered on the outcome.

The life span of a cricket is short, stretching from early summer to the first heavy frost—giving us not many months in which to enjoy the music of this energetic little instrumentalist!

Doodlebug

In sandy areas of the country, miniature craters with occasional spurts of soil flying from them are not an unusual sight. Though children very often play with their small architects, few intimate facts are generally known about them.

The excavator of these funnel-shaped pits is an insect commonly dubbed the "doodlebug." Actually, it is the larval form of the ant lion.

The ant lion does not go abroad in active search and capture of food. It combines stratagem and patience to accomplish this end. Crawling repeatedly backward from a central point and constantly moving in a circle, the ant lion tosses loose sand out of the way with its jaws. A pit is gradually formed with steeply graded sides, measuring an inch or more in diameter and 1 inch in depth. The ant lion conceals itself under loose sand at the bottom, with only its sicklelike jaws protruding. Here it resolutely awaits the approach of an unwary or curious ant. This is the moment when dirt flies! The ant lion flings up the sand, causing small-scale avalanches on the sloping walls. Caught in the dirt slides, the ant is swept to the bottom, where it is seized by the ambusher's jaws. Long and curved, they act as hypodermic needles to inject the body of the prey with potent venom, reducing its interior to liquid, which is then sucked up through the hollow jaws. In order to dine in leisurely fashion, the ant lion feeds, undisturbed, beneath the sand. When the victim's body has been siphoned dry, it is cast from the pit, and the ant lion resumes its silent, expectant waiting.

When the ant lion first emerges from the egg its mother has laid in the sandy dust, its tiny dimensions dictate that it restrict itself to the capture of equally tiny prey. In keeping with its constantly increasing size, it constructs bigger craters and traps larger insects.

Eventually, the fully grown larva is ready for the pupal stage. Skillfully a cocoon of sand and silk is fashioned while the little creature is under the sandy soil. Several months later the pupa breaks from confinement and heads for the world above. Along the back a rent in the skin appears, and the mature ant lion crawls forth. Once its wings spread and harden in the air, it is somewhat similar to the dragonfly in appearance. Unlike the dragonfly, however, it is not a strong flyer. The adult ant lion never eats. Whatever it consumed during its youth in the pitfalls must suffice it now and for the rest of its days.

Ant lion pits can usually be found in places somewhat protected from rainfall, such as close to barns or under rock outcroppings. Country children enjoy watching the unusual behavior of these insects. Sometimes they keep them as temporary pets in jars of sugar or salt to observe close at hand their excavating technique.

Dragonfly: Colorful Aerialist

Many a fisherman out on a lake or along the bank of a stream has been pleasantly surprised at the sight of a dragonfly alighting on his rod, its long jewel-toned body and glassy wings glinting in the sun. Though a common insect, it is, nonetheless, remarkably unique.

The dragonfly begins life as a drab mud-colored nymph, denizen of an underwater world. The squat body creeps along the muddy bottom on six spindly legs or climbs amid small-scale jungles of aquatic plants. The bloodthirsty dragonfly nymph is stalking prey. The means for capture is singular in Nature. A jointed underlip, half the length of the insect's body, shoots out, impaling the living food with two sharp inward-curving claws at the tip. Just as quickly does it drag the victim back to the waiting mouth, equipped with powerful teeth. When not in use, the jointed lip folds conveniently beneath the body, the turned-up end fitting over the lower face like a mask. The nymph's food ranges from invisible one-celled animals to small minnows and tadpoles. However, the insect is cannibal as well as carnivore, devouring its own kind at the first opportunity.

When frightened, the nymph escapes by lifting its legs from the silty bottom and flashing forward in quick bursts of speed, using the legs as oars. It achieves such swift forward locomotion by rapidly sucking in water and expelling it from the rectum, combining breathing with jet propulsion. If captured, a nymph will play possum, simulating death. When an appendage becomes tangled in vegetation or is caught by an enemy, it is shed, enabling the insect to make its escape. Protective coloration is another form of defense; the brown body is inconspicuous in the muddy stream bed. The nymph is capable of making a shrill sound by rubbing its hind legs over a serrated area on either side of the body. The noise is generated when the insect is alarmed and is, perhaps, a defense mechanism.

Dragonflies of some species complete their aquatic life in one year; others need two years for fulfillment; and some remain in their watery realm for five years. Gradually the nymph's form and size are altered by repeated molts.

At last, when darkness settles over the water, the nymph creeps out and ascends a plant, hanging on with hooked feet. Gradually a split lengthens down its back, and eventually the insect, no longer water-breathing, partially emerges from its former sheath. Motionless, it waits until the legs become firm before freeing them. The wings begin to expand and harden; often several hours pass before they are fit for flight. During this time the dragonfly's dazzling hues are heightened. Depending upon the species, it may be copper brown, vivid green, azure blue, lavender, ultramarine, scarlet, lilac, or ivory.

A strong, swift flyer, the dragonfly has no aerial equal in speed or grace. Its well-designed wings permit it to shoot forward or upward, to dive, and even to fly backward. They are so timed that as the front wings move upward, the back wings beat downward. Thus each pair of wings encounters undisturbed air, making for efficiency of flight. With wings throbbing at a rate of 1,600 times per minute, the dragonfly speeds through the summer air to capture insects. It sometimes catches them with its jaws but more often uses its legs. The spiny legs are bunched forward, forming a sort of net for scooping up insects, whence they are transferred to the mouth. Of insatiable hunger, the dragonfly consumes quantities of horseflies, bees, moths, butterflies, and mosquitoes. Because of its voracious appetite for the last, it is sometimes called the mosquito hawk.

The large, mobile head, capable of pivoting, is set with great compound eyes that can see in all directions simultaneously. The upper part of the eyes serves for long-distance vision; the lower part is suited for close viewing. With such acute sight the dragonfly is able to detect moving insects several hundred feet away.

When dragonflies are seen darting over trees and fields, they are on a hunting trip. Their presence over streams and ponds means that mating time has arrived. Male dragonflies fix territorial boundaries, remaining ever vigilant to intruders, who are forcefully driven off. During mating the insects often stay linked for some time, flitting about in tandem.

Female dragonflies of those species which produce elongated eggs slip beneath the water after mating, their closed wings entrapping an air bubble to sustain breathing during submergence. The eggs are inserted into slits in the stalks of aquatic plants. Those which lay rounded eggs drop them on the water's surface; dragonflies of still other types fasten their eggs to plants above water. In certain dragonfly species the females deposit their eggs while yet attached to the male.

So responsive are these insects to sunshine that a small cloud temporarily darkening the sun will cause them to alight on the nearest perch. At twilight dragonflies seek cover amid rank growth. Few species are about at dusk's end.

Strong wing muscles enable the dragonfly to cover amazing distances at high speed. In the fall, larger specimens migrate considerable distances to the south. Mass migrations of dragonflies were recorded as early as the end of the fifteenth century. Winds and storms take their toll, as do living enemies: swifts and swallows, bats, frogs, fish, and water snakes. Sharp vision and swift wings are the dragonfly's only defense.

The dragonfly can boast of ancient ancestry, for it is one of the oldest and largest insects of the world. Scientists tell us that skies were punctuated by its darting flight before the advent of dinosaurs. The gigantic ancestors flashed over ageless forests on wings spanning 2 ½ feet. Today the wingspread varies from 1 inch to 7 ½ inches.

Among country folk the dragonfly has been known by various names due to prevailing superstitions. Some called it the horse stinger, despite the fact that it is incapable of stinging. Perhaps its most common nickname is the Devil's darning needle. People believed that the insect could sew up children's ears. Another superstition held that the insect doctored and fed snakes; hence it was often referred to as the snake doctor.

Although the dragonfly occasionally feasts on honeybees, it benefits man by its consumption of vast numbers of gnats, flies, and mosquitoes. Even as a nymph it devoured mosquito larvae, and it was itself an important fish food.

As the days begin to cool, the dragonfly's activity diminishes. The first frost brings death.

Ladybug: Friend to Man

Rare is the child, playing in the summer countryside, who hasn't delighted at the sight of a ladybug. Somehow he senses, whether because of the insect's inoffensive appearance or through knowledge passed along by grandparents or parents, that it will do no harm. Indeed, this tiny domed beetle, lacquered scarlet with black polka dots, is an invaluable friend to man.

In spring, farmers justifiably predict a good crop upon the arrival of ladybugs. During their larval and adult stages, they wage unrelenting war against scale insects, aphids, and other plant-eating lice. Not long after the Civil War, scale insects ravaged citrus groves. In the late 1800's a particular species of ladybug with a ravening appetite for such destructive pests was imported from Australia, with favorable results. This was an early example of the biological control of harmful insects.

Ladybugs, in both immature and adult form, relish the eggs of other insects. Where farmers specialize in potato-growing, they serve them by devouring innumerable eggs of the potato beetle.

However, farmers did not always appreciate the efforts of ladybugs. Spotting them continually among plant lice, they wrongly concluded that ladybugs were the parents of the destructive insects. So ladybugs and lice were eradicated simultaneously. Their true offspring, also found amid insect pests, met the same fate.

The ladybug picks out a protected site—the underside of a leaf or a crevice in bark—for depositing her eggs. When the young emerge from the eggs, they look like miniature alligators. Their insatiable appetites immediately spur them to hunt and consume plant lice. They suck the vital fluids from aphids and gobble up the hollow bodies. A tiny ladybug larva is not hard put to devour some forty aphids within an hour. Such an intake of food means rapid growth, and the lizardlike larva is busy changing its skin to keep pace. Upon attaining full size, it suspends itself by the tail from a leaf and becomes a chrysalis. When the days as a pupa are fulfilled, the shell splits, and into the world comes the winged beetle. After the polka-dotted wing covers are moved forward, the folded rear wings are exposed. Fanning the air approximately ninety times per second, they launch the ladybug on its first flight.

The adult, having reached full size, eats somewhat less than the gluttonous larva, but still has an immense appetite for insect eggs and plant lice. As ladybugs and their young assault a cluster of aphids, however, they are often driven away by ants. Aphids have no form of self-protection and would be easy prey except for these defenders. When ants are collecting honeydew, a sweet substance secreted by aphids, they are most anxious to protect its source against any threat.

Late in autumn, ladybug beetles begin their unusual hibernating practices. They tend to be social, massing together on rocks. Sometimes so many converge on a boulder that their closely packed bodies color it scarlet. For hibernation they select almost any spot that affords shelter: beneath bark, under shingles, in haystacks, or in woodland mold. During winter thaws they sometimes creep out to enjoy the temporary warmth. The common two-spotted variety often seeks the interior of farmhouses for overwintering.

The most dramatic massing of these colorful beetles occurs in the West. On late autumnal days millions of ladybugs fly up from the valleys into the mountains, where they pass the winter months in rock crevices. Their habit of mass hibernation gave rise to a new and unusual occupation, that of ladybug prospecting. After searching out great conglomerations of the insects, prospectors shovel them into sacks and refrigerate them for the remainder of winter. With the arrival of spring, they are marketed. Farmers and orchardists are guided in their purchasing by the standard recipe for successful insect control: 2 ounces of ladybugs for 1 acre of ground. (Approximately 1,500 ladybugs equal 1 ounce.)

Should you chance upon the empty shell of this little beetle, it will mean that the assassin bug has been abroad. Through a vulnerable spot, between body and head, in the ladybug's armor, the bloodthirsty insect forces its beak to suck out the juices until nothing but the brightly polished shell remains.

Two stratagems are employed by the ladybug to foil most enemies. By contracting its body, it so forcefully constricts its blood that the skin breaks at weak points. The drops discharged are repellent as to both taste and smell, discouraging presumptuous assailants. When confronted by too disproportionate an enemy, such as man, the tiny insect resorts to playing possum. Falling over as though dead, it lies motionless.

From generations past, many names for the ladybug have come down to us: ladybird, ladycow, ladyfly. They evolved from the fact that the ladybug was consecrated to Our Lady, The Virgin Mary. Superstition as well as religion is associated with the insect. Country girls catch a ladybug, place it on their palms, and expectantly wait for it to cross. Its reaching the other side before winging away is believed to make marriage a certainty before the year is out. During pioneer days a ladybug discovered passing the winter in the homestead was an omen of good luck. Farmers claim that ladybugs bring good weather and that the sight of them, come spring, means abundant crops. The ladybug was believed to possess medicinal properties as well. Rural folk recommended reducing the seven-spotted variety to pulp and placing it in the cavity of a tooth to relieve the ache.

Strange as it may seem, the infamous boll weevil is kin to the invaluable ladybug.

Ingestion of Insects

Eating insects for survival, a thought that might make one's flesh crawl when one is comfortably at home, could prove the only way to preserve that flesh were one lost in the wilderness, without knowledge of safe, edible plants or means to hunt and fish. Bees, beetles, caterpillars, cicadas, leeches, locust, maggots, termites, and many other insects and their eggs are excellent nutritional sources.

Bees

Not native to the Americas, bees were brought to our continent in early colonial days by Spanish and British settlers. Black bees, obtained from a bee colony owned by Pilgrims in

Holland, were the first to be introduced. They were brought to Massachusetts in the 1600's and soon escaped to the forests. In William Penn's time, bee trees were numerous in the woods of eastern Pennsylvania. Until about 1750 bees had not yet traveled beyond the Susquehanna River.

During the 1800's they swarmed across the Mississippi as far as the Rockies, always maintaining a 100-mile lead over the ever-westering frontier. The Indians noted the advance of bees with apprehension, recognizing that the "white man's fly" was a precursor of the invader's intrusion into new territories. The bees progressed over the countryside at a rate of about 10 miles per year, lured westward by flower-blanketed prairies and hollow cottonwood trees.

By the early 1800's, bee trees extended some 600 miles up the Missouri River. Gathering honey soon became a trade, some trees containing 8 to 10 gallons each. Colonial settlers and frontiersmen were not alone in collecting honey; black bears quickly became adept at pilfering it from bee trees. Previously, cornstalks had been the sweetest food in the western Indians' diet. Now they, along with black bears, rapidly developed a zeal for honey. Black bears stole honey from the bees; the Indians robbed the men collecting it.

Even if bees produced no honey, they would perform a valuable service in their role as pollinators. In addition to pollinating flowers, bees fertilize many of our most important agricultural crops—among them alfalfa, cucumbers, melons, and almonds.

Most persons associate bees with pollination and honey-making; few regard the bee itself as a food. However, some primitive people consider roasted bees (and wasps) a delectable dish.

Beetles

In Mexico people are fond of eating a particular beetle, the *jumil*. It is high in iodine content.

Leeches

The word *leech*, from the Old English *laéce*, originally meant "one who practices healing; a physician." As the application of aquatic blood-sucking worms by leeches, or physicians, became widespread in Europe late in the eighteenth century, the name *leech* was gradually transferred from the doctor to the worm itself. By the mid-1800's, France was importing over fifty million leeches a year, and leech farming was a very profitable business.

Though seldom used for bloodletting in modern times, leeches still render valuable services. Their saliva contains a blood coagulant, hirudin, used to treat humans. An unusual purpose for leeches is their function as a barometer. Country folk keep them in a bowl of water with dirt in the bottom. Weather is predicted by the degree of their elevation in the water.

A fact unrecognized by the general public is that leeches can provide life-sustaining nourishment in times of dire need. They afford high-quality protein; in order to preserve this protein, leeches should be eaten raw. Walleyes, imbued with the instinctive selection of a nutritious diet, prefer leeches to worms or minnows and thrive on them. Should circumstances dictate, humans could survive on them.

Locusts

Locusts, rich in protein, are an important edible insect in certain desert areas. We read in the Bible that John the Baptist, while sojourning in the wilderness, fed on locusts and honey.

Shore Flies

Adult shore flies abound near tide pools and are often seen walking on the water's surface. Their larvae are marine insects living in sea water and brackish pools. Those shore flies which breed in western salt lakes are called "brine flies." They are so numerous there that great clouds of them hover over the lakes. Indians were familiar with brine flies. They gathered large numbers of them in their immature form to use as food.

Termites

Little-known vitamin T is an important factor in good health; it maintains stamina and increases resistance to stress and shock. A source of vitamin T for human consumption is sesame seed and its oil. Emergency rations for soldiers of former times consisted of cakes made from sesame seed and honey. It was found that a man could march farther on a given amount of that food than on any other. In areas where sesame-seed products have always been part of the national diet, the stamina of the people is exceptional. The fact that so many of them survive to a ripe old age has been attributed to the effect of sesame seed with its vitamin T content.

It is because this substance was first discovered in termites that it was designated vitamin T. There are many tribes of people that dine on termites, preferring them in a pickled state. These insects contain more protein than fish.

Water Boatmen

Water boatmen are common aquatic bugs resembling miniature submarines, propelled by oarlike legs. They fasten their eggs to water plants; some kinds glue them to crayfish. So plentiful are the eggs of water boatmen in Mexico that, it is said, people gather them for a nutritious food.

Wood Borers

The body fluid of wood borers contains carbon compounds and a good many minerals. As the days of autumn chill, the fluid thickens. A sweet alcohol, called glycerol, starts to form, acting as a kind of antifreeze against the increasing cold. The flavor of wood borers has been likened to that of vanilla ice cream. Professor Roscoe Hawley of Indiana says that they are particularly delicious by November, when the accumulation of the syrupy-sweet glycerol is greatest.

Both animals and primitive peoples have found wood borers to be nutritious and tasty fare. Bears and skunks especially relish them.

So it is readily seen that in addition to whatever other functions insects may perform in the world, whether harmful or beneficial to man, they can serve him as survival food. The thought that these small creatures can be lifesaving—just in case—is comforting.

8
Boughs, Bark, and Blossoms

Of all man's works of art, a cathedral is greatest. A vast and majestic tree is greater than that.
—H. W. Beecher
Proverbs from Plymouth Pulpit
1870

In olden times trees played an even more vital role in the lives of people than they do today. Perhaps because they provided so many of man's basic needs, people revered them and were more acutely aware of their individual beauty and characteristics.

Some trees were considered sacred, and to them many powers of good and evil were attributed. Delving into the past, we find fascinating legends about them that developed over the ages and were handed down from one generation to the next. Centuries ago people discovered which tree furnished wood most appropriate for a particular purpose.

Learning the ways that trees were used in the past, legends

and superstitions concerning them, and their uses today can enhance our appreciation of these wonders of Nature, too often taken for granted.

Ash

The ash is unique in being the only tree in the world to produce black buds.

Through the centuries, supernatural powers have been attributed to it. Country people would split an ash sapling and then pass a sick infant through the opening to waiting hands on the opposite side. This procedure was repeated three times. The opening was then smeared with mud and bandaged. If the young tree healed, the baby would recover; if the wound failed to close, the child would die. When cattle developed sore limbs, it was believed that a shrew had scampered over them. As a countermeasure a shrew was put into a cavity in an ash tree and the hole stopped up, the tree thereafter being called a shrew ash. The mere touch of a branch from a shrew ash was supposed to cure the animal suffering from painful legs. The tree was also said to have an adverse effect on snakes, and its leaves were considered a cure for their bites.

The ash was thought to have medicinal properties as well as supernatural powers. A tea made of the leaves was advocated in cases of gout and rheumatism and was prescribed for longevity.

White ash timber is valuable for its dual qualities of strength and elasticity. From the earliest ages it was used for weapons of war. It was favored for making wheels, shafts, and other articles that are required to be light and springy. Today ash wood goes into staircases, kitchen furniture, and bedroom furniture, especially dressers. Because of its toughness and flexibility, baseball bats, polo mallets, hockey sticks, tennis-racket frames, shovel and hoe handles, oars, and swing seats are manufactured from it. Ash wood is also used for butter tubs, baskets, boxes, and crates. The roots of the tree, being beautifully veined and receptive to high polish, are prized by cabinet-makers.

From the bark of the blue ash, early settlers of North America extracted a pigment which was used to dye cloth blue.

Indians customarily used splints from the black ash to fashion pack baskets; hence the tree became known as the basket tree.

Sassafras

Early colonists of North America had great faith in the healing powers of the sassafras tree. All parts of it have a spicy taste. A tea made from the roots' bark was used to reduce fever and treat dropsy and skin diseases.

The oil from sassafras roots is used for flavoring candies and medicines, for perfuming soap, and occasionally for making the glue on stamps.

Southerners thicken their soups with the dried and powdered sticky new leaves of the tree together with the pith from its smaller branches.

Many a country child, strolling home from school, has eaten sassafras buds or chewed on a bit of fragrant bark dug with a pocketknife from the tree's roots.

Rural folk find sassafras timber useful for their fence posts, because it does not rot easily in soil. In days gone by they made ox yokes and barrels from it.

Oak

There are many species of oak trees varying greatly in appearance, but they have one thing in common: all of them produce acorns. Centuries ago, oak trees marched over half of England. Pigs were fattened on their acorns. Country people, when referring to the size of an oak forest, mentioned the number of swine it could sustain rather than the number of its trees or acres. When famine plagued the land, people ate acorns, too.

The acorns of America's white oak are relished by jays, wild turkeys, squirrels, deer, and other creatures. The Indians and many white settlers ground them into meal for breadmaking. You can roast them to make acorn coffee, which is not a stimulant and is reputed to benefit people with poor digestion.

Certain insects lay their eggs in the oak tree's bark. Each egg is surrounded by a drop of irritating liquid, causing the bark to swell and form a gall, resembling a miniature apple. The juicy contents of oak galls are used in dyes and medicines, in photographic work, and to make black ink.

The oak's bark is much in demand by tanners. It is rich in the tannin that transforms soft skins into leather. Long ago the bark's lining was soaked and then pounded to produce a thin material for ladies' garments. The padding of the bark provides cork for bottle stoppers, life jackets, and buoys.

Much of the furniture in country homes of the past was made of the oak's heavy, hard, firm wood. Of oak wood, too, are many of the beautiful old carvings in churches and mansions of bygone days. Generations ago rural people in America preferred it for well buckets, wash tubs, kegs, and barrels for containing liquids. Mindful of its strength and durability, early seagoing traders constructed their vessels of it, and Americans chose it for bridges, beams of barns, agricultural implements, wagons, fence posts, railroad ties, and mine props.

Even the sawdust of oak trees serves a purpose. Brown and yellow dyes are made from it. When combined with water and vinegar, it is excellent for cleaning bottles.

The oak is said to be struck by lightning more frequently than any other tree. Country folk, wise in the ways of Nature, never seek shelter from a storm under its branches.

Beech

In literature of the past, one finds many references to the carving of letters on the beech tree's bark. Its extreme smoothness, which is maintained throughout the tree's life, seems to invite such action.

Pigs are as fond of beechnuts as they are of acorns. Indians valued them for their oil; it is slow to become rancid, and they favored it for cooking purposes. American pioneers fattened their Thanksgiving turkeys on the nuts. Some people claim that eating beechnuts can cause headaches.

Many years ago country folk picked small leaves from beech trees to use as mattress stuffings. They give off a pleasant aroma and do not become brittle and musty as fast as straw.

Because beechwood has no detectable odor or taste, barrels and other wooden containers for food are made from it. The beech tree provides the woodsman with the finest firewood. Its timber burns with a hot flame, eventually leaving a bed of long-lasting embers.

Linden

Honey made from the flowers of the linden tree is ranked by many as the most delicious of all varieties. Rural households steep the blossoms, using the resulting tea as a remedy for coughs, indigestion, and nervousness.

In ancient times the tough inner bark was used for writing tablets and its fibers for tying garlands. During the days of the old oaken bucket, well ropes were made of these fibers, as was a coarse cloth. Fishermen made nets from them, and gardeners used them for biding bouquets and for making mats to protect plants. In generations past, poor people fashioned footwear from the bark, using the outer part for soles and the bark lining for the tops. When a tree had been stripped of its bark, it was used for charcoal.

During winter, the tiny nuts and buds of the linden tree have often meant survival to a lost and starving trapper.

The soft white wood of the linden is used in papermaking, woodenware, paneling, and cabinetwork. The sounding boards of pianos are made of it, and its smooth grain renders it ideal for carving and wood engraver's blocks.

Redbud

Legend has it that the Old World relative of the redbud was the tree from which Judas hanged himself after his betrayal of Jesus. The tree is said to have blushed with shame, and hence the pinkish-red hue of its flowers. The story was brought to America by colonists and applied to this country's species.

Some folks enjoy the young pods and flowers of the redbud tree as fritters. The acid flowers are used in pickles and salads.

The tree's inner bark furnishes an ingredient long used in cough medicine.

Sycamore

The sycamore is known as the buttonball tree because of its fruit, which resembles small balls suspended on stems. The tree's life span is a long one, some sycamores reaching the age of five hundred years or more.

Their trunks are frequently hollow, providing havens for owls, dens for raccoons, and sometimes an abode for man. In the 1700's two men were reported to have lived in the wilderness for three years with the hollow trunk of an immense sycamore serving as their home.

The hard wood has an interlocking grain, making it difficult to split. It is excellent for butcher's blocks and is used for flooring, furniture, boxes, barrels, crates, and handles. Many a violin owes its existence to the wood of the sycamore. Berry boxes and baskets are made from its veneer.

Black Gum

The pioneers tried in vain to split the wood of the black gum tree to make rail fences. The wood's twisted, interlocking grain defied their axes. So they sawed hollow trunks of the black gum into short sections and converted them into bee-hives. The tree became commonly known as the "bee gum."

Today black gum timber is used for egg crates, berry boxes, barrels, furniture, and gunstocks.

Elm

During lean times of the past, the inner lining of elm bark was ground into meal for making bread. Country people fed elm leaves to cattle, which seemed to prefer them to oats.

A certain variety of elm was thought to have magical prop-erties. Dairymaids fastened a twig of it to their churns, believ-ing that butter would form only in its presence.

Elm wood is excellent for articles subjected to moisture, such as keels of ships, water wheels, and troughs. Before iron piping came into use, water pipes were made of it. The hard, tough wood of the elm goes into coffins, boxes, barrels, bas-kets, crates, some furniture, vehicle parts, the frames of sad-dles, and dairy, poultry, and apiary supplies. The inner bark is twisted to form a coarse rope.

Country boys on their ramblings often chew a twig or piece of inner bark from the slippery elm. It contains a slimy, palat-able mucilage, which accounts for the tree's name. The sticky bark lining served as nourishment for the Indians, as an ap-peaser of thirst among the pioneers, and as a valued medicine of frontier days. Many rural households still use it for coughs and fevers and in poultices for boils and sores.

Saguaro

The saguaro is a giant tree cactus. Over the centuries, south-western Indians have used the woody interior skeleton of this immense cactus as a framework for their homes.

Indian women dry the fruits of the saguaro and make preserves and syrups from it. The fruit is often eaten raw and is enjoyed by wild creatures as well as humans.

Birds excavate nesting places in the cactus. The exposed sap dries, forming a lacquerlike coating on the hole's interior. When the rest of the cactus falls to decay, this bowl-shaped vessel remains, to last for years. The Indians store the preserved fruit of the saguaro in it.

Today fences and rafters for ranch houses are often made from the woody skeleton of the saguaro.

Horse Chestnut

The horse chestnut tree (which is not a true chestnut) originated in the mountains of Asia. Its nuts (which are not true nuts) are unpalatable to man, but deer relish them, and when they are boiled poultry will eat them. In some areas they are fed to horses and are used to fatten sheep. The American Indians tossed ground horse chestnuts into the the waters of their favorite fishing sites. Fish, intoxicated by the narcotic properties of the nuts, rose to the surface and were easily scooped up in nets.

Horse chestnuts are used in veterinary practice. The tree's bitter, astringent bark has been used in treating fevers.

Both nuts and roots contain a substance that can be worked into a lather as a substitute for soap. It serves as a bleach for linens. An adhesive paste and a very good starch are made from the seeds. Years ago, candles were made from horse chestnut flour and tallow. They burned longer than ordinary candles, but less brightly.

The soft, easily worked wood of the horse chestnut is used in the manufacture of small objects. Throughout the United States it is planted as a shade tree.

The state tree of Ohio is one of our native horse chestnuts, the buckeye. It is so named for its large, polished seed, which somewhat resembles the eye of a male deer. Superstitious people keep one in their pocket as a defense against rheumatism.

Country boys used to gather the shiny brown nuts to play the game of "conquerors." They tied horse chestnuts to both ends of a string, whirled them rapidly around, and let them fly to land on telegraph wires, where they hung indefinitely.

Cabbage Palmetto

A bud resembling a cabbage sprouts in the middle of the cabbage palmetto's crown. The Indians of Florida relished it, and Spanish explorers pronounced the large, tender bud palatable. Today's people have developed a taste for it, which proves detrimental to the tree: removal of the bud often causes its death.

In colonial times the trunks of the cabbage palmetto were valued for docks and wharf pilings because of their resistance to shipworms. A fort built of the wood was reported to withstand cannon balls. Florida's Seminole Indians build their houses of the trunks, thatching them with the tree's fan-shaped leaves.

Whisk brooms and brushes are manufactured from fibers of the leaf stalks; the leaves go into hats, mats, baskets, and other woven articles.

Flowers of the cabbage palmetto furnish bees with nectar, and the tree's sweet fruit is enjoyed by the Seminoles. Birds and raccoons share the Indians' fondness for it.

Maple

Early settlers of North America were amazed to find that the Indians made sugar from the maple tree's sap. The news was carried to Europe, where it was hailed as an outstanding scientific discovery. The colonists quickly adopted the practice, making both sugar and syrup.

The smooth yellow wood of the maple tree is hard, strong, and uniform in texture. When polished, it gleams like satin. From colonial times it has been considered one of the finest woods for furniture and flooring. Spools and bobbins, handles, boxes, crates, shoe lasts, and agricultural implements have been manufactured from it. In the past, before steel took the place of wood, ships' keels were made of it.

Bird's-eye maple is a favorite wood with cabinetmakers and is used for gunstocks and the backs of violins. Certain chemicals are distilled from it.

When used for fuel, maple burns with a steady, clear flame.

Rowan Tree

The rowan tree is often called the mountain ash, though it is no relation to the ash.

In olden times supernatural powers were associated with it. If cattle were thought to be in danger of the evil eye, country people protected them by fastening rowan branches to cowsheds and stables. As an extra precaution, farmers drove their cows with a rowan stick. Crosses made from such wood were believed to ward off evil spirits.

A type of beer is made from the tree's astringent bright scarlet berries, and they are used for making jelly.

Long ago, slender branches of the rowan tree served as wood for archers' bows.

Elder

Young shoots of the elder tree were a source of fun for country boys generations ago. Their soft, pithy interior was easily removed with a pocketknife, resulting in a quickly made popgun. In earlier times, flutes were fashioned from these hollow stalks.

The elder was valued for its medicinal properties. At a time when country people concocted many home remedies, elder buds were brewed for a tea to reduce fevers; a skin ointment was also made from the flowers; and they were used to add flavor to vinegar. Sleep could be induced through the medicinal qualities of both flowers and leaves. A decoction of elder leaves was said to destroy insect pests on other vegetation. Farmers put garlands of ill-smelling elder leaves on their horses' heads to drive away annoying flies. A healing salve was prepared from elder bark to treat burns. Many a rural household made elderberry wine, regarded as a good cold remedy as well as a pleasing drink. Regular imbibing of this was believed to ensure a long, healthy life. Some folks even used the berries to dye their hair.

The timber of the elder has been employed in the making of boxes, toys, and shoemaker's pegs. Butchers prefer skewers of elder wood, claiming that they never taint the meat.

Willow

Indians used the lining of willow bark to make fish nets and lines. In spring, pioneer farmers cut strong, supple willow stems to bind together fence rails; as they seasoned, the knotted willow wands hardened, lasting year after year.

In some parts of the world, the down from willow seeds was used to stuff mattresses and pillows. It was also made into paper.

One type of willow, the osier, has tough, flexible branches appropriate for basketmaking. Centuries ago, boats were woven from slender osier branches and covered with animal skins. Warriors made light but sturdy shields in the same fashion. When firearms required black powder, the willow's high-grade charcoal was utilized.

The lightweight wood of the black willow goes into baskets, furniture, coffins, boxes, and crates. From its bitter bark medicines are made.

Redwood

Seeds of the mighty redwood are so delicate and minuscule that roughly eight thousand of them would not exceed an ounce in weight. The redwood tree was regarded as sacred by the Indians. It was called "sequoia" in honor of Sequoyah, the Cherokee Indian who developed an alphabet for his people.

The hard, strong timber of the sequoia is particularly resistant to both decay and harmful insects. It is useful for construction, siding, doors, and sashes. The wood's long-lasting quality makes it ideal for outdoor furniture, silos, tanks, garden trellises, greenhouses, and fences. The bark is excellent for insulation purposes.

Shagbark Hickory

The Indians made a sweet, milky liquor from the nuts of the shagbark hickory. The name "hickory" was derived from the Indian word for this drink.

In the old days, country folk gathered hickory nuts in the fall to put into candies and cakes. The bitter, astringent inner bark of the tree was used to treat indigestion and fevers. Its tough, strong wood went into the rims and spokes of wheels for buggies and wagons and was made into buggy shafts and whippletrees.

Today it is used for tool handles, ladder rungs, agricultural implements, furniture, and archer's bows. Hickory is considered the best wood for smoking meat.

Pecan

To the Indians the pecan tree represented the Great Spirit. They relished the nuts of wild pecan trees.

Hard, tough pecan wood goes into flooring, furniture, tool handles, and boxes and crates. It is used widely for smoking meat and provides a good fuel wood.

The pecan is the state tree of Texas.

Holly

Have you ever wondered what wood goes into black piano keys? They are usually made from the hard, easily dyed wood of the holly tree. The wood is also used in riding switches, whip handles, and furniture inlays. However, its chief use is in the making of musical and scientific instruments.

The holly tree contains a fragrant resin that has medicinal properties. A tea made from the leaves has served as a remedy for rheumatism and fevers.

Country dwellers used faggots of holly to sweep their chimneys. Many believed that holly branches would protect a home from lightning and its residents from witchcraft.

Poplar

The down of black poplar seeds has been manufactured into cloth and paper, but neither has proved very satisfactory. Poplar bark is so light in weight that in water it is extremely buoyant. For that reason fishermen prefer strips of poplar bark to string for tying their nets. Because the wood does not ignite easily, it is chosen for flooring but shunned by campers as firewood.

When celebrating their independence from England, Americans planted poplars as symbols of freedom, calling them "liberty trees."

The white poplar acts as a sort of weather gauge. When the white undersides of its leaves are uplifted, a storm is in the offing. Its wood is used for toy-making, and at one time bakery ovens were heated with it because of its slow-burning quality.

The United States utilizes the soft wood of the balsam poplar as pulpwood for paper and to make boxes and crates. From the fragrant resin of the tree's buds, an ointment and cough medicine are made. Indians pressed the aromatic wax from the buds and used it to waterproof the seams of their birch-bark canoes.

Hornbeam

The wood of the hornbeam is tougher than that of any other tree. In early times objects requiring strong, hard wood were made from it, such as rake teeth, cogs of mill wheels, and yokes for oxen. Because of its durability when in contact with soil, it is frequently used for fence posts. In addition, tool handles, levers, and mallets are manufactured from it.

Its bark is utilized in homeopathic medicine and, being rich in tannin, is used in tanneries.

Hornbeam timber provides good firewood. Torches made of it burn with a bright, candlelike flame.

For its qualities of solidity, toughness, and strength, the hornbeam has been referred to as the ironwood tree.

Black Walnut

Pioneers of the North American continent derived a dye from the hulls of black walnuts. With it they colored their homemade cloth brown.

Colonists used the hard but easily worked wood of the black walnut tree for furniture and staircases in both town and country homes. Recognizing the durability of the timber, they made fence rails and barn beams from it.

Since black walnut trees are scarce today, their wood is usually limited to furniture veneer. It is particularly sought for gunstocks, because it sustains shock without splintering and retains its beautiful finish through long use.

Birch

In the days of the country schoolhouse, the first thing to come to mind at mention of the birch tree might have been the birch rod. However, over the ages the birch has been put to many and varied uses other than the schoolmaster's disciplinary stick.

Birch bark is extremely durable—almost everlasting—and waterproof. The tree turns its sap into an aromatic oil, which it stores in the bark.

The sole tree to grow in Lapland is the birch. Being waterproof and long lasting, it was used as roofing material. After removing a large section of bark from a tree and cutting a hole in it big enough for their heads to go through, people wore it as a moistureproof covering. From bark they fashioned waterproof shoes and boots, baskets, cords, and mats. Their torches, made from twisted bark strips, burned brightly because of the oil stored there. When food was scarce, the natives ground the bark's lining into flour for making bread.

In some areas the birch produces clumps of twigs among its branches, often referred to as witches' knots. Years ago people employed birchwood for making footwear and even their houses.

Being easily separated into delicate layers, birch bark was used in the past for papermaking. The bark and leaves of some types of birch are used as a remedy for skin diseases.

Country people tap birch trees for their sap, which they call "birch water" or "birch blood." Each spring they collect a supply to use medicinally for curing skin afflictions and rheumatism. The sweet sap is sometimes made into a wine similar to champagne.

One kind of birch, the paper birch, was put to good use by northern Indians. They used it as a covering for their shelters and in making lightweight canoes, utensils, and containers for food storage. Today it finds its way into shoe lasts, clothespins, spools, toothpicks, and pulpwood.

The hard, strong, straight-grained wood of the birch is used to advantage in flooring, interior finish, furniture, veneer, baskets, boxes, crates, and hoops for casks. Certain chemicals are derived from it through distillation. It makes excellent fuel, burning fiercely with a bright, clear flame. Because the oil of the birch makes it both waterproof and flammable, woodsmen seek it for their campfires, particularly when the forest is soaked with rain.

Butternut

Country dwellers almost everywhere are familiar with the white walnut, or butternut tree. Women gather the nuts while they are yet soft and pickle them with vinegar, sugar, and spices.

The Indians made sugar from the sap of the tree and from its nuts extracted oil. A gentle cathartic can be made from the roots' inner bark. Pioneer women used husks of the butternut and the bark lining to dye their homespun fabric brown or tan. During the Civil War days many a soldier's uniform owed its color to butternut dye.

Butternut wood is beautifully grained, and when polished takes on a satiny glow. The altars of some of America's old churches were made of it. Today it is used for furniture and paneling.

Persimmon Tree

Persimmons are a favorite food of wild creatures. They were enjoyed, either fresh or dried, by southeastern Indians, who also ground them into meal for breadmaking. Not only a kind of beer but an indelible ink can be made from the fruit. Both bark and unripe fruit have been utilized in the treatment of fevers. The pioneers made a drink from persimmon seeds as a substitute for coffee. A very good tea can be made from the leaves, which have a high content of vitamin C.

The persimmon tree's hard wood is used in golf-club heads, rollers, and shuttles in textile mills.

Cottonwood

During pioneer days on the western expanses of prairies and plains, cottonwood trees were of exceptional importance, their presence determining the site for a homestead. They provided cooling shade in summer and in winter furnished firewood. Homes and stockades were constructed from their timber. Livestock was nourished with cottonwood leaves.

Today the soft, easily worked wood of the cottonwood is used for papermaking, excelsior, baskets, crates, and boxes.

Eucalyptus

Because the eucalyptus tree soaks up tremendous quantities of water, it has been planted in marshy areas that were considered breeding places for fevers. Thus it became known as the "fever tree."

A tea made from its leaves has been used to treat fevers, colds, respiratory troubles, and various infections. The dried leaves, when smoked in cigarette form, are said to benefit asthma sufferers. Eucalyptus wine is considered an aid to digestion.

Over a century ago the eucalyptus tree was imported from Australia by railroad men, who planned to use the hard wood for track ties. However, the wood proved too difficult to cut for profit.

Since that time the wood has been put to many other uses. Able to endure drought, eucalyptus trees serve as fine windbreaks in arid regions. A medicinal oil has been extracted from the bark. The tree also provides nectar for honey, tannin for leather-tanning, and good fuel for warmth. In some areas of our country, sweet-scented smoke curling from the chimney at a house probably means that slow-burning eucalyptus logs are flaming on the hearth.

Cedar

Indians steeped small branches of the northern white cedar in boiling water, making a tea that cured scurvy. The sap of the tree has been found to contain vitamin C, which no doubt was responsible for the treatment's success. A fragrant oil from the leaves and branches of this cedar has been used in medicines.

The timber, being resistant to decay, is made into poles, posts, railroad ties, tanks, shingles, buckets, and boats. The lightweight wood makes good floats for the nets of fishermen.

Alaskan Indians use red cedars for carving their totem poles. From the trees' massive logs, they hollow out their canoes, known as dugouts.

Pine

In the past the Scotch pine provided wood for strong ship masts. Its cones have been used to flavor wines.

Turpentine and its oil, yellow rosin, wood tar, and pitch are processed from the tree's juices.

During times of scarcity, country folks made a bread from the inner lining of the bark. The leaves of the tree, mixed with wool, became stuffing for mattresses.

The eastern white pine formerly served many purposes. Its even-textured, easily worked wood was used for covered bridges, barns, houses, furniture, coffins, and matches.

Indians were reported to have included the inner bark in their diet, and even today it is sometimes used in cough remedies.

The extensively used eastern white pine soon became scarce, and the western white pine took its place in building construction. It is used, too, in the manufacture of matches, crates, sashes, doors, frames, and foundry patterns.

Over the centuries, the seeds of the piñon pine were a staple food of southwestern Indians. The timber of the tree makes excellent fuel and charcoal. Its wood sometimes goes into mine timbers, poles, and posts.

The hard, resinous wood of the longleaf pine is widely used for boxes, crates, and poles. Its pulpwood is manufactured into cartons, bags, and wrapping paper. Turpentine and rosin are made from its sap.

The ponderosa pine's somewhat soft, even-grained wood is used chiefly for lumber but also for railroad ties, mine timbers, posts, poles, and veneer. Finer-quality ponderosa pine goes into cabinets, paneling, trim, doors, and sashes; inferior grades become boxes and crates.

Saplings of the lodgepole pine provided the Indians with poles for their tepees or lodges—hence its name. Today its wood is used for railroad ties, mine timbers, poles and posts, pulpwood, and lumber.

Dogwood

The bitter bark of the dogwood tree was made into a tea by the Indians to treat fevers. The pioneers used it as a remedy for malaria. When the South was unable to get quinine during the Civil War, dogwood bark served as a substitute. The Indians made a dye from it, which they used to color their feathers scarlet. Sometimes the leaves and unripe fruit of the dogwood were used as tonics and astringents.

Today the tree's tough, close-grained wood is used for mallets, tool handles, jeweler's blocks, meat skewers, bobbins, and spools. It is especially suited for the shuttles of textile mills, because it retains its smoothness under constant use.

Spruce

Eons ago gummy sap oozed from spruce trees and congealed into transparent stones which today we value as amber. Country people have brewed beer from tender sprouts of the spruce tree. Planks for flooring are made from its wood.

The easily worked, hard wood of the red spruce is used for papermaking, ladder rails, and general millwork. Parts of violins and the sounding boards of pianos are often made from it.

The black spruce brings cheer to many a home during the yuletide as a Christmas tree. Its wood goes into canoe paddles and oars, ladder rungs, boxes, and crates. The white fibers of the wood require so little bleaching that they make excellent pulpwood.

North American Indians used the pliable roots of the white spruce to weave baskets and to lace their birch-bark canoes.

The state tree of Alaska is the Sitka spruce. Its timber goes into boats, ladders, doors, sashes, furniture, boxes, crates, and sounding boards for pianos. In our modern times, the chief wood used in aircraft construction has come from the Sitka spruce.

Yew

Because the leaves of the yew are poisonous, the tree is never planted in fields or along roadways where cattle might eat them.

Before the advent of the gun, bows were made from the yew tree. Today its strong, fine-grained wood is still used for archer's bows and for canoe paddles, posts, poles, cabinetwork, and inlaying.

State Trees

A good many of our states have adopted state trees. They are listed here:

- BALSAM POPLAR Wyoming
- BLUE SPRUCE Colorado, Utah
- CABBAGE PALMETTO South Carolina, Florida
- DOUGLAS FIR Oregon
- EASTERN HEMLOCK Pennsylvania
- EASTERN REDBUD Oklahoma

- EASTERN WHITE PINE Maine, Michigan, Wisconsin
- ELM Massachusetts, North Dakota, Nebraska
- FLOWERING DOGWOOD Missouri
- LIVE OAK Georgia
- LONGLEAF PINE Alabama
- NORTHERN RED OAK New Jersey
- OHIO BUCKEYE Ohio
- PECAN Texas
- PIÑON PINE New Mexico
- PONDEROSA PINE Montana
- RED PINE Minnesota
- SHORTLEAF PINE Arkansas
- SINGLE-LEAF PIÑON Nevada
- SITKA SPRUCE Alaska
- SOUTHERN MAGNOLIA Mississippi
- SUGAR MAPLE New York, Vermont, West Virginia
- TULIP TREE Indiana, Kentucky, Tennessee
- WESTERN WHITE PINE Idaho
- WHITE OAK Connecticut, Maryland

Tree Growth

In a period of ten years, trees grow approximately as follows:

TREE	HEIGHT (FEET)	DIAMETER	
Birch	17	8	inches
Elm	17	8	"
Butternut	17	8	"
Black walnut	17	8	"
Chestnut	17	8	"
White ash	17	8	"
Larch	21	6½	"
Ash-leaf maple	17	5–6	feet
White maple	17	5–6	"
Yellow willow	29	1¼	"
White willow	33	1¼	"

9
Flowers, Herbs, and Shrubs

The Infinite has written its name on the heavens in shining stars, and on the earth in tender flowers.
—Jean Paul Richter
Hesperus, XXV
1795

Flowering plants do more than brighten our world with their myriad hues and diversify the landscape with an infinite variety of silhouettes and textures. Through countless generations of experiments and accidental experiences, man has discovered the special properties of each plant and its specific value in his life. Plants have been used as food, drink, and flavoring, as perfume, cosmetics, and dyes, and in medicine, religion, and myths to account for earthly life. This relationship with plants that share our environment multiplies our appreciation of the interlocking associations among all of God's creations.

Hundreds of years ago herb gathering was an essential pursuit in life. Herbs were the chief source of dyes (chemical dyes were not developed until the mid-1800's), cosmetics, and medications. Medicinal herbs and the medicines obtained therefrom were called "simples," because each plant was believed to possess its individual virtue and so to embody a simple remedy. The herbalist who collected simples was known as a "simpler," or "simplist."

People of those times believed that effective medicine must have an offensive smell and bitter taste. Often medicinal plants were chosen at first because of their rank odor and found later actually to contain tonic properties—horehound being one such plant.

For the relief of headaches, aromatic flowers were held to temples and forehead. Some were applied to wounds to hasten their healing. Bay leaves in bath water were found to have a soothing effect on sore and aching bodies. Powdered leaves of alehoof, camomile, peppermint, sneezewort, sweet flag, thyme, and woodruff were used as snuff to cure head colds and relieve depression. As protection against disease, people fumigated their houses with many kinds of fragrant substances, such as aloes, rosemary, sage, angelica, cinnamon, and thyme. Rue was particularly popular because it repelled fleas, considered bearers of the plague. The powdered seeds of love-in-a-mist were sprinkled in the hair, their scent being loathsome to lice. Sufferers from insomnia slept on pillows stuffed with hops; besides exuding a pleasant scent, the hops exerted a gently narcotic influence, inducing sleep.

Strongly aromatic leaves and resins are said to possess antibiotic properties. Plants produce aromatic substances, known as essential oils, which are their waste products. As a general rule, oils taken from the leaves have stronger antiseptic powers than those extracted from the petals. So potent is the antiseptic quality of the oil from thyme leaves that in the past it was applied to soldiers' uniforms to protect them from vermin. Doctors customarily carried aromatics at the upper tips of their walking sticks, which they frequently raised to their noses as discreetly as possible when tending the sick.

The odor of herbs and flowers was used to combat odors of

a less pleasant variety. Known as "strewing herbs," such plants as thyme, sage, camomile, basil, lavender, and hyssop were scattered on the floors of churches and other places where people, usually unbathed, congregated in large numbers. In courts of law, judges were presented with aromatic flowers to counteract the offensive odors of unwashed prisoners. Potpourris were an old-fashioned way of scenting musty houses. Mixtures of rose petals, lavender, rosemary, thyme, cloves, and dried, powdered orange peel were placed in potpourri jars of china or wood, holes in their lids releasing the aroma. A properly made potpourri was said to maintain its perfume for fifty years or more. Housewives used lavender and peppermint to freshen bedrooms with fragrance as well as to cool them in summer. Aromatic foliage is actually capable of lowering air temperature; as the essential oils in the leaves oxidize, an invisible haze forms that impedes heat rays.

The emotional response to floral fragrance influenced a good part of folk medicine, flower healing, and herbalism. Certain flower scents (for example, white jasmine) were alleged to produce sensual effects, some to evoke changes in temperament (sweet basil being used to incite feelings of good cheer), and others (for instance, withering strawberry leaves) to engender an exhilarating atmosphere conducive to creative work.

Early perfume consisted of the dried parts of aromatic plants, among them cinnamon, iris, sweet marjoram, myrrh, saffron, spikenard, sweet flag, carnation, narcissus, rose, lotus, lily, and dill. Perfumed powders were sprinkled in bedding to be absorbed by the skin during sleep. Saffron was spread on floors, the aroma being released as it was trodden upon. Dried crocus petals and the leaves of agrimony and woodruff provided fragrant stuffing for pillows and cushions.

The distillation of flowers and leaves for perfume began at the start of the seventeenth century. Sweet waters were concocted from balm, marigold, sage, tansy, lavender, and rosemary. They were used for personal cleanliness, medicine, and cooking.

The most fragrant flowers are white. In general, with the

increase of pigment in the petals, perfume lessens. Experience taught that the most favorable time to gather flower petals was just before the morning sun rose to evaporate their oils.

The floral kingdom provides some four thousand aromatic substances for perfumery. To deter the too-rapid evaporation of the scent of perfume, a fixative assumes this role formerly fulfilled by the plant's resin or wax. From earliest times animal secretions were considered the best fixatives. Castor from the beaver, musk from the musk deer, the civet of the civet cat, and ambergris from the intestines of a species of whale were valued as perfume fixatives. However, plant resins and sweet gums were used too, such as the oils of sandalwood and cedarwood.

Early settlers of America were concerned with the basic necessities for sustaining life. Perfume was frowned upon as frivolous. Indeed, young women discovered using scent to entice a member of the opposite sex were liable to dunking, according to the law.

Colonists used the wax enclosing berries of the wax myrtle shrub to make their candles. By continually rubbing furniture with balm, the herb melissa, they gave it both scent and luster. To impart sheen and pleasant aroma to oaken floors, they polished them with the seeds of sweet fern. The calycanthus shrub of the Carolinas was found to have flowers redolent of apple scent, bark with the odor of cinnamon, and roots that smelled like camphor. Colonists used the bark as a substitute for cinnamon and fumigated their houses by burning the dried roots.

The following are some of the flowers, herbs, and shrubs that have served man in a variety of ways through the centuries. You will notice that among them are plant names ending in *wort*, such as "sticklewort." *Wort* is a word from the Old English meaning "root," "herb," or "plant."

Agrimony (Sticklewort)

Because the fruits of agrimony possess tiny hooks which serve in seed dispersal as they catch in the fur of passing animals, the plant is known also as sticklewort.

Colonists brought it to North America for medicinal purposes. They used it to doctor snake bite. Lemonade containing its flowers was a standard remedy for colds.

Early country folk made a tea of agrimony leaves to treat sore throats, kidney and bladder trouble, and disorders of the liver. The wounds of humans and animals were ministered to with the leaves boiled in wine. The seeds were used in salves and balms and in wine as a cure for dysentery.

A yellow or gold dye can be made from the agrimony's yellow flowers.

Centaury

Herbalists sought the centaury for its tonic properties. Internally it was used to fight contagious disease, cure jaundice, lower fevers, and kill worms. Externally it was employed to treat ulcers and wounds and to stop the falling of hair.

Elecampane

The mucilaginous roots of elecampane are sometimes made into sweetmeats and for centuries have been employed as horse medicine. The plant has been used as a home remedy to treat respiratory ailments, kidney and bladder problems, and indigestion. Elecampane wine was taken as a cough syrup, diuretic, and tonic.

Yellow Gentian

The life of the yellow gentian sometimes spans more than fifty years.

During earlier times the plant's roots, collected in the fall and steeped in water, were used as a cure-all for disorders of the bowels, liver, stomach, and heart. It was believed that the gentian's particular medicinal properties could prolong life and render poisons ineffectual. Vinegar made from the plant was a remedy for fevers and a safeguard against communicable diseases.

Today it finds its way into alcoholic beverages—aperitifs and liqueur—and is used to treat stomach problems, general weakness, and nervous conditions.

Lady's Bedstraw (*Cheese Rennet*)

The scent of lady's bedstraw has been likened to that of honey or lime blossoms. In times past the plant afforded a pleasant stuffing for mattresses and so acquired its descriptive name. It is frequently called "cheese rennet" because its flowers were once used as a substitute for rennet to curdle milk during cheese making.

Formerly the plant was prescribed as a cure for epilepsy. It is used in treating dropsy, obesity, skin ailments, and illnesses of nervous origin. A lotion from the boiled stems is recommended for soothing sunburn and removing freckles.

A drink can be made from bedstraw seeds that is an excellent alternative to coffee. The plant has been used to fashion crude sieves for straining milk. At one time Scotsmen colored their tartans with the roots' red dye.

Meadowsweet

Meadowsweet has properties similar to those of aspirin. It is a natural remedy prescribed for kidney and bladder problems, dropsy, gout, fevers, and insomnia. A brew made of its leaves benefits ulcers and sores, the tannin content of the leaves causing them to dry up quickly.

The roots of meadowsweet are a source of black dye.

Bouncing Bet (Soapwort)

Early settlers brought bouncing Bet from Europe as much for a domestic convenience as for a garden bloom. Its bruised leaves, stems, and roots make a lather for washing delicate fabrics and cleaning woolens just before dyeing. Because of these cleansing properties, it is known too as soapwort. Ladies particularly favored it for shampooing hair and for laundering dainty undergarments. For this reason it acquired the name "my lady's washbowl."

A decoction of the plant's leaves is said to be a good remedy for itch. Long ago it was prescribed for ulcers, leprosy, and venereal disease.

Marjoram

Marjoram has long been used as a flavorful herb in cooking and as a home remedy. It was considered soothing to liver and stomach pain and was used to treat asthma, catarrh, bronchitis, whooping cough, head colds, migraine, insomnia, and rheumatism. The leaves, dried and powdered, were taken like snuff to evoke sneezing and thus clear a stuffy nose.

Goldenrod

Medicinally, goldenrod has been used to treat skin diseases, arthritis, rheumatism, and dropsy and to stimulate the liver and kidneys.

A pigment extracted from the plant dyes cloth in shades of lemon yellow to warm gold.

Wild Rose

A honey found on the fluff surrounding seeds of the wild rose has been used to combat intestinal worms in humans as well as animals. Country people dry and powder the seeds as a home cure for kidney stones. From the hips enclosing the seeds, they make a tonic to purify the blood in springtime. The hips possess a goodly amount of vitamin C and are considered an aid to resisting infection and a remedy for diarrhea and bleeding gums.

Yellow Dock

Yellow dock has nutritive and medicinal value. Its leaves are often used as edible greens.

For generations country families have made yellow dock into salves, tonics, and laxatives. The roots, being high in iron content, have been prescribed for weakness, anemia, rheumatism, and skin disorders. When dried and powdered, the roots are said to provide an acceptable dentifrice.

Blackberry

The blackberry bush is sometimes referred to as the "mother of the oak" because new trees sprout best beneath its sheltering branches.

While gathering blackberries for jam and syrup, country people learned that the crushed leaves would quickly stop bleeding from thorn scratches. An excellent tea can be brewed from the dried leaves. Long ago blackberries were believed to be a cure for loose teeth and protruding eyes. Considered beneficial to mucous membranes, they are employed as a mouthwash and gargle for sore throats.

A dye for coloring fabric a pale gray can be extracted from the berries.

Alkanet

Alkanet was brought to North America by some of the first settlers for use in medicine and as a dye.

Medicinally it was employed to treat rheumatism and kidney problems and to induce perspiring in cases of fever.

Sap from the roots of the plant yields a red coloring used to dye paper and cloth. Cosmetically it served as a rouge for the cheeks.

Eyebright

The small herb eyebright blossoms but once, on a sunny day. Country people believed that the linnet used it to improve its eyesight.

As a rural remedy it was recommended for conjunctivitis, watering eyes, and poor vision. It was also a treatment for head colds, coughs, and indigestion.

Broom (Genista)

As its name implies, the broom shrub provides material for broomsticks. In medieval times witches were reputed to ride such brooms. Paradoxically, the plant was believed to keep witches away. Its branches have furnished firewood for baker's ovens and potter's kilns and material for constructing huts. Yarn and strong rope can be made from the bark.

Medicinally it has been used as an antivenom, a heart tonic, and a diuretic and in the treatment of rheumatism and malarial fever. Country people drink wine containing ashes of the broom shrub to cure dropsy.

The plant gives a good yellow dye.

Comfrey

For centuries comfrey has been employed as an aid in healing wounds and mending broken bones. In compress form it is used to relieve the pain of burns, sprains, gout, and phlebitis.

Marsh Marigold (American Cowslip)

Because the marsh marigold had been dedicated to the Virgin Mary, it was used in church ceremonies throughout the Middle Ages.

Country people cook tender young marigold plants for table greens. The buds are added to sauces as a substitute for capers.

The plant is a source of yellow dye.

Wood Betony (Lousewort)

At one time country dwellers believed that sheep which fed on wood betony risked developing a skin disease caused by a louse, and so the plant is sometimes called "lousewort."

It is claimed that betony's aromatic scent often makes its collectors dizzy. Rural folk gather the leaves and flowers for a tea brewed as a remedy for inflammation and congestion of the respiratory tract. The leaves, dried and steeped, are used in compresses to aid the healing of ulcers and wounds. In powdered form they act as a decongestant in cases of head colds by provoking sneezing and are also used to stop hiccups. Wood betony has also served as a treatment for stomach, kidney, and liver discomfort, brain disorders, rheumatism, sciatica, gout, and shortness of breath.

The ancients prescribed it as a medicine for women in prolonged labor. According to prevailing superstition, the plant would protect journeyers by night from all harm, even witchcraft.

Thyme

The Egyptians and Etruscans employed thyme in embalming procedures. Greeks burned it for incense when worshiping their gods. Both Greeks and Romans used the herb in the preparation of food. For Roman women it was a beauty aid.

Over the centuries thyme has been used to improve circulatory, digestive, and respiratory functions and to relieve insomnia, exhaustion, coughs, chills, and anemia. As a scalp tonic it is recommended for preventing and stopping hair loss. The plant's dried and powdered leaves, when used like snuff, are said to act as a decongestant for the respiratory tract and to check nosebleed.

Calamus (Sweet Flag)

In times past calamus was regarded as a medicinal plant. Chewing its roots was a remedy for stomach disorders and a means of sweetening the breath.

Over the years country lads have enjoyed munching on the hot, sweet roots of calamus, or sweet flag.

Lesser Celandine (Figwort)

An irritating element contained in lesser celandine was once used by country people to poison rats. Beggars used the substance to intentionally create sores as a means of gaining sympathy and alms. In olden times doctors prescribed it for wens and hemorrhoids.

Greater Celandine (Swallowwort)

According to an old legend, swallows brush the eyes of their young with a twig of greater celandine, or swallowwort, to protect them from blindness. The name *celandine* comes from the Greek word for "swallow," because the plant first appears when that bird arrives and fades when it departs.

The yellow-flowered herb was believed to have supernatural powers. Wearing a sprig in the shoes was supposed to cure yellow jaundice. Carrying celandine on the person, along with a mole's heart, would ensure a favorable outcome in lawsuits. People believed that the plant sang when an ailing man was on the verge of death; if he was destined to get well, it would weep. Various illnesses were treated with the plant: blindness, cancer, dropsy, and plague.

Honeysuckle

For hundreds of years honeysuckle was used in treating wounds. A tea made from the leaves is an old country cure for constipation, kidney stones, and coughs. A drink concocted from its bark and roots has been used as a tonic and remedy for liver disorders and gout.

Barberry

A first fruit carried to the New World by early colonists was the barberry. They used it for medicine as well as food. It was a remedy for indigestion, dropsy, jaundice, and rheumatism. Fevers were reduced with a tea made from the red berries, which were also made into jelly.

All parts of the plant yield a yellow dye for coloring cloth and staining wood. It imparts a tawny gloss to leather when used as polish.

Fennel

Fennel has been used for centuries in preparing food. Wet nurses partook of it to maintain milk production. It was prescribed as an antidote for scorpion stings and snake bite and as a treatment for failing eyesight.

A great deal of superstition was associated with the herb. Hanging twigs of fennel from the rafters was supposed to force harmful spirits from the house; a few seeds placed in the keyhole would prevent ghosts from entering.

In rural areas fennel has been employed as a home remedy for the following conditions: kidney and gall bladder disorders, anemia, weakness, bronchitis, poor appetite, headaches, indigestion, and eye problems.

Buckthorn

The stems of the buckthorn, being flexible, are used to advantage in making wicker furniture.

During colonial times housewives brewed tea with its leaves, thus avoiding England's tea tax. A drink made from the plant is said to alleviate constipation and the berry juice, used in compresses, to ameliorate skin problems.

Pokeweed

New leaves of pokeweed are sometimes boiled and served as table greens, especially in the southern United States.

The plant's dried fruit and roots possess a property used in diminishing the swelling and caking of cows' udders. Farmers blend it with wool oil and apply it to the afflicted udders.

In days gone by, country children made a red ink from pokeweed berries.

Burdock (*Beggar's Buttons*)

Burdock serves as both food and medicine. Its young, tender leaves are a tasty addition to salads; the roots are palatable when boiled and buttered; and the stalks, stripped of their skin, provide a food reminiscent of asparagus. Sometimes the nutritious stalks are candied.

The plant has been used medicinally to treat the following ills: skin afflictions, arthritis, colds, falling hair, measles, respiratory ailments, and rheumatism. It has been used as a diuretic and laxative.

Country children fashion baskets and chains of the flowering burrs.

Camomile (*Mayweed*)

An aromatic but bitter tea brewed from camomile flowers has been taken over the years as a blood purifier and tonic. Camomile has been employed as a home remedy to treat skin infections, inflamed eyelids, rheumatic pains, fever, indigestion, and insomnia. Used as a shampoo, it enhances blond hair with golden highlights.

The scent of camomile flowers is said to discourage bees from stinging collectors of honey.

Daisy

In former times daisy leaves were cooked as a vegetable or served in salads. Rural folk make a tea from the whole daisy plant, including its flowers; taken every spring, it is considered a tonic for cleansing the blood of impurities accumulated during the winter months. A decoction of the leaves and flowers is used as a home remedy for pains of rheumatism, respiratory troubles, general stiffness, and skin ailments.

Hop

In ancient times the yellow powder found on the female flowers of the hop vine was used in treating ulcers and tumors of the liver and spleen. It was also prescribed in cases of depression. Today it is used as a tonic, diuretic, sedative, and aid to digestion.

Brewers employ it to give aroma and flavor to beer. Because of the sedative properties of the female flowers' dried ripe cones, pillows stuffed with them benefit those suffering from insomnia and nervousness.

Wild Touch-me-not

The stems of wild touch-me-not are engorged with juice. This juice is a boon to poison ivy sufferers, for when applied to affected areas it affords almost instantaneous relief. A complete cure is said to take place in a period of twenty-four hours.

Dandelion

The dandelion provides both food and drink. Its leaves furnish palatable table greens, and wine can be made from the plant.

The white sap is used as a treatment for eye afflictions, problems of the kidneys and bladder, rheumatism, diabetes, circulatory trouble, and jaundice. The roots are employed in liver medicine and tonics for aiding digestion and cleansing the body of waste material. The flowers can be steeped to produce a lotion that is said to remove freckles.

Long ago it was believed that if the white sap was rubbed on the entire body, all of one's desires would be granted. Country maids wistfully figure the number of years until their marriage by counting the breaths needed to blow away the dandelion down. Children puff on the fluffy balls to tell the time of day.

The vireo chooses the down of the dandelion to cushion the interior of its nest.

Crane's-bill

Country people have used crane's-bill to treat a great many ills: tonsillitis, diabetes, gastric ulcers, diarrhea, cancer, and bone fractures. It was given to nursing mothers to help them retain milk. A compress of crane's-bill was applied to skin irritations and inflamed eyes. Country dwellers crush the leaves to drive away mosquitoes with their odor.

Black Currant

In the past, black currants were regarded as a veritable elixir of life. People supposed that frequent partaking of them would preserve youthfulness and ensure longevity. They were used as a remedy for dropsy, diarrhea, bladder and kidney ailments, inflammation of the stomach, and chronic fatigue.

Their juice dyes cloth in hues of deep lilac to purple.

Valerian

Only the roots of valerian are used medicinally. They constitute one of the earliest treatments for nervous conditions. Formerly the plant was used in treating epilepsy. Today it is used as a calmative for nervousness, breathlessness, palpitations, hysteria, convulsions, insomnia, migraine, and dizziness.

Valerian has a powerful effect upon cats, sending them into paroxysms of delight.

Sage

Through the centuries sage was valued as a healer of all ills. People believed that it helped to create life and protect it; so the herb was prescribed for those wanting to conceive and for those already with child.

Chewing a sage leaf before dining has been recommended to avoid indigestion. As a seasoning it not only flavors food but is said to prevent spoilage. In tonic form sage is felt to increase circulation and aid in convalescence. Sage tea is used to treat bronchitis and vertigo. A decoction of the herb is advocated for sore throats, inflamed gums, and dental abscesses. Added to rum and applied to the scalp, it is used to cure dandruff and check hair loss. Sage salve is employed for relieving the discomfort of muscular pains, rheumatism, sciatica, and gout. Asthma victims claim to find relief by smoking the plant's dried leaves. Sage leaves allowed to smoke on hot coals in the fireplace or boiled in an open vessel have been employed as a disinfectant for sick rooms.

Balm (*Melissa*)

Balm is a favorite plant of bees.

In the past, a drink distilled from the flowers and leaves was used to alter human temperament in cases of depression, mania, and lethargy and to treat apoplexy and epilepsy. It was also regarded as an elixir of youth.

Red Rose

The red rose is thought to be the flower earliest cultivated by man. Many religions have used it symbolically.

People have long feasted on foods flavored with roses, such as rose cakes and rose jams. Wines have been infused with the flowers. Ladies scented themselves with rose powder and added luster to their eyelids by applying rose oil. They perfumed their breath with candies of myrrh and rose petals mashed in honey.

Medicinally the red rose was used to treat tuberculosis and other lung afflictions. Sore throats were soothed with rose honey. A lotion made from the plant's dried leaves was a remedy for eye inflammations.

Bloodroot

North American Indians extracted a dye from the orange-red juice of bloodroot to color porcupine quills. Finding it so quick to stain whatever it encounters, they employed it as war paint.

An old-fashioned country cure for children's head colds was a lump of sugar saturated with the juice of bloodroot.

Hawkweed

Long ago, people believed that birds of prey fed on hawkweed to make their eyesight keen; hence its name.

The plant is said to be an efficacious treatment for infectious abortions among cattle and for undulant fever in humans. It has been used as a remedy for various other ills: dropsy, jaundice, hardening of the arteries, fevers, gall bladder ailments, and kidney disorders.

Rosemary

Rosemary has been used for centuries in cooking as a seasoning for meat and sauces.

In olden times it was an ingredient in salves to heal wounds and assuage pains. The herb was used in treating loss of memory, vertigo, general weakness, and jaundice. It was recommended that it be eaten with salt the first thing upon rising for strengthening eyesight. Its candied blossoms were considered a good defense against plague. Rosemary wine was said to aid digestion and benefit the kidneys. An infusion of the plant was employed in compresses to ease the pain of contusions and rheumatism.

It was a cherished belief in those early days that homes scented with rosemary would be safeguarded against harm.

Hollyhock

The hollyhock originated in China and the Mediterranean area and was introduced to Europe in the sixteenth century, thence to North America.

A drink made from the hollyhock was advocated as a remedy for bronchitis and coughs and as a mouthwash for ulcers of the mouth. A lotion concocted from the plant was prescribed for facial blotches and general redness. Wine was tinted with its dark purple flowers.

Chicory

Chicory came to North America from Europe. It makes excellent hay, said to be superior to alfalfa.

The dried roots often serve as a coffee substitute or an additive. Tender new plant shoots can be used in salads.

Medicinally chicory is said to purify the blood, stimulate the appetite, and cure anemia, indigestion, arthritis, dropsy, liver problems, and constipation. A massage with alcohol containing chicory root is advocated as a treatment to check the withering of paralyzed limbs.

Horsetail (*Mare's-tail*)

Horsetail is a plant of very ancient lineage. Over the eons it created deep layers of coal.

The ancients valued it as a general tonic. It has been prescribed for anemia, tuberculosis, kidney complaints, skin disorders, and weak fingernails. A tincture made from horsetail is said to remedy perspiring feet. Because a high percentage of silica and other minerals are stored in the plant, it is considered a strong remineralizing substance when taken internally.

The tender shoots of horsetail make good salad greens. Country housewives scour vessels of wood, brass, and pewter with the plant. Furniture makers have used it for polishing wood.

Horsetail furnishes a yellow-greenish dye.

Climbing Ivy

The climbing ivy was at one time considered a preventive against inebriation. With that thought in mind, craftsmen carved goblets of the ivy's wood from which to sip wine.

A drink of ivy berries steeped in wine was prescribed to ward off the plague. Country folk have used the berries as a purgative. Poultices of crushed ivy leaves were placed on sores and wounds to hasten healing. It was said that injured animals in the woodland rolled amid ivy to cure their wounds. Country mothers fashioned caps of ivy for babies whose heads were afflicted with impetigo. A tea made from the leaves was a remedy for inflamed mucous membranes, bronchitis, whooping cough, rheumatic pains, and neuralgia. Ivy juice rubbed on temples and forehead was recommended to relieve headaches.

Basil

Basil originated in India, where it figures in religion. Long ago the plant was regarded as sacred, and offerings of flowers and rice were made to it. People believed it was a guardian spirit.

According to prevailing superstition, a pounded twig of basil placed under a stone would become a scorpion. Strangely enough, the herb was considered an antidote to the sting of a scorpion.

Early settlers, noting basil's tranquilizing properties, employed it as a cure for epilepsy, nervousness, insomnia, vertigo, migraine, and stomach disorders. Folk medicine advocates the putting of several drops of juice from the leaves into an inflamed ear.

Nettle

In some countries nettles are eaten as a cooked vegetable. Newly sprouted plants make flavorful salads. In the 1800's a popular drink was an herbal tea brewed from nettle leaves.

Formerly the leaves were put in the feed of swine and poultry, and they were employed as a scouring agent in cleaning dairy utensils. To induce hens to lay more eggs, nettle seeds were added to their mash. After being steeped, the stems furnished a strong yarn for the nets and ropes of fishermen.

The plant was thought to have magical powers. To overcome fear one had only to hold a sprig of nettle and yarrow in the hand. Country people believe that coating the skin with nettle and tarragon juice would render one capable of seizing fast-swimming fish with the bare hands. As a love potion the seeds were swallowed in wine.

The nettle was used as a tonic, an aid to digestion, and a rejuvenator of the blood. It was recommended for treating diabetes, rheumatism, and dropsy. The plant was a classic rural remedy for bed-wetting. Applied to the scalp in lotion form, it was said to combat dandruff and check hair loss.

A greenish-yellow dye can be extracted from the nettle.

Tansy

Tansy was so highly regarded as a heal-all in Europe that early colonists felt obliged to bring it to the New World. Tansy tea was used as a remedy for indigestion, head colds, and intestinal worms. The leaves, fresh or dried, discourage the presence of bedbugs and fleas; country folk scattered them amid the bedding and sprinkled them in the straw of dog kennels. Country lasses steeped the leaves in buttermilk for more than a week and used the wash to improve their complexions.

In the past tansy was used in cookery. Its leaves were an ingredient in cakes known as tansies. Tansy pudding was traditionally served at the end of Lent.

The plant's flower heads give a yellow dye.

Periwinkle

Because the periwinkle retains its green leaves throughout the year, it is identified with immortality.

Long ago this creeping plant was used in magic rituals. Casting it into a fire with other herbs would cause the ghosts of loved ones to arise in the smoke. To render a snake bite harmless, the wound was rubbed with the periwinkle while mysterious formulas were repeated. Women wore it about their thighs as a safeguard against miscarriage. It was also used as an ingredient in love potions.

From the herb's astringent property came the belief that it could check any kind of bleeding. Crushed leaves placed in the nostrils are said to arrest bleeding from the nose. The periwinkle has been used to treat fever, tiredness, tonsillitis, mouth ulcers, sores, and wounds. A rural remedy for pleurisy consists of a mixture of one-half glass of white wine and one-half glass of periwinkle juice.

Bilberry (Blueberry)

Bilberries are excellent for making brandy, jam, and pies.

Country people value them as a treatment for bladder inflammation, diarrhea, and skin diseases. They are also reputed to improve night vision.

Bilberries yield a dye which colors cloth in shades ranging from pink to purple.

Ground Ivy

During long sea voyages of the past, leaves of the ground ivy were put in beer as a preservative.

When cockfighting was legal and popular, the owner of a bird with an eye injury would chew several ivy leaves and spit the juice into its eye to promote healing. The plant in lotion or compress form is used to treat sores and wounds. Sniffing ivy juice into the nostrils is said to relieve migraine and long-lasting headaches. Several drops of ivy oil in an aching ear are supposed to check pain.

Used as a dye, ground ivy produces colors of yellow-green or greenish gray.

Knotgrass

An old superstition once prevailed that the juice of knotgrass would stunt the growth of young farm animals and children.

For the ancients the plant was a cure for the spitting of blood. Rural folk have long used its stems as a home remedy for diarrhea. In veterinary medicine knotgrass has been similarly used to treat farm animals. A decoction of the plant is said to alleviate gout, skin diseases, varicose veins, and arthritis. It has also been employed as a tonic for those suffering from tuberculosis. The plant's juice, rich in tannin and silicic acid, is reported to stop nosebleed when squirted into the nostrils and to staunch the flow of blood from wounds.

A blue dye can be extracted from the knotgrass leaves.

Madonna Lily

At one time an antiseptic was produced from petals of the madonna lily as an aid in healing burns and sores. The boiled bulb of the plant was made into poultices for chapped skin, abscesses, and carbuncles. The uncooked bulb, when mashed, is said to rid the feet of corns. Lily water is supposed to remove blotches from facial skin.

Lavender

For countless years lavender has been used as perfume, sedative, tonic, disinfectant, and healer of wounds.

Ladies of long ago scented their bath water with lavender, and closets and chests were perfumed with sachets of it.

A tea brewed from the plant's blue flowers had sedative properties and was taken in cases of migraine and indigestion. It was also used to treat asthma, bronchitis, whooping cough, and chills. A tincture of lavender applied as a lotion was said to strengthen hair. It was employed as a compress for bruises and as a massage for rheumatic pain.

Oil of lavender was smeared on bedsteads to discourage bedbugs and rubbed into children's hair to destroy lice and their nits.

It was utilized to further the healing of burns and wounds. When hunting hounds became victims of snake bite, the punctures were quickly treated with crushed lavender leaves. Lavender oil is felt to be a strong antiseptic and neutralizing agent of poison.

Nasturtium

In olden times the nasturtium was used more as table fare than as medicine. Tender new leaves and the flowers served as a substitute for water cress in salads. The buds and green seeds were often used like capers.

The plant was later recognized as having powerful antibiotic properties. It was believed to possess aphrodisiac and youth-restoring elements, too. The fruits were employed as a purgative. Because of the nasturtium's high content of sulphur, it is said to check hair loss, foster hair growth, and benefit the scalp.

Marsh Mallow

The ancients esteemed the marsh mallow for its medicinal properties. Every part of this mucilaginous plant was used. The roots were made into a salve for softening the skin. In the days when people endured trial by red-hot iron, the sap combined with egg white and the seeds of the plantain was rubbed in the hands as a protective unguent—enabling the accused to better bear the pain and prove his innocence, because the burns would not be severe. Early-day Georgia swamp dwellers smeared oil from crushed marsh mallow seeds on their bodies as a defense against snakes.

Internally the marsh mallow has been used to treat bronchitis, laryngitis, head colds, gastritis, and constipation. As a gargle it is said to soothe sore throats and tonsillitis, and as a mouthwash to relieve gum inflammations and dental abscesses. It is made into healing compresses for boils and sores. Country mothers give teething babies a piece of marsh mallow root to suck on.

When the plant's petals have fallen, a ring of seeds is revealed at the flower's center, resembling a small flat cheese. Many a country boy has munched on such cheeses while they are yet soft and fresh.

Lily of the Valley

From spring through summer the leaves of lily of the valley yield a yellow dye; in the fall when they turn yellow, the dye extracted is of a bronze-gold hue.

A tea made from the flowers was a standard country remedy for a weak heart. The dried flowers in powdered form, used like snuff, are supposed to ease a prolonged headache.

Mullein

The roots of mullein were used by colonists of North America to treat hoarseness and lung afflictions. The herb was also a remedy for gout and hemorrhoids. Long ago it was believed to be a cure for leprosy. A tea made from mullein produces a sedative effect. It is said that asthma sufferers experience relief by smoking the plant's dried leaves.

Mullein is sometimes called "candlewicks" because country people collected the quantities of hair from its leaves to make wicks for their candles. Hummingbirds also filch the minute hairs that cover the plant, using them to line their tiny nests. The lightweight but sturdy stalk provides an excellent walking cane, especially when the root has grown in a curved fashion to form a handle.

Rural maids massage their faces with the velvety leaves to impart a glow to their cheeks. Country boys delight in smoking them, for they resemble the tobacco used by grown men.

Vervain

For centuries superstition and religion have been associated
with vervain. Hung over a doorway, along with dill and a
horseshoe, it was a standard safeguard against witchcraft. Because of its brushlike structure, it was used in churches to
sprinkle holy water.

Perhaps as a result of vervain's religious use, people developed faith in its healing properties. They employed it in treating pleurisy, bronchitis, and bladder troubles. The bruised
leaves are reputed to relieve the pain of earache, headache,
and rheumatism. The plant is used externally in hot compresses
on bruises, sprains, and wounds.

Vervain also found its way into cooking. The minced leaves
were included in soups and in stuffing for roasted meats.

Being mostly stems, the plant provides excellent swatters
with which country boys do battle with bees while pilfering
their honey. Through the ages both Indian and white boys
have used the tough slender stalks of vervain as arrows for
their bows.

10
Farm Foods

The cities may have their little mobs and riots, but the farmers will plow and sow and reap and feed their stock, and go forth to their labors until the evening. The farmers have ever and always been the hope of the world.
—Elbert Hubbard

Many of our commonest farm foods have histories stretching far back in time. In addition to their use in nutrition, they often served in other ways—to remedy bodily ills, to enhance beauty, and to fulfill superstitious beliefs. Here are some uncommon facts about some common foods.

Asparagus

Asparagus was cultivated as food before the Christian era in Persia and Arabia. It is a delicious vegetable rich in vitamins A and B.

The plant has no true leaves. Its so-called foliage consists of a great many slender branchlets, looking like green threads, which emerge from a tiny scale leaf at the tip.

Long ago, people believed that they could grow asparagus by planting the crushed horn of a wild ram. Its stalks were thought to have medicinal value. A broth made of them was said to relieve the pain of toothache and sprains. A drink of the plant's roots boiled in wine was administered to victims of snake bite.

In years past asparagus was known as "looking-glass weed." Before the use of window screens, its feathery sprays were draped over bedroom mirrors for flies to alight on. Walking very cautiously, one might succeed in reaching an open door or window with a spray still black with flies!

Carrot

All carrots sprang from a common ancestor—that beautiful wild flower Queen Anne's lace.

In the early 1500's the English were cultivating carrots in their gardens. Besides providing a delicious vegetable for tables, carrots furnished an adornment for women. In autumn their delicate, feathery foliage takes on a red or purple hue. Ladies used to pick the leaves and wear them on hats or in their hair instead of feathers.

Today a yellow pigment derived from the carrot is sometimes used to give butter a richer color. Furriers use the oil from this orange root on pelts to protect them from moths. Carrots also serve as nutritious food for livestock.

Cheese

A camel is supposed to have been responsible for the world's first cheese. Thousands of years ago, legend has it, a camel driver used a lamb's stomach as a container for fresh milk. The fermenting action of the enzymes remaining in the lamb's stomach, plus the constant swaying motion of the camel's gait, transformed the milk into cheese.

Cheese was said to have provided David with nourishment and strength when he challenged Goliath. It was brought to Europe by Crusaders returning from the Holy Land. Early Britons, in addition to getting subjugation from Caesar, got cheese. The eighteenth-century Italian lover Casanova advocated cheese and wine as a means of hastening love's blossoming.

Speaking of love, if you are a lover of cheese, you're known as a turophile.

Garlic

Garlic, that odoriferous member of the lily family, was native to southwest Siberia.

In olden times its odor was considered so intolerable that those guilty of heinous crimes were punished by being forced to eat garlic. Because animals as well as humans were believed to be offended by its strong smell and taste, domestic fowl were sprinkled with garlic juice to keep them safe from weasels and other predators.

The ancients valued garlic for its medicinal qualities. It was prescribed externally as a treatment for the bite of beast or insect and internally as an antidote for poison. Garlic was supposed to improve eyesight. When cattle lost their vision, farmers hung roots of it about their necks. A very ancient use of garlic was as a disinfectant in the cremation of corpses. During the First World War, when antiseptics were scarce, garlic oil was used as an acceptable substitute.

Magical protective powers were attributed to garlic. Throughout ancient times it was considered a sure defense against the influence of the evil eye. Hung on doors and around windows, it was supposed to provide protection against vampires. Midwives kept garlic cloves handy to place about a baby's neck immediately following birth or after baptism to guard him from harm. Country dwellers fastened garlic around their cows' necks to deter goblins from stealing milk in the night. To prevent a snake from crawling out of its hole, a clove of garlic was laid at the entrance.

A very practical use for garlic was to keep heavy drinkers from becoming intoxicated. Putting a few crushed cloves at the bottom of their sizable wine pitchers was supposed to do the trick. In Europe, garlic accompanied by chunks of coarse dark bread was a standard breakfast for peasants. In the United States, it is used chiefly for flavoring. High in iron content, it may eventually be regarded as a staple food in the American diet.

Meanwhile, rural folks claim that it's a dependable corn cure. Kermit Zog of North Carolina says to rub a pesky corn with a crushed clove of garlic every night before going to bed, or to bind a sliver of it on the corn with a plaster. This procedure should be repeated until the corn drops off, usually within eight to ten days. Kermit cautions that you may find yourself sleeping alone!

By the way, if you're fond of garlic, you're an alliophiliac.

Honey

In olden times honey affected people's lives virtually from cradle to grave. Regarded as pure, it was the first food given to newborn infants. Marriage contracts often specified a quantity of honey that the groom was obliged to give his future wife every year of their married life. Marriage ceremonies were sticky affairs. In addition to honey's being served in food and drink, it was smeared on the bride's ear lobes, forehead, eyelids, and lips. Its purity served as a kind of talisman to protect the couple from evil and ensure their happy future.

Honey became known as an aphrodisiac and was the chief

ingredient in love potions designed to increase virility. People believed it could influence fertility in women, cattle, and crops.

Esteemed for its nutritional value, it formed part of the daily diet. The ancients considered it an elixir of youth and predicted longevity for faithful users of honey as nourishment.

Since it was felt to be a magical substance, soothsayers used it in their ceremonies. It was regarded also as sacred and was generally included as a sacrificial offering during religious rites.

Over the centuries honey has been considered a cure-all for internal and external woes: gastric disorders, respiratory troubles, inflammation of the kidneys, epilepsy, labor pains, skin diseases, and inflammation of the eyes and eyelids. It has been used for dressing wounds, to spread on the skin of small-pox victims, and to treat obesity, typhoid fever, pneumonia, rheumatism, and insomnia. Because of its antiseptic quality, it was recommended as a gargle.

Peasants paid their taxes in honey. As a widely accepted medium of barter, it served as purchasing power.

Country folks valued it not only as a stimulant for the appe-tite and an aid to digestion, but as a supernatural agent to protect their cattle. Honey fed to cows and applied to their eyes were sure to guard them against pestilence. Rural folk added honey to their wells so that the water would not be-come contaminated. It was regarded as a cure for persons of disagreeable temperament and for those poisoned by mush-rooms, bitten by snakes, or attacked by rabid animals. Used externally, it was said to kill lice and nits. Country people maintained that lightning never struck where there were honey and bees.

At life's end honey continued to play a role. Since honey represented eternal bliss, vessels of it were placed near the coffin and later in the tomb. Outstanding members of society were embalmed in honey. The belief prevailed that the souls of those whose bodies were preserved in it would be rein-carnated.

Nowadays honey might be associated with a country breakfast of hot biscuits spread with butter and honey or the aroma of split acorn squash baking in the oven, honey and spices steaming in the hollows. Yet among country dwellers today, honey is often mixed with hot lemon juice and used as a cold remedy or administered, combined with roasted onions, as a poultice for congested lungs.

To all the uses for honey down through the ages there has been added a modern one. Because of its low freezing point, honey mixed with an equal amount of water has been utilized as an emergency substitute for antifreeze.

Jerusalem Artichoke

Though the Jerusalem artichoke is a true native of North America, facts about it are not widely known. It is not an artichoke but a member of the sunflower family, having a thick, fleshy root. North American Indians ate the root raw, boiled, or roasted. In the western part of the country the plant grew wild, but Indians in the East cultivated it along with other crops of beans, maize, and squash.

French explorers carried it back to their homeland, where it was favorably received as table fare and used as feed for livestock. Upon reaching Italy, it was called *girasole*, the Italian word for sunflower. The English mispronunciation of this word brought about the first part of the name "Jerusalem artichoke"; a comparison of the tuber's flavor to that of the artichoke accounts for the latter part. After its introduction to the English, it was looked upon initially as an unusual delicacy. Since the Jerusalem artichoke grows prolifically, it was soon considered common and shunned.

The plant is similar to other small wild sunflowers but grows to a greater height. During the summer months the edible root grows very little, because the lengthening stalk and maturing flowers consume most of the nourishment. Fortunately, the Jerusalem artichoke is resistant to frost, since its chief growing season extends through the cool months, from October to June. This vegetable is more widely cultivated in Europe than in America, its homeland.

Lettuce

In ancient times travelers from the Mediterranean area eastward were guided by the "compass plant." This plant was wild lettuce. Along its tall stalk climbed upturned leaves whose edges pointed due north and south. One's direction could be determined by it as surely as by the sun. Thirsty journeyers could rely upon its juicy leaves for refreshment, and so it became known as the "water plant."

Not long afterward the leaves, cooked as greens, were found to be a wholesome, palatable food. From then on—and that was probably three thousand years ago—lettuce was a cultivated plant.

Partaking of lettuce salad at the beginning of a meal, it was believed, would stimulate the appetite; eating it at meal's end would prevent inebriation from the wine imbibed while dining.

Because lettuce has a white juice similar to that of opium poppies, it was thought to have narcotic and sedative properties and was recommended as a treatment for pain, fevers, and insomnia.

Onion

The onion is one of the world's earliest-cultivated plants. The Bible relates that it was a food much craved by the Israelites in the wilderness.

Egyptians were said to have placed their right hand on the onion as they took an oath. They sometimes used it as a sacrificial offering to their deities. Divine honors were bestowed upon one variety, and it was depicted on Egyptian monuments. The nutritional value of the bulb was appreciated by Egyptians, who fed it to slaves erecting the pyramids as a defense against scurvy. In later centuries ships of other lands, destined to be long from home port, put to sea with holds laden with onions for the same purpose.

The onion reached the New World through the West Indies, where it was introduced by the Spanish. It spread throughout the Americas and was grown by early colonists and a little later by the Indians.

According to folklore, the onion was an aphrodisiac. From this belief developed the custom of carrying onion soup to a newly married couple.

In the past it was believed that various ailments could be remedied by the onion. A few drops of onion juice in the ear would cure deafness or ringing. Onion juice applied to bald areas of the head would rejuvenate hair growth. For the relief of gout, the juice mixed in a tea of pennyroyal should be spread with a feather on affected areas. Onion juice blended with capon grease was recommended as a cure for blisters on the feet. Today country people of America use raw onion to draw out the poison from a bee sting.

Parsley

Long ago parsley was used for both the living and the dead.

It was considered a healthful food for man and other creatures. The herb was used in meat dishes, poultry stuffing, omelets, soups, salads, and gravies. Eating parsley was said to benefit the brain and memory, beautify the skin, and counteract the effects of a mad dog's bite. One variety boiled in ale was a drink prescribed for the bite of a poisonous spider. Ailing fish were cured, it was believed, if parsley leaves were tossed into their ponds.

Victors of athletic games were crowned with chaplets of

parsley. As for the dead, their graves were customarily spread with it, for parsley was long regarded as the death herb.

To account for parsley's tendency to germinate slowly, legend said that it is the property of the Devil and must make seven trips to him before sprouting. During the Middle Ages it was believed that an enemy would meet sudden death if one uprooted parsley while repeating his name. To this day there are those who avoid transplanting the herb, fearing it might cause bad luck.

Potato

The potato grown in this country, often called the "Irish" potato, followed a rather circuitous route in reaching us. Though its history is spotted with unauthenticated information, there is general agreement that its original home was Chile.

From Indians in the Andes of South America, potato cultivation spread to other tribes, gradually finding its way to the West Indies and, to what is now Virginia, even before colonial days. Sir Francis Drake's ships, bearing supplies for settlers there, returned to England with potatoes obtained by barter from the Indians. These curiosities were presented to Sir Walter Raleigh, who planted them on his estate in Ireland. When the English imported them from that country, they became known as "Irish" potatoes.

Grain was the chief crop of Ireland at that period, and it was a long time before the potato was established as a staple food. By many it was regarded as unfit for human consumption. Its denouncers organized the "Society for the Prevention of Unsatisfactory Diets." From the initials of this group came the word "spud," used for the potato.

The potato was rejected in Scotland as a product of the Devil, since no mention of it could be found in the Bible.

Spaniards became acquainted with the vegetable when they invaded South America early in the sixteenth century. They carried it to Spain, from which country it spread to other parts of Europe.

For a considerable time the French would not accept the potato, believing it was poisonous because of its membership in the nightshade family. It was also believed to cause leprosy. Later, however, it was found to be a cure for scurvy on long sea voyages. In Germany it became a chief crop food as a result of a grain failure. Eventually the potato won its way into the hearts and stomachs of most of the civilized world.

The potato is actually the enlarged tip, or tuber, of an underground stem. In addition to their nutritional value for both humans and farm animals, potatoes are utilized in manufacturing potato flour, starch, alcohol, glucose, and syrup. Country dwellers use the potato as a remedy for lumbago by carrying a small one in the pocket, replacing it when it becomes dried out.

The most reliable written record shows that potatoes were first cultivated on a large scale in New Hampshire from a stock of "Irish" potatoes brought from Ireland. To do its ancient lineage justice, the potato should actually be called the "Chilean" potato.

Radish

The radish was cultivated so long ago that there is conjecture as to where it originated. In ancient times it was food for the people of China, Japan, India, and southern Europe.

The plant is believed to have been cultivated at first for its leaves along Mediterranean shores. Constant tending caused its root to enlarge, providing a second vegetable. Possibly its ancestor was the wild radish of Europe, credited with the power of detecting the presence of witches.

Medicinal properties were ascribed to the radish. Taken internally, it was believed to quicken mental capacities; used externally, to cure bruises. Mixed with honey vinegar, it served as a soothing gargle for tonsillitis. The radish was also considered efficacious in the event of snake bite. Cosmetically, it was recommended for renewal of hair growth and the removal of freckles.

In addition to the pleasantness as food of the crisp, pungent root of the radish plant, its pods are enjoyed when pickled.

Raspberry

Old-timers attached much importance to raspberries when hunting season arrived. Bears are particularly fond of them. When the fruit ripened, bears were easily located.

In olden times people believed that vinegar made from raspberries was a good protection against plague. The juice of the berries was used to dissolve tartar on the teeth and to treat scrofula.

Rhubarb

Rhubarb, usually served as a dessert, is a vegetable of the buckwheat family. Its origin was the Mediterranean area.

In ancient China a variety of rhubarb was cultivated for the use of its roots in medicine.

Benjamin Franklin, in the late 1700's, was responsible for introducing rhubarb to America. While in England, he sent a gift of it to a friend in Philadelphia. Its popularity soon spread. Only the stalks were used for pies and wine making; hence rhubarb is often called "pie plant" and "wine plant." The leaves are discarded because of their poisonously high content of oxalic acid, which can cause a skin rash.

Rice

Rice was probably a native crop of India some five thousand years ago. It soon spread and was cultivated throughout Asia.

The Greeks and Romans did not plant this cereal grass but imported it. Rice cultivation was introduced to the Mediterranean area by Arab armies in the seventh and eighth centuries, and by the fifteenth century it was raised in Italy and France.

On his second voyage to North America, Columbus brought rice from Spain, but its growth was not successful. Then late in the seventeenth century, a storm-tossed ship sought safe harbor along the coast of South Carolina. Some of its cargo was unhusked rice from Madagascar. The captain gave a quantity to a plantation owner, who cultivated it with good results. It was the start of a new money crop for the South. Today the states of Arkansas, California, Louisiana, and Texas produce most of America's rice.

Long ago rice was prescribed as a treatment for hemorrhages and lung disease. Powdered and mixed with milk, it was used as a poultice for skin inflammations. Today a standard country cure for diarrhea is rice water.

Soybean

One of the very earliest food crops grown by man was the soybean. It was a common food among the ancient Chinese well before the Christian era; yet not until the seventeenth century did it find its way to Europe.

In the United States, soybeans were first cultivated to a limited extent in the late nineteenth century, and by the early 1900's home-grown soybeans were processed for the first time.

In China, superstition clings to the soybean. One wearing a concealed necklace of the beans is supposed to be capable of great feats. Diviners are able to predict future events by consulting soybeans that have been soaked in sesame oil for three days.

Besides being a nutritious food containing ten times the protein of milk, soybeans provide oil that is important in the finishing of automobiles.

Spinach

Spinach was first cultivated in ancient Persia and surrounding areas. Not until the Christian era did the plant become widespread. It was introduced to China in the seventh century. Moors were responsible for carrying it to Europe in the twelfth century. For generations a variety of spinach was grown in secluded monastery gardens of Europe.

Finally, in the early part of the sixteenth century, colonists transported the plant to North America. Today Arkansas and Texas produce our major spinach crops.

Nature included an acceptable amount of oxalic acid in spinach. However, with man's constant hybridization of the plant, the acid content has been substantially increased and can cause formation of small stones of calcium oxalate in the body. Eaten occasionally and in moderate amounts, spinach is a good source of vitamin B_2.

Recently the plant has been processed to form a film of chlorophyll which produces electricity when under the sun's rays. The resulting energy is stored in batteries. So spinach has twofold potential energy: food power and electrical power.

Tomato

Spanish padres are credited with the initial dissemination of the tomato plant. Peace following the conquest of the Aztecs permitted them the leisurely pursuit of examining plants in Mexico used by the natives for food and medicine. The Indians cultivated tomato plants on their floating gardens and ate the red fruit. Tomato seeds were among the first sent by the monks to Spain for planting in monastery gardens.

Some years later a Moorish visitor to Mexico, intrigued by the plant's beauty, carried seeds to Morocco. It was here that the bright fruit caught the eye of an Italian sailor. He took the *pomo dei Mori*, the apple of the Moors, to his homeland, where it spread quickly. The French received it from Italy and cleverly changed the name to *pomme d'amour*—the apple of love. The tomato reached England from France and continued being called the "love apple" for centuries.

The tomato plant of those times differed considerably from that of today. The fruit was very much smaller and deeply furrowed. Considered poisonous because it belongs to the nightshade family, it was cultivated not in the vegetable garden but amid flowers, solely as an ornamental plant. Stalks of the shiny red fruit were kept in vases as colorful centerpieces for dining tables or as decorative touches for fireplace mantles. Because of the supposed poisonous quality of tomatoes, they were thrown to marauding wolves, along with poisoned meat chunks.

During the days when tomato plants were relegated to flower beds, ketchup was made from English walnuts. By the mid-1800's, however, walnut ketchup had lost favor to ketchup made from tomatoes. The Italians extracted an oil from the seeds, which they used in making soap. Today tomato-seed oil, along with other oils, is still incorporated in soaps.

After centuries of cultivation the tomato has developed into the large, smooth-skinned sphere of red we know today, delicious to eat and nutritious as a source of vitamin C. We think of the tomato as a vegetable; actually it is a berry.

The tomato really came into its own as a food in America just about the time that hoop skirts went out of style. Resourceful country housewives used discarded hoop-skirt frames as improvised trellises for training tomato vines.

11
Old-time Receipts

RECIPE FOR A HAPPY HOME

½ cup friendship
1 cup thoughtfulness

Cream together with a pinch of tenderness; very lightly beat in a bowl of loyalty, a cup of faith, a cup of love, and one of charity.

Be sure to add a spoonful of gaiety that sings, and the ability to laugh at little things. Moisten with the sudden tears of heartfelt sympathy. Bake in a good-natured pan, and serve repeatedly.

—Anonymous

Dandelion Wine

Put 4 quarts of dandelion heads and 4 quarts of water into a crock. Cover it and let stand for 9 days. Strain out the dandelion blossoms, pressing out the liquid. Add 1 yeast cake, 3 sliced lemons, and 3 pounds of honey to the liquid. Allow to stand for 9 days. Strain it into a jug. Cork the jug only after the wine has stopped working.

Mead

4 quarts water	1 tablespoon grated lemon
2 cups honey	peel
½ cup brown sugar	2 tablespoons lemon juice
2 egg whites, beaten	½ yeast cake
1 teaspoon powdered cloves	1 tablespoon lukewarm water
1 teaspoon powdered ginger	

Mix water, honey, and sugar. Heat. Add egg whites. Simmer until the sugar dissolves. Skim and cool. Add the spices and the lemon peel and juice. Dilute the yeast in the warm water and add. Let the mead stand in a large crock for several days until it stops working. Bottle and cork it. Drink after 6 months.

Root Beer

Take ½ ounce each of burdock, dandelion, hops, sarsaparilla, spikenard root, and yellow dock. Bruise them. In a gallon of water, boil them for 20 minutes. Strain the mixture while it is hot. Add 10 drops each of oils of sassafras and spruce. When it is somewhat cool, add ⅔ of a pint of molasses and 2 teaspoons of yeast. Put the mixture in a jug with a cloth over it. Allow it to stand for 2 hours. Bottle the root beer, and keep it in a cool place.

Marrow Dumplings

Beat 1 egg, a pinch of salt, and a little nutmeg into ½ cup of marrow. Add some flour, and shape dumplings the size of a hickory nut. Roll them in flour, and drop them into boiling stock.

Mutton Broth

Put 3 pounds of scrag (neck of mutton) into 3 quarts of water. Add 1 celery stalk, a small turnip, and 1 large onion. Cover the pot and allow to boil until the meat shreds. Strain the soup; return it to the vessel. Add a gill of rice, and boil the soup till the rice is done. Season with salt and pepper.

Old-fashioned Split-pea and Fish Soup

Soak 2 cups of split peas in 6 cups of water for 12 hours. Drain them. Put them in a pot with 12 cups of water and fish heads, fins, and tails. Simmer covered for 3 hours. Add 1 cup of chopped celery, including the leaves, and ½ cup each of chopped carrots and onions. Simmer covered for 1 hour more. Put the soup through a colander. Chill it and remove the grease, reserving 2 tablespoons. Melt this, and blend it into 2 tablespoons of flour. Slowly add the soup mixture. Cook and stir it until the boiling point is reached. Season the soup to taste.

Potato Bread

Boil 8 large and fully ripe potatoes; mash them fine while hot. Add 1 quart of sweet milk, ½ cup of white sugar, a pinch of salt, and ⅓ cup of yeast. Prepare a pan of sifted flour. (The amount of flour seems to be left to the cook's discretion.) Make a hole in the center, and stir in the ingredients. Do this at 6 P.M. If the dough becomes light before you go to bed, stir it down, sprinkle flour over it, and allow it to stand until morning. Stir it down again. When it is light the third time, shape the dough into loaves and bake.

Skillet Bread

Place 6 short strips of bacon in the bottom of your skillet, arranging them like wheel spokes. Make a dough of the following ingredients:

2 cups flour	powder
½ teaspoon soda	1 teaspoon salt
2½ teaspoons baking	1½ cups sour milk

Sift the dry ingredients together thoroughly. Quickly stir in the milk. Spread the dough evenly over the bacon. Cover the skillet, and cook slowly for 10 minutes. Pour off excess grease. Turn the bread over and cook for 10 more minutes.

Sourdough Starter

Put the following into an earthenware crock: 4 cups flour, 2 tablespoons sugar, 1 teaspoon vinegar. Add just enough water to make a light, creamy batter. Cover it with cheesecloth. Put it in a warm place. The dough should be ready for use in 7 to 10 days.

Sourdough Bread

Place all but one cup of the starter mix in a large bowl. (The cupful you reserve will be used to continue the starter.) Add 1 tablespoon of cooking oil, a pinch of baking soda, and sufficient flour to make a bouncy dough. Knead it very little. Form loaves, and put them in a warm place until the dough rises. Bake at 375 degrees for 45 minutes or until the crust is brown and the bread has a hollow sound when tapped.

Cucumber Catsup

Grate 3 dozen medium-sized cucumbers. Sprinkle with salt and pepper and spoon into jars. Put a small white onion in each. Pour hot cider vinegar in to cover. Close the jars, and pour melted wax over their corks.

Gooseberry Conserve

4 quarts gooseberries   *10 cups sugar*
4 oranges   *1½ pounds seeded raisins*

Wash the berries; remove the stem and blossom ends. Add the chopped peel of 4 oranges, their pulp, and their juice. Boil the mixture until almost tender. Then add 10 cups of heated sugar and 1½ pounds of seeded raisins. Boil the conserve for 30 minutes more.

Honey of Roses

Country people considered this recipe a sure-fire cure for tuberculosis:

1 pint honey   *1 pint red rose petals*

Bring the honey to a boil. After removing any scum, put in the rose petals. Place the pan in a vessel of hot water. Boil for 30 minutes. After 15 minutes, more petals may be added. Allow to stand for 10 minutes. Strain while hot. This confection may be preserved in sterilized jars.

How to Make Honey Vinegar or Patience Is a Virtue

Vinegar made from honey is superior in quality to any other vinegar, especially for making pickles. Washings from honey barrels, honey cans, etc., which would ordinarily go to waste, are excellent for making vinegar.

Put honey washings into an open barrel or barrels. To determine whether the water is sweet enough, drop in a whole fresh egg. If the egg floats, leaving a spot above the surface of the liquid about the size of a ten-cent piece, it is about right. Cover the top of the barrel with cheesecloth, and keep it in a warm place where it can work and sour. In winter put it into the cellar.

It will take from 1 to 2 years to make good vinegar.

Milk Jelly

Clean well 2 calf's feet. Put them in a crock. Pour over them 1 quart of fresh milk and the same amount of water. Add lemon peel and a little sugar. Cover and bake in a moderate oven for 3½ hours. Chill and remove the fat.

Pickled Lily (*Piccalilli*)

Finely chop 1 peck of green tomatoes, 1 head of cabbage, 12 onions, and 6 peppers. Put in a kettle and add mace, cinnamon, mustard seed, salt, and a little sugar. Cover with vinegar and boil for 2 hours.

Pumpkin Butter

After removing the seeds from a pumpkin, cut it into small pieces, and boil them until soft. Chop up 3 more pumpkins and boil them separately. When they have reached a soft consistency, put them in a coarse bag and squeeze out the juice. Add the juice to the first pumpkin and allow to boil for 10 hours or until it attains the thickness of butter. Stir frequently to avoid burning. If the pumpkin butter is too sour, add brown sugar to taste. (This makes a good substitute for cow's butter or apple butter.)

Worcestershire Sauce

4 ounces asafetida	1 pound coriander seed, powdered
1 gallon brandy	
15 gallons white wine vinegar	½ pound mace, powdered
10 gallons walnut ketchup	½ pound cinnamon, powdered
10 gallons mushroom ketchup	
5 gallons Madeira wine	4 gallons soy sauce
1 pound allspice, powdered	25 pounds table salt

Dissolve the asafetida (an ill-smelling gum obtained from certain plants of the carrot family) in the brandy. Now mix all the ingredients together and allow to stand for 2 weeks. Then boil 20 pounds of hog liver in 10 gallons of water for 12 hours. Renew the water when necessary. Remove the liver, chop it fine, and mix it with the pot liquor in which it was boiled. Put it through a sieve. Thoroughly blend it with the strained liquor that has been standing for 2 weeks. Let it settle for 24 hours. Pour off the clear liquor and bottle for use.

Because of the generous amounts of recommended ingredients, this recipe was doubtless intended for commercial production. For family use we suggest that it be reduced considerably.

Bear-meat Marinade

Mix the following:	
1 chopped onion	2 tablespoons orange juice
2 diced celery stalks	1 tablespoon lemon juice
1 diced carrot	1 mashed garlic clove
1 teaspoon paprika	1 bay leaf
1 cup cider	a dash of mustard

Boil for 5 minutes in an enamel pan. Soak the bear meat in this mixture overnight; then roast it.

Grilled Woodchuck

After skinning a woodchuck, soak it in well-salted water for 4 hours. Cut it into pieces. Put them in boiling water, adding a dash of celery salt, a pinch of minced onion, and a bit of freshly ground black pepper. Simmer 15 minutes per pound. Remove the meat when tender; dry it. Baste the woodchuck with a meat sauce and grill on an open fire. Turn to brown.

Hardtack

Hardtack, used for generations by outdoorsmen as a convenient, palatable source of energy, was made by the following recipe:

5 cups flour	*1 teaspoon sugar*
1 teaspoon salt	

Mix the dry ingredients thoroughly, gradually adding enough water to make a stiff dough. Roll it out to ¼-inch thickness. Cut into sections. Bake on a greased pan until bone dry. Allow to cool.

How to Remove the Wild Flavor of Duck

After drawing and picking the duck, put it in vinegar with allspice, bay leaf, and onion. Soak it overnight. At cooking time, skin it and cut it up. Sprinkle the pieces with salt, pepper, and flour; brown them in fat. Tenderize the duck in the oven.

Jerky

Making jerky is a very old but practical way of preserving meat.

Cut lean meat along the grain in strips ½ inch wide. The meat can be flavored by marinating in a mixture of spices: onion salt, garlic salt, soy sauce. (Use less spice than in normal cooking.) Soak the meat for 24 hours.

Dry the pieces and string them on wire, taking care to leave space between each strip and the next. Construct a 3-foot-high frame of small green saplings. Build a fire of hardwood beneath it. When the wood of the fire is reduced to hot coals, suspend the wires from the frame. Place a few leafy branches over the bed of coals to generate smoke. Maintain a hot, smoking fire for 10 hours. Do not allow it to flame up more than 12 inches. Be alert to the right time to remove the meat: when the jerky is chewy but not brittle.

Muskrat Meat Loaf

1 muskrat	*¼ onion, minced or grated*
1 cup milk	*⅛ cup dry crumbs*
2 eggs, beaten	*1 teaspoon salt*
1 teaspoon Worcestershire sauce	*¼ teaspoon pepper*
	¼ teaspoon thyme

Put the muskrat in 1 quart of water to which 1 tablespoon of salt has been added. Soak it overnight. Remove the meat from the bones, and grind it. Combine the meat with all other ingredients. Place it in a loaf pan and set the pan in a container of hot water. Bake it in a 350-degree oven for 2 hours.

Old-time Rabbit Sausage

Remove cleaned rabbit meat from the bones. Coarsely grind the rabbit meat and an equal portion of fresh pork. Add sausage seasoning, blend, and form into patties. Fry slowly until done.

Place them in layers in a stoneware crock. Pour the hot grease over them to cover; heat additional lard to add if necessary. Cover the crock, and keep it in a cool place. The sausage will be preserved through the winter. Remove the patties as needed, finish browning, and pour over them milk gravy made from the drippings.

Pigs' Ears

At one time pigs' feet, fried, broiled, or pickled, were a standard country dish. Their only drawback was the time required for cooking—some 4 hours.

Many considered pigs' ears more delicate fare than the feet, with the added advantage of their being tender after only 2½ hours of cooking. Served as a nice complement to the pigs' ears were sliced tart apples, fried until brown in a mixture of butter and pork drippings.

Possum with Chestnuts

Skin and dress a possum. Scrape it clean, and scald it in hot water. Rub it, inside and out, with salt and pepper. Stuff the animal with a mixture of applesauce, bread crumbs, and chestnuts in equal amounts. Place slices of sweet potatoes on top. Pour over all a mixture of 1 cup of boiling water with ½ cup of lemon juice. Bake in butter until tender. Baste frequently.

Potted Beef Tongue

Boil a salted beef tongue with 1 pound of veal. Skin the tongue and chop it and the veal fine. Pound the meat. Add 4 tablespoons of butter, mace, nutmeg, cayenne, and ground cloves.

Mix thoroughly and press into jars. Pour melted butter over the top to help preserve the meat. It may be served cold or fried in butter.

Rabbit Hash

1 good-sized rabbit	*1 garlic clove, minced*
½ gallon water	*1 diced onion*
salt	*2 cups cubed potatoes*
pepper	*1 cup cubed dry bread*

Boil the rabbit until the meat falls from the bones. Put the meat in a skillet. Flavor it with salt, pepper, and garlic. Add onion, potato, and sufficient broth to simmer them until tender. Immediately before serving, add the bread cubes to soak up the excess broth. (Sage may be substituted for the garlic.)

Roast Skunk

Skunk meat is white, tender, and palatable. It was considered a delicacy among Indians.

Skin and dress a skunk. Remove the scent glands. Parboil in salted water for about 15 minutes. Put the meat in fresh water, and steam for 1 hour or until tender. Roast in a 375-degree oven, adding 1 cup of broth, 2 sliced carrots, and 1 teaspoon of onion juice. Cook uncovered for about 2 hours.

Roast Snipe

Dress birds and wipe thoroughly. Season with salt and pepper. Toast as many slices of bread as you have birds. Butter them, and put them in a meat pan. Dredge the birds in flour, and place them on the toast. Bake for 20 minutes, basting frequently with butter.

Roast Woodcock

Sauté 1 small sliced onion in butter. In this brown a whole woodcock on all sides. Add 1 or 2 jiggers of sherry. Simmer for 5 minutes. Coat the bird with wild currant jelly, and add another jigger of sherry. Put it in a 350-degree oven for 10 to 20 minutes, according to your preference. Baste with more sherry while it is roasting.

Scrapple

Soak several hogs' heads in water overnight. The following morning clean them thoroughly, and cut out the eyes and ears deeply. Boil the heads until tender. Take them from the water and allow to cool. After removing the bones, chop the meat fine. Strain the pot liquor to get out bits of bone. Reheat the liquid. Season the chopped meat, return it to the kettle, and add enough water to half-fill the vessel. When the water commences to boil, thicken it with corn meal until the mixture reaches the consistency of mush. Put it into pans while hot, smoothing it on top. When it is cold, pour melted lard over it. At mealtime cut it in ½-inch slices and fry in butter until brown; turn and brown the other side.

Squirrel Stew

Cut a cleaned squirrel into 6 pieces. Drop them into 2 quarts of boiling water along with 1 cup of corn, 2 potatoes, 1 cup of lima beans, half an onion, and salt and pepper. Cover and simmer for 2 hours. Add 1 spoonful of sugar and 2 cups of tomatoes. Simmer 1 hour more. Add ¼ cup of butter and 1 cup of red wine. Then simmer for 10 minutes.

Terrapin

Soak 2 black terrapins (about the size of bread plates) in a tub of cold water for 1 hour to clean them. Next drop them into a pot of boiling water and allow to boil for 15 minutes. Now submerge them in cold water so that you can easily remove the skin. Return them to boiling water and cook until the meat is tender. In order to remove the shells, place them again in cold water. (Care must be taken not to break the gall bags.) Cut the meat into small pieces. Put in a pan with ½ pound of butter. Sprinkle flour over it and season with cayenne pepper. When it is heated, moisten with 4 tablespoons of sherry, and scatter chopped hard-boiled eggs on top.

Venison Meat Loaf

1½ pounds ground venison	½ cup minced onion
½ pound pork sausage	1 teaspoon salt
3 eggs	½ teaspoon pepper
1 cup soft bread crumbs	½ teaspoon minced garlic
1 cup milk	1 teaspoon sage

Combine the venison and pork sausage with the other ingredients. Form the mixture into a loaf; place it in a baking dish. Bake at 350 degrees for approximately 1 hour or until done. It may be served with mushroom sauce.

Hot Slaw

Put a chunk of butter the size of a hen's egg in a skillet. Add finely chopped cabbage. Beat the yolks of 2 eggs, and stir them into ½ cup of milk with 1 teaspoon of salt, ¼ teaspoon of pepper, a level teaspoon of dry mustard, and 3 tablespoons of vinegar. Pour the liquid over the cabbage, and stir continually until it heats well through.

Making Hominy

Remove the kernels from 12 ears of corn. Put them in a vessel with more cold water than is needed to cover them. In the center submerge a sturdy muslin sack containing 1 quart of ashes. Let the kettle boil until all the strength is out of the ashes; then remove them. As the water boils off, replenish it with more boiling water. Boil gently and steadily. When the outside starts to come off the kernels, they are done enough. Drain them, and empty the corn into a tub of cold water. Using a clean broom, swish the corn about in the tub. Drain and add fresh water, repeating the cleaning procedure 3 times. Drain again, and place the tub where it will freeze overnight. In the morning put the corn in cold water and boil slowly until cooked. Never stir hominy; instead, occasionally lift the kettle and whirl the contents about to prevent settling and burning. Allow to boil until the kernels swell and burst. Remove from the fire. Leave the corn in its liquor and cover till cold. To serve, cook the hominy in meat fryings with a little of the pot liquor.

Parsnip Stew

Cut ½ pound of salt pork into slices and 1 pound of beef into small pieces. Scrape, wash, and slice a bunch of parsnips. Peel and cut 6 medium-sized potatoes in halves. Stew all ingredients in a covered pot of water for ½ hour or until tender. Then add a bit of butter, pepper, and flour. Cook a few more minutes until the flour has made gravy of the liquid.

Samp

Generations ago country people relied upon samp (a coarse meal of Indian corn) as a cheap but satisfying dish. Older folks can still remember pounding corn in the samp mortar to remove the outer husk of the kernels.

Here's the way samp was prepared, usually served for a Sunday dinner.

Soak 1 quart of samp and 1 cup of white beans overnight. The following morning add a pig's foot (two pounds of salt pork or a ham bone may be substituted), and simmer all day. When the beans are like pulp and the mixture is thick, the samp is done.

It was brought to the table hot, with a pitcher of chilled milk.

Squash Pie

Stew a medium-sized squash. Strain the soft part through a colander, and add the following: ½ pound of butter, 1 pint each of cream and milk, 2 cups of sugar, 12 well-beaten eggs, and 1 teaspoon each of cinnamon, nutmeg, mace, and salt. Put into a thick piecrust and bake in a moderate oven.

Dried-apple Cake

Soak 2 cups of dried apples overnight. Chop them, and boil them in 1½ cups of molasses with spice. Mix 1 cup of cream and milk, 1 cup of butter, 3 eggs, 1½ cups of sugar, 4 cups of flour, and 1 teaspoon of saleratus (baking soda). Add molasses and apple mixture. Bake.

Gingerbread

1 cup butter	*1 tablespoon allspice*
1 cup sugar	*1 tablespoon cinnamon*
1 cup molasses	*a wineglass of brandy*
3 eggs	*1 teaspoon soda*
3 cups flour	*1 cup sour milk*
1 tablespoon ginger	

Mix the butter and sugar to a cream. Add the molasses, eggs, flour, spices, and brandy. Dissolve the soda in the sour milk and add to the batter. Bake.

Grandmother's Suet Pudding

1 teaspoon baking soda	1 cup suet, chopped fine
½ cup sour milk	1 cup bread crumbs
1 teaspoon salt	1½ cups flour
1 teaspoon cinnamon	1 cup seeded currants
1 cup honey	

Add the baking soda to the milk. Mix in the remaining ingredients. Put into a well-buttered pudding mold. Cover with buttered paper, and tie the cover down. Set the mold on a rack in a kettle of boiling water 1 inch below the paper cover of the mold. Place a lid on the kettle, and steam the pudding for 3 hours. Turn out of the mold and serve with honey topping.

Henry Chalmers of New York State admired his landlady's suet pudding and once asked her how she made it. "Oh," she answered, "suet pudding is very to make. It takes me, and *I* can hardly."

Grits Pudding

Mix 1 cup of hominy grits with 1 pint of milk in the top of a double boiler and cook over boiling water for 1 hour. Beat ½ cup of sugar into 6 egg yolks. Stir them into the hot milk and grits. Remove from the fire and add 1 pint of cream and 1 teaspoon of vanilla. Put into an ice chest. When it is frozen, stir in an additional pint of whipped cream.

Persimmon Pudding

Sieve about 1 quart of ripe persimmons, or enough to yield 2 cups of pulp. Add a little water if the persimmons are too dry. Beat in 3 eggs. Add the following ingredients:

1 ¼ cups sugar	½ teaspoon salt
1 ½ cups sifted flour	½ cup melted butter
1 teaspoon baking soda	2 cups whole milk
1 teaspoon baking powder	1 teaspoon vanilla

Bake in a greased pan at 325 degrees for 1 hour; the top should then be crusty and brown.

Pie-plant Pie

Make crust, leaving enough for strips on top. Prepare 1 ½ pints of rhubarb, unpeeled but sliced thin. Mix the following ingredients well:

1 beaten egg	1 tablespoon flour
¼ teaspoon salt	1 cup sugar
⅛ teaspoon grated nutmeg	

Blend this mixture with the rhubarb and pour into the bottom crust. Cover with the crisscross strips. Bake at 450 degrees for 10 minutes. Reduce temperature to 350 degrees and continue baking for 30 minutes more.

Salt-pork Pudding

Slice enough salt pork to fill a large cup. Soak it overnight in milk; then chop it fine. Stir 1 teaspoon of saleratus (baking soda) into 1 cup of molasses, and add it to the pork. Mix separately ¾ cup of sweet milk, 1 cup of currants, and 1 teaspoon each of ground cinnamon, cloves, and nutmeg. Add sufficient flour to achieve the consistency of pudding. Combine all ingredients and steam in a cloth for 4 hours.

Vinegar Pie

1 cup sugar	*2 tablespoons butter*
1 cup cold water	*1 whole egg*
4 egg yolks	*5 tablespoons vinegar*
3 rounded tablespoons flour	*2 teaspoons lemon extract*

Mix the ingredients, boil until thick, then bake in one crust. Beat the whites of the 4 eggs to a stiff froth. Beat in 4 tablespoons of sugar and spread over the baked pie. Return it to the oven for browning. (This is a less expensive and more easily made substitute for lemon pie.)

Long ago recipes were sketchy, leaving a great deal to a seasoned cook's experience. The following are good examples of three such "receipts":

Cookies with Ammonia

1 pound lard	*caraway seeds*
5 cups sugar	*pinch of salt*
1 quart milk	*flour (to make dough stiff*
1½ ounces carbonate of am-	*enough for rolling out)*
monia	

Mix the lard and sugar. Add to it the milk in which the ammonia has been dissolved.

Hickory-nut Cake

One cup of sugar, ½ cup of butter, 2 eggs, ½ cup of sweet milk, 1 teaspoon of cream of tartar, 1 teaspoon of soda, 2 cups of flour, 1 pint of nuts.

Ladyfingers

One and ¼ pounds of sugar, 12 eggs, 1 pound of flour. Run it through a bag on paper, and grease the pan.

Kitchen Tips from Times Past

BAKING POWDER

To make a good baking powder, thoroughly mix the following: 4 ounces of flour, 5 ounces of bicarbonate of soda, 10 ounces of cream of tartar, and 1 ounce of tartaric acid.

CRANBERRY DOUGH

Use dried wild cranberries to make dough for tarts and pie-crusts. It is said that the Pilgrims, when celebrating harvest time, baked dough cases with dried cranberries.

TO CLEAN CURRANTS

To clean dried currants, shake them about in a sieve with a little flour until only the currants remain. Wash them thoroughly, and remove any twigs. Spread them on a flat surface in some warm spot to dry. Don't use the currants until you are sure that they are completely dry, else they will sink to the bottom of your puddings and cakes.

FIRM BUTTER

Butter can be made firm during hot weather in this way: Mix 1 teaspoon of powdered alum with 1 teaspoon of carbonate of soda. At churning time put this mixture into the amount of cream that will produce 20 pounds of butter.

FLAVORING EXTRACTS

Homemade flavoring extracts are found to be more delicious than those that are bought. To make lemon extract, put 1 pint of good alcohol in a jar and add 1 ounce of lemon oil and the peel of 2 lemons. Allow it to stand for a week; shake it 3 times each day. Now take out the peel, and bottle the liquid for use. All essences can be made according to the same proportions as the lemon-flavored extract.

COOKING FRUIT

Fruits of an acid nature should be cooked in tin, brass, or porcelain vessels.

HERBS

Gather herbs on a sunny day of low humidity. To dry them, you may spread them in the shade on such a day, or hang them near a stove, or place them in an open moderate oven. When the herbs are very dry, powder and sift them. Store them in bottles with snug corks or in air-tight tins to preserve their flavor.

PRESERVING APPLES

First pile apples in a heap to sweat. Then pack them in barrels or boxes in hemlock sawdust. In this manner they can be kept fresh until Nature provides new fruit in the spring.

PRESERVING EGGS

To keep eggs fresh, follow this procedure: Gather new-laid eggs, and coat each with salt butter so that the shell is completely sealed. Dry some bran in the oven. Place a layer of the bran in a box, and pack the eggs in it with their small ends down. Continue to fill the box with alternating layers of bran and eggs. Keep the box in a cold, dry place, and the eggs will remain fresh for 10 months.

PRESERVING ROOT VEGETABLES

Put root vegetables into a large box. Pack them in such a way as to leave a space of an inch or more around the sides of the box. When it is filled to within 6 inches of the top, shake in sand or dry road dust and cover with a layer of fresh earth. This will nicely keep vegetables—especially beets and turnips—for winter use.

TO COLOR SOUPS

To impart an amber color to soup, add finely grated carrot. If a reddish color is desired, use red tomatoes, straining out their skins and seeds. Press the juice from spinach; dry and powder the leaves. To give soup a green color, add both the juice and the powdered leaves. For brown soup a clear stock should be used.

SOUP FLAVORING

Wash the large leaves of 5 celery stalks. Boil them in 1 quart of water until the liquid is reduced to ½ pint. Allow it to cool, strain out the celery leaves, bottle the liquid, and store it in a cool place. Use it as a flavoring for soups, gravies, and stews.

SUBSTITUTE JELLY

If jelly is desired and fruits are not available for its making, the following method will produce a satisfactory substitute: Boil ½ ounce of powdered alum in 1 quart of water for 3 minutes. Put in 8 pounds of white sugar; boil for a few minutes, and strain. Add any preferred flavoring.

RESTORING TAINTED MEATS

To remove the odor from tainted (not rotten) meat, prepare this solution: Boil 1 quart of water, and allow it to cool. Then add 1 ounce of permanganate of potash. Put the liquid in a tightly closed bottle and shake well. Into a container of water sufficient to cover the ill-smelling meat, put 1 tablespoon of the solution. Stir it with a long stick to avoid staining hands or clothing. Submerge the meat and allow to stand for 10 minutes. Then rinse well, and all trace of unpleasant odor will be gone.

VINEGAR USES

- When cooking rice, add 1 teaspoon of vinegar to the water. This will keep the grains whole.
- You can make lettuce and other greens clean and crisp by soaking them for 5 minutes in water with a little vinegar added.
- Put vinegar in the water for boiling eggs. This will keep the whites from running out if the shells crack.
- Add a few drops of vinegar to uncooked icing during the mixing, and it will remain softer.
- To keep cheese fresh, wrap it in a cloth moistened with vinegar.

12
Things Homemade

Idleness is the only sin. A blacksmith singing at his forge, sparks a-flying, anvil ringing, the man materializing an idea—what is finer!

—Elbert Hubbard

In the old days few wants were "store bought." Country people supplied themselves with life's essentials by tediously making at home everything from hair dye to fire extinguishers. Here are some homemade items of the past and their methods of production.

CEMENT FOR BROKEN CHINA AND GLASS

▪ Beat egg whites until frothy. When they have settled, beat in quicklime and grated cheese. Mend china or crockery by applying it to the broken edges.

▪ In boiling water (enough to fill a wineglass) dissolve gum acacia. Add sufficient plaster of Paris to produce a thick paste. Use this almost-colorless mixture to cement broken china.

▪ Combine 1 pint each of vinegar and milk. Remove the whey, and beat it well with 5 egg whites. Add enough finely powdered quicklime (you may substitute burned oyster shells for the lime) to form a thick paste. It is excellent for mending glass or china.

CEMENT FOR LABELS ON TINS

Boil glue in vinegar. Thicken the liquid with flour to make a paste for sticking labels on tin boxes.

CEMENT FOR PAPER

To make a white, almost transparent paste for fancy paper work that calls for a strong but colorless cement, mix a little cold water into powdered rice. While stirring constantly, slowly add boiling water until the proper consistency is reached. Then boil for 1 minute.

CEMENT FOR BOOTS AND SHOES

Combine 1½ ounces of sulphide of carbon and ¼ ounce of gutta-percha. Bottle it for use in applying patches to boots and shoes.

WHITE PASTE

▪ In 3 cups of warm water, dissolve 1 ounce of alum. When the liquid is cold, stir in enough flour for a thick consistency and add 6 drops of oil of cloves and 1 teaspoon of powdered resin. Boil. Used while fresh, this will make a good paste for general use.

▪ Dissolve 2½ ounces of gum arabic (gum acacia) in 2 quarts of water. Stir in 1 pound of flour until the mixture is pastelike. Heat, and add 1½ ounces of sugar of lead (dissolved in water) and 1⅓ ounces of alum. Stir until the boiling point is reached. Remove it from the stove, and add 7 drops of carbolic acid. This is a strong, all-purpose paste.

PASTE FOR STAMPS, LABELS, ETC.

Put 5 ounces of glue into 20 ounces of water to soak for 1 day. Dissolve 9 ounces of rock candy and 3 ounces of gum arabic in this liquid. It makes a particularly good mucilage for the labeling on bottles to be stored in damp cellars.

WALLPAPER PASTE

Add enough water to 2 cups of flour to make a thin dough, without lumps. Stir it into 1 gallon of boiling water. When it again reaches the boiling point, pour the hot batter into a tin bucket. Let it stand for 24 hours. Strain it through some coarse muslin. Use the paste as an adhesive for wallpaper.

LAUNDRY SOAP

Put 1 pound of quicklime into 1 gallon of very hot water. Stir occasionally over the next 2 hours. Allow it to settle. Pour off the clear liquid into a large vessel, and add 5 gallons of soft water, 4 pounds of bar soap, and 3 pounds of washing soda. When the soap and soda are dissolved, stir in 2 ounces of salt. After the mixture has cooled a bit, pour it into jars or half-barrels. Store covered for use. This amount of half-solid soap will wash four times as much laundry as the bar soap alone would do.

HARD SOAP

Put 6 pounds of washing soda, 3½ pounds of quicklime, and 4 gallons of soft water into a kettle. Boil. Stir until the soda is dissolved and the quicklime slaked. Allow it to settle; then pour off the clear liquid. Rinse the kettle, and boil in it 6 pounds of liquid grease (during the winter save drippings from ham, mutton, etc. for soapmaking) and ½ pound of borax until soap begins to form. Empty it into a tub to cool.

When hard enough, it can be cut into bars and placed on boards to dry. This is a good laundry soap; with the addition of a little perfume, it becomes a nice complexion soap. Scent it with oil of sassafras or oil of caraway, using 1 ounce to 10 gallons of soap. Stir it in well when the soap is fairly cool.

SCOURING SOAP

Put 1 pound of borax and 3 pounds of washing soda into 3 gallons of soft water. When they are dissolved, add 10 pounds of yellow soap shaved fine and 1 pound of tallow. Heat to melt. Then sift a quantity of lime to remove the lumps, slake it, and add as much to the mixture as you can stir in well. This soap is good for difficult cleaning jobs, such as removing grease or tar from the hands.

MEDICATED SOAP

Cut a 1-pound bar of hard white soap into slivers and put them into a jar. Set the jar in a basin of water and heat it over the fire until the soap dissolves. Stir in well 1 ounce of flour of sulphur, and pour it into a wooden box to cool. Cut into squares and let dry. To make tar soap, use the same formula as the sulphur soap, stirring in ¼ ounce of creosote. These are excellent soaps for irritated skin.

RENOVATION SOAP

Put 3 drams of camphor gum into 1 ounce of alcohol and reserve. Put 1 dram of powdered pipe clay into 2 ounces of beef gall and reserve. Reduce ¼ ounce of saltpeter and ¼ ounce of borax to powder; mix them and 1 teaspoon of common salt with ¼ ounce of honey and reserve. After 3 hours shave ¼ pound of good soap (such as used by barbers) into a porcelain vessel. Add the gall mixture and stir over a low fire until the soap is dissolved. Remove from the stove and allow to cool somewhat. Put in the other ingredients, stirring well. Quickly pour the mixture into glass jars, where it will harden. Store them covered in a dark closet until needed for renovating soiled garments. To use, spoon out ½ ounce, and dissolve it in 1 quart of boiling soft water. Scrub soiled areas of jackets, trousers, etc. with a scouring brush dipped in this solution.

WASHING FLUID

Dissolve concentrated lye (potash) in 1 gallon of rain water. Put 2 ounces each of muriate of ammonia and salts of tartar into another gallon of soft water. Combine both solutions in a 2-gallon stone jug. Cork and shake. Use ½ cup of the fluid for each boiler of dirty clothes.

WASHING POWDER

Pulverize 1 pound of borax, 2 pounds of washing soda, and 2 ounces of salts of tartar. Mix them, and add 1½ ounces of muriate of ammonia. Bottle and cork. Use 1 rounded table-spoon of the powder in each boiler of laundry.

GRAFTING WAX

Melt 1 pound of rosin, and blend in 4 ounces of mutton tallow and 6 ounces of beeswax. Cool the mixture a bit in cold water; then work it until it is pliable. It not only makes a good graft-ing wax, but also serves as a salve for cuts you may sustain while climbing and sawing among tree branches.

SEALING WAX FOR FRUIT JARS

Melt 1 pound of beeswax, 4 pounds of rosin, and 1 pound of orange shellac. Dip a brush into this mixture and paint the corks of fruit jars to seal them effectively.

BLACK COPYING INK

Mix thoroughly ⅛ pound of soft brown sugar, ⅛ pound of gum arabic, ⅜ pound of powdered nutgalls (nut-shaped tumors found on oaks and other trees, formed by irritation due to insects), and ⅛ pound of copperas. Let the mixture steep in 1 gallon of rain water for 2 weeks, shaking it occasionally. This procedure will result in a good black copying ink.

INDELIBLE INK

Dissolve a strong solution of Prussian blue in water. Add it to a quantity of gall ink. While being used in writing, the ink is green. When dry, it will be black and indelible.

PERMANENT BLACK INK

Boil 1 ounce of logwood chips in 1 gallon of soft water. Cool and strain. Add more hot water to compensate for evaporation, and bring it to a boil. Pound ¾ pound of blue nutgalls into a coarse mash. Put them into the kettle with 3 ounces of purified copperas, ½ ounce of verdigris (acetate of copper), ½ ounce of pulverized sugar, and 4 ounces of gum arabic. Remove the mixture from the fire, and let it stand until it attains the desired blackness. Strain and bottle. This ink will not fade and consequently is excellent for keeping records.

SCHOOL INK

Dissolve 10 grams of bichromate of potash and ½ ounce of extract of logwood in 1 quart of hot rain water. When it is cold, bottle it. Leave it uncorked for 7 days; it will then be ready for use. It is a good black ink for school purposes, one that will not leave a permanent stain on clothing.

COPYING PAD

Soak 2 ounces of glue in a dish of water. When it is soft, drain off the water. Put the dish into a pan of hot water and let stand until the glue melts. Mix in 1½ ounces of hot glycerine. Add a few drops of carbolic acid. Pour the mixture into a shallow square pan to cool. It can be used as a copying pad after 12 hours. Write what you want to reproduce on a sheet of paper with a sharp pen and aniline ink. When the ink dries, put the paper, writing down, on the pad. Press lightly. Remove the paper; an impression will remain on the pad. You can make a duplicate of the original writing by placing another paper on the pad. When the required number of copies have been made, wash the pad with a sponge and cold water.

BLACKBOARD

The wood for a blackboard must be completely smooth. Fill in all holes in the boards and the cracks between them with plaster of Paris mixed with water. Smooth with sandpaper. For slating, pour liquid gum shellac into a container, and add enough lampblack to make a thick paint. Spread the gloss on the boards with a clean brush.

WHITEWASH

To make whitewash, slake ½ bushel of lime in a barrel. Add 1 gallon of sweet milk, 1 pound of common salt, and ⅓ pound of sulphate of zinc.

WHITE PAINT

You can make a beautiful white paint by mixing the following: 9 ounces of slaked lime, 2 quarts of skimmed milk, 6 ounces of linseed oil, 2½ ounces of Burgundy pitch, and 3 pounds of Spanish white.

MACHINE POLISH

To make an excellent polish for machinery, blend 3 parts of oil of turpentine, 3 parts of blood coal, and 1 part of stearine oil. Dilute this mixture with alcohol, and brush it onto the machine parts to be cleaned. When the alcohol has evaporated, rub the coaling with crocus (powdered iron oxide) or some other polishing agent.

PIANO POLISH

To make a good piano polish, mix ⅔ cup of vinegar, 1 cup of turpentine, and 1 cup of boiled linseed oil. Using a flannel cloth, rub the polish well into the wood. Finish by polishing the piano with a chamois skin.

BOOT AND SHOE POLISH

For a good shoe polish, combine the following in a saucepan: 1 pint of soft water, 1 quart of cider vinegar, ¼ pound of clear glue, ½ pound of logwood chips, and 2 teaspoons each of powdered indigo, isinglass, and soft soap. Boil for 10 minutes. Strain when cool. First clean boots or shoes, and then apply the polish with a swab.

WATERPROOF BLACKING

Melt and stir 16 parts of beeswax and 1 part borax to form a jelly. In another pot, stir the following mixture: 13 parts of oil of turpentine, 1 part asphalt varnish, 1 part of melted spermaceti. Add to this the contents of the first vessel. For coloring put in 5 parts of ground Berlin blue and 12 parts of vine black. This waterproof blacking may be perfumed with 1 part of nitrobenzole. Store it in boxes. Apply it to boots and shoes with a rag; then brush them.

HARNESS BLACKING

Reduce to powder 1½ ounces of blue nutgalls. Put the powder into a bottle, and add 1 pint of soft water, ½ pint of alcohol, and 2 ounces each of tincture of muriate of iron and extract of logwood. Allow to stand for several days; shake the bottle twice daily. When the extract of logwood is dissolved, the harness blacking is ready for use.

AXLE GREASE

To make a good axle grease, put 2 pounds each of rosin and tallow, 1 pound of beeswax, and 1 quart each of castor oil and linseed oil into a kettle. Heat well and stir to blend. Continue stirring until the mixture cools.

ICE CHEST

Select 2 boxes, one sufficiently smaller than the other so that there is a space of 4 inches on all sides when the smaller box is placed in the larger. Pack the free space between the boxes with sawdust. Make a cover for the larger box that fits snugly inside the top. Insert a small pipe in the bottom of the chest for drainage of waste water. This will make an efficient ice chest.

MAKING ICE

Into a cylindrical container pour $1\frac{1}{3}$ ounces of water, $3\frac{1}{2}$ ounces of sulphuric acid, and 1 ounce of powdered sulphate of soda. Set a vessel of water in the middle of this. The water will freeze. To make more ice, insert another vessel of water.

FIRE EXTINGUISHERS

Dissolve 5 pounds of salimoniac and 10 pounds of common salt in $3\frac{1}{3}$ gallons of water. Pour the liquid into bottles of thin glass that will easily break. Keep one in each room. When a fire starts, hurl the bottle into the flames forcefully enough to shatter the glass. The contents will extinguish the fire.

OILED CLOTH

Over a low flame mix 2 ounces of lime water with 4 ounces of linseed oil. Beat separately 1 ounce of egg white and 2 ounces of egg yolk. Blend them into the other ingredients. Stretch close-textured white cotton cloth on frames, tacking it well. Apply the mixture with a brush. As each coat dries, brush on another. The oiled cloth will be waterproof after 3 coats.

BUSHEL BOXES

Make bushel boxes 17½ inches long, using lath for the length and bottoms. Use common pine wood for the ends, the boards to be 12 inches wide and 14 inches long. Plane the boards on both sides. Cut holes in them for the hands. With an inch bit bore 3 holes, and trim them with a pocketknife. An average wagon bed will accommodate from 32 to 36 of these bushel boxes. Potatoes, apples, and other produce packed in them will be less bruised than those in a loose load.

MATS

Wash a fresh sheepskin in warm water and strong soapsuds to which has been added a tablespoon of kerosene. Scrub it thoroughly on a washboard. Repeat the washing in fresh soapy water. When the wool looks clean and white, submerge it in cold water. Dissolve ½ pound of alum and ½ pound of salt in 3 pints of boiling water. Pour this mixture over the skin, and allow it to soak for 12 hours. Then hang it over a fence to drain. Next nail it on the side of the barn to dry, with the wool side against the wood. When it is almost dry, rub 1 ounce each of saltpeter and powdered alum into the skin for an hour. Rub it daily for 3 days or until completely dry. Scrape all impurities from the skin with a stick, and rub it with pumice stone. Trim it to a satisfactory shape. It will make a serviceable mat and can be dyed if color is desired.

SCARECROWS

A stuffed coat and pants propped upright is customarily used to frighten crows from crops. Another means of keeping off these marauders is to string kernels of corn on long horsehairs and scatter them over the cornfields. Upon swallowing them, the crow will make such a raucous noise as he tries to free his throat of the corn that other birds will be driven away— sometimes, it is said, for the season.

A well-recommended method involves reflected sunlight. Fasten 2 small mirrors back to back; hang them on a cord from a pole. As the glass dangles, sunshine is flashed over the field. A crow will leave as quickly as one of the startling flashes strikes him.

The following plan is efficacious in ridding fields not only of crows but of smaller birds and even domestic fowl. Make an imitation hawk, using a large potato and long turkey feathers. Stick the feathers into the potato in such a manner that they resemble the spread tail and wings of a hawk. Suspend it from a tall, bent pole. The wind will lend it realism by agitating it.

BUTTER

Before churning cream, let stand 12 hours to ripen. Warm it in the churn with sweet skimmed milk that is at a temperature of 62 degrees. Wash the butter 3 times in brine, not water. Weigh it, and allow ½ ounce of salt to each pound of butter. Work the butter slowly until the salt is evenly absorbed. Never touch it with the hands; use spatulas and paddles only. Let it stand for 24 hours, and then work it enough to remove surplus brine and all buttermilk. Form it into rolls, and store them for 24 hours until they are firm. Dip cloth in brine, wrap the butter rolls, and store them.

To keep your table butter fresh during hot weather, invert a clean flowerpot wrapped with 3 thicknesses of wet cloth over the dish of butter. The butter will be as firm as if kept in an ice chest.

TOOTH POWDER

Mix ½ ounce of powdered borax with 3 ounces of precipitated chalk, adding a few drops of oil of wintergreen to make a good dentifrice.

HAIR DYE

A good black hair dye can be made as follows: Mix 1 dram of pyrogalic acid into 6 ounces of rain water. Apply the mixture to your hair, and allow it to dry. Meanwhile, blend 2 drams of nitrate of silver crystals, 1 ounce of gum arabic (dissolved in a little water), and 1 ounce of aqua ammonia. Apply after the first application has thoroughly dried. The beard can also be colored in this manner.

HAIR TONIC

Into 1 pint of good alcohol put 4 ounces of oil of sweet almonds, 2 drams of oil of bergamot, and 1 dram of oil of citronella. Then add 8 ounces of rye whiskey, 4 ounces of aqua ammonia, and ½ ounce of gum camphor. Mix well. Shake before using as an excellent hair tonic.

SHAMPOO

A good hair wash consists of 1 ounce each of powdered borax, aqua ammonia, and salts of tartar mixed into 1 quart of clear rain water. To make another good shampoo, dissolve 2 ounces of powdered borax in 1 quart of sage tea.

POMADE

Melt 1 ounce of spermaceti in 4 ounces of oil of sweet almonds. When it is cool, perfume it by stirring in oil of neroli (the oil of orange blossoms) or oil of lemon grass. Put the pomade in a large-mouthed bottle for easy access by the fingers. Keep it corked. It is a fine pomade for hair or for chapped hands and lips.

13
Cleaning Methods of Yesteryear

Cleanliness and order are not matters of instinct; they are matters of education, and like most great things—mathematics and classics—you must cultivate a taste for them.
—Disraeli
Speech at Aylesbury
Sept. 21, 1865

Old-fashioned procedures for removing spots, stains, and odors are as effective today as they were in times gone by. Here are some cleaning methods that were used generations ago to maintain spic-and-span households.

ACID STAINS

Wrap the stained area around some pearlash (potash) and tie with twine. Boil the cloth in soapy water until the stain is gone.

BAKED-ON FOODS

Scour baked-on foods from pans by using a paste of ½ flour moistened with a little vinegar and ½ salt.

BARRELS

Dissolve 2 pounds of baking soda in 4 quarts of hot water. Pour this into a barrel of water and let stand for 12 hours. Empty the liquid and let the barrel stand for 2 hours, and it will be free of odor. All wooden vessels can be treated in this way.

BEDS

A good way to shine unvarnished brass beds is to rub them with half a lemon dipped in table salt. After washing them in hot water and drying them well, rub the brass with rotten-stone.

BOOTS AND SHOES

For a fast shine, cut a lemon and rub it over your leather boots or shoes; wipe off quickly with a soft cloth.

BOTTLES AND JARS

To remove odor from bottles and jars, fill them with a solution of water and dry mustard. Let stand for several hours and rinse in hot water.

BRASSES

Crush onion with a little damp earth for cleaning brasses.

BREADBOARD

Using a piece of pumice, scrub breadboards and carving boards clean with a mixture of borax and salt.

CARPETS

Cut the heart of a cabbage in half. Using it like a brush, go over the entire carpet to clean and renovate it.

COCOA STAINS

Soak the article stained with cocoa in a mixture of water and borax to remove discoloration.

COPPER

To remove the tarnish from copperware, clean it with half a lemon dipped in a mixture of 1 tablespoon of salt and 1 table-spoon of vinegar.

CRUST

To prevent a crust from forming in water kettles, keep a large marble or an oyster shell in them.

DUST MOP

Clean a dust mop by boiling it in water to which have been added 2 tablespoons of paraffin and 1 tablespoon of baking soda.

FAUCETS

Lime deposits around faucets can be removed by rubbing with a cloth dipped in vinegar.

FEATHER BEDS

To satisfactorily clean feather beds, spread them on tall grass during a heavy shower. Be sure to turn them so that both sides will be soaked. Place them on slats across chairs in the full sun to dry. Beat them with a stick to fluff up the feathers.

FIREPLACE

When the fire is burning strongly, toss in a handful of salt. It will act as a cleaning agent and aid in preventing chimney fires.

FLATIRON

Wrap a piece of beeswax in a coarse rag. When the iron is almost hot enough to use, rub it with the beeswax cloth to remove starch or rust.

FLOORS

Clean varnished floors and woodwork with cold tea to bring out their shine.

FLYSPECKS

Soak a bunch of chopped leeks in a half bucket of water for a week. Strain the resulting infusion and use for washing paintings, mirrors, lampshades, etc. to protect them from being dirtied by flies. To remove flyspecks from varnished furniture, clean with a mixture of half cold water and half skimmed milk.

FRUIT STAINS

Hold cloth stained by fruit over a piece of burning sulphur. Wash thoroughly.

GLUE

Use a cloth dipped in vinegar to remove glue from fabrics.

GOLD ARTICLES

Make a paste of cigar ashes and water to polish gold articles.

GREASE SPOTS

Stale grease can best be removed with wood alcohol. Rinse the garment, scrub it with yellow soap, then give it a thorough rinsing in hot water.

GREASY POTS AND PANS

Wipe out greasy pots and pans with paper; then scour them with corn meal.

GRINDSTONE

When your grindstone gets coated with dirt and oil and will barely sharpen an ax or knife, clean it easily by holding a piece of ice to the stone while you slowly turn it.

INK ON CLOTH

To remove ink stains from white cloth, rub them with freshly picked sorrel. Wash with soap and water, and if necessary repeat the procedure.

INK ON PAPER

To remove writing in ink from paper, add 2½ drams of muriate of tin to 4 drams of water and apply with a camel's-hair brush. When the writing has disappeared, dip the paper in water and allow to dry.

IRON STAINS

Soak the cloth with iron stains in buttermilk. Dry it in the hot sun. Then launder in cold water.

KID GLOVES

Clean kid gloves by rubbing them with cream of tartar.

KNIVES

To clean rusty knives, insert the blades in an onion and let stand for a half hour. Rust will quickly disappear when this is followed by washing and polishing.

LACE

Put 1 rounded teaspoon of borax in 1 pint of warm soapsuds. Let soiled lace soak in this for 1 hour. Rinse 3 times, adding 1 teaspoon of sugar to the last rinse water.

LAMP GLOBES

To remove smoke stain from lamp globes, soak them in hot water in which washing soda has been dissolved. Then wash the globes with a good stiff brush in a pan of warm water to which has been added 1 teaspoon of powdered carbonate of ammonia. Rinse them in cold water and dry.

LAMPS

To prevent a lamp from smoking, soak the wick in vinegar; allow it to dry thoroughly before using it.

LEATHER ARTICLES

Clean leather articles by rubbing them with equal parts of vinegar and boiled linseed oil. Then polish with a soft cloth.

LEATHER BOOKBINDINGS

Brighten leather bookbindings by rubbing them with egg white.

LINOLEUM

To clean and preserve new linoleum, wash it with beer, and wipe it dry. Do this daily for the first week. Then clean it weekly with warm, clear water. When it is dry, sponge with beer. Washing linoleum with milk will also help to preserve it.

MILDEW

Rub soap on mildew; then apply salt and lemon juice to both sides of the material. Wash and hang in the open air to dry.

MUD STAINS

Remove mud stains from black cloth by first brushing the garment well and then rubbing the stains with half of a raw potato.

ODOR

If clothing has a musty odor, restore it to freshness by placing charcoal in the folds.

PAINT BRUSHES

To soften and clean hardened paint brushes, insert them for a few minutes into boiling vinegar. Then wash them in warm soapy water.

PAINT ODOR

A pailful of water placed in a freshly painted room will eliminate the offensive paint smell.

PIANO KEYS

Clean piano keys by using a piece of silk cloth barely moistened with alcohol.

PICTURE FRAMES

To bring luster to the gold leaf of picture frames, rub them with boiled onion juice and wipe dry. Gilt frames can be cleaned and brightened by washing with a mixture of 2 egg whites and 1 ounce of soda.

POTS AND PANS

Boil apple peelings in aluminum pots and pans to brighten the metal.

PRIVIES

Three spoonfuls of spirits of turpentine in a pail of water is an effective cleaner for eliminating odors in privies.

RUGS

Sprinkle a generous amount of corn meal on a rug where there are grease spots. Gently brush it into the rug, and leave it for 24 hours before removal.

RUST ON CLOTH

To remove rust stains from white cloth, put a slice of lemon between two layers of cloth on the stain; apply a very hot iron. Repeat until the stain has disappeared.

RUSTY POTS

Remove rust stains from iron pots by boiling water and clean hay in them. Allow to stand for 10 hours and boil again with fresh water.

SAUCEPANS

Boil a few pieces of rhubarb in water to remove lime in saucepans.

SCORCHES

Clothing that has been scorched during ironing should be laid in the bright sunshine.

SHADES

Dirty window shades can be cleaned with a piece of rough flannel dipped in flour.

SHAWLS

Spread a clean cloth on the table and sift dry white corn meal over it. Place the soiled shawl on this and sprinkle more corn meal on top. Roll it up tight. After 7 days dust away the meal, and the shawl will be clean.

SILVER

Clean tarnished silver by soaking it in potato water for 2 hours. Use a soft brush and silver polish to remove any lingering tarnish.

SINK DRAINS

To keep sink drains free of unpleasant odors, pour into them 1 gallon of water to which has been added ⅓ pound of calcium chloride.

SKUNK ODOR

Soak clothing in milk, vinegar, or tomato juice to remove the odor of skunk. If this fails, bury the garments.

SMOKE

Put vinegar in an open vessel to eliminate the odor of smoke.

STAINS

Apply glycerine to wine and fruit stains. Let it remain for 5 minutes and rinse.

STEEL MACHINERY

Heat 1 pound of lard. Dissolve ½ ounce of powdered gum in it. Add enough black lead to make the mixture the color of iron. Rub this on steel or iron machinery, and leave it for 24 hours. Then rub with a soft rag. This method will prevent rust from forming on sewing machines, coffee grinders, etc.

STICKY IRON

Run a hot iron over salt sprinkled on a piece of paper to remove sticky spots from its sole.

STOVEPIPES

The best way to clean stovepipes is to put a piece of zinc on the coals in the fire.

TAR ON CLOTHING

To remove tar, rub the clothing with lard, and leave it for an hour or more. Scrape off the lard, and scrub the garment with hot water and soap. If this is not completely successful, apply turpentine.

TAR ON SKIN

Take tar from your hands by rubbing them with lemon or orange peel and then wiping them off.

TEA STAINS

Mix 1 tablespoon of salt with 1 cup of soft soap. Use it to rub the tea stains. Spread the cloth on the grass in a sunny spot. Leave it for 2 days and then launder.

VASES

Put soapy water and crushed eggshells into vases or bottles that are difficult to clean because of narrow openings. Shake well and rinse.

WALLPAPER

To remove grease spots from wallpaper, rub them lightly with a piece of flannel dampened with spirits of wine.

WAX

To remove candle-wax drippings, place a blotter on the spot and hold a hot iron over the blotter.

WINDOWS

Add 1 tablespoon of kerosene to 1 gallon of water for washing windows. This solution will prevent the glass from streaking. To make windows shine, add a little vinegar, or rub them with newspaper.

WOOD

Remove stains from wood surfaces with ½ ounce of vitriol in 4 ounces of water. Use a cork instead of a cloth for rubbing.

WOODWORK

To clean oak woodwork, wash it with warm beer. Next boil 2 quarts of beer, 1 tablespoon of sugar, and a piece of beeswax about the size of a walnut. Brush the wainscoting with this mixture. When it is dry, polish it with flannel.

WOOLENS

Remove stains from black or colored woolens by soaking them in water in which a handful of ivy leaves has been boiled for 15 minutes.

WROUGHT IRON

Clean wrought iron with a drop of paraffin on a soft cloth.

14
Pest Purges
of the
Past

Bedbugs are all right—except when acting in their official capacity.
—Elbert Hubbard

Here are some old-time means, passed on from generation to generation, for ridding both house and garden of various pests.

Ants

■ Place small sponges soaked in sweetened water wherever in the house ants have been seen; the ant-covered sponges can be collected periodically and plunged into hot water.

■ Paint the floor with paraffin oil in areas that ants most frequent.

■ Mix 3 ounces of powdered fennel, 3 ounces of chrysan-

been seen. This solution is effective against roaches, ants, chintz bugs, and other pests.

■ To discourage crawling insects, spread walls and cracks with a solution of 2 pounds of alum boiled in 3 quarts of water.

■ Cayenne pepper will keep your pantry free of roaches, ants, and other pests.

Crickets

■ To destroy crickets, put Scotch snuff into their holes.

Fleas

■ Tansy leaves, fresh or dried, will keep away fleas.

■ You can eradicate fleas in the kennel by mixing dried walnut leaves with the straw.

■ To free your cat or dog from fleas, saturate a string with oil of pennyroyal, and tie it about the animal's neck.

Flies

■ Mix the following: 5 ounces of sugar, 1 ounce of arsenate of potassa, ¼ ounce of red lead. Bottle for use. Put suitable amounts moistened with water in dishes, and place them where flies congregate. The mixture will destroy these insects quickly.

■ To keep the house free of flies, put dishes containing oil of bay leaves on window sills. Or paint door and window casings with paint to which 4 per cent of bay oil has been added.

■ Melt 6 ounces of rosin, and add 2 ounces of shortening. When cold, this mixture will have the consistency of molasses.

Spread it on small pieces of wood, and place them about the house. Flies are attracted to it and will be held fast.

Garden Insects

- Steep ¾ pound of tobacco leaves in 1 gallon of boiling water. Strain it after 15 minutes. Pour this solution over your garden plants to drive away harmful insects.
- Several bugs that are attracted to roses and some vegetable plants can be lured away to marigolds planted near them.
- If you have a little kitchen garden in the back yard, plant hot peppers among tomatoes and other vine crops to protect them against insects.

Grasshoppers

- Make traps for destructive garden grasshoppers by half-filling deep jars with a solution of water and molasses.

House-plant Parasites

- To effectively destroy parasites on house plants, place containers of steaming soapsuds close to them 3 times a week. Once a week wash the leaves to keep them free of insects.

Insect Eggs

- Wash corners of drawers and closets with scalding potash water, 1 teaspoon of potash to ½ gallon of water, to destroy insect eggs.

Lice

■ Sprinkle sulphur under the wings of your chickens and pet canary to rid them of lice.

Mice

■ Mix tartar emetic with any favorite mouse food. After eating it, mice will sicken and leave.

■ Mint, particularly pennyroyal, strewn on floors and placed in beds, in sacks, and near cheeses will keep mice away because of its odor.

Mites

■ To rid a pantry of mites, empty it and fumigate it with sulphur. Afterward, scrub it thoroughly with kerosene emulsion.

Mosquitoes

■ To keep mosquitoes off your person, apply hemlock oil to the hands and face.

■ Burning pyrethrum powder in the house will discourage mosquitoes.

■ Make traps for mosquitoes in the form of boxes that can be easily closed. Line them with black or dark blue cloth, to which these insects will be attracted.

■ A freshly cut sprig of pennyroyal placed in the room will keep away mosquitoes.

Moths

■ Clean garments before storing, and wrap them in linen with lumps of camphor to protect them from moths.

■ Combine cloves, lavender, tansy, and wormwood as a substitute for camphor to discourage moths.

■ To protect clothes from moths, hang bunches of woodruff in closets. The herb will also serve to scent the linens.

■ Steep walnut leaves in cold water for 2 hours. Bring gently to a boil and continue boiling for 2 minutes. Then allow the leaves to steep for 15 minutes. Wash cupboards with this solution, and moths will stay away.

■ As protection against moths place small muslin bags filled with cedar shavings or camphorwood shavings among the clothing, or sprinkle the clothes with allspice berries.

■ Hang sachets of dried lemon peel inside cupboards and closets to keep moths away.

■ To safely store fur or hair wraps against moths, add a quantity of black pepper to powdered camphor.

■ Thoroughly mix 1 dram of flour of hops, 4 ounces of cedar sawdust, 2 ounces of Scotch snuff, and 1 ounce each of black pepper and powdered gum camphor. When scattered among stored woolens and furs, it will keep moths away.

■ Grind the following to a fine powder: 3 ounces of orris root and ½ ounce each of tanguine leaves, caraway seeds, cinnamon, cloves, mace, and nutmeg. Blend them thoroughly, and put the powdered mixture into small cloth bags. Place these among clothing to protect them from moths.

■ Sprinkle salt around the edges and over the entire surface of the rug while sweeping as a preventive against moths.

Rats

■ Put powdered potash near the holes of rats. It will encourage them to go elsewhere.

■ To exterminate rats, mix 2½ ounces of carbonate of barytes with 1 pound of grease. Since this mixture produces intense thirst, put some water close by. (It is a deadly poison; be sure all other animals are kept away from it.)

■ Spread slices of bread and butter, and sprinkle them with arsenic and sugar. Press the arsenic and sugar into the bread with a knife to prevent their falling off. Cut the bread into small squares, and put them in rat holes. As soon as some rats begin to die, others will depart.

■ Lure rats to one particular spot by leaving quantities of cheese there for some days. When they are accustomed to gathering at this place, affix a piece of cheese to a fishhook suspended about 12 inches from the floor. The first rat to leap at it will be left hanging; his example will put the other rodents to flight.

■ Mix well equal amounts of unslaked powdered lime and rye meal. Put this on pieces of board where rats are most frequently seen. Place containers of water close by. When they have eaten the mixture, thirst will drive them to the water, which slakes the lime. The resulting gas will kill them.

■ Add 2 parts of bruised squills (squill is the dried bulb of a plant belonging to the lily family) and 3 parts of chopped bacon to enough meal to make a firm mass. Form into small cakes and bake. Put them about the premises as food to exterminate rats. It is thought that the action of the squills is responsible for their death.

■ Using a piece of lead pipe as a conduit, introduce 2 ounces of sulphite of potassium into holes occupied by rats outside the house.

Silverfish

■ Mix boric acid and sugar. Sprinkle it in areas affected by silverfish.

Slugs and Snails

■ Pour several inches of stale beer into a shallow vessel. Place it where slugs and snails are damaging garden plants. These pests will be attracted to the beer and drown.

15
Country Cures

It is part of the cure to wish to be cured.

—Seneca

So-called cures and remedies were handed down among country folk, from generation to generation, usually by word of mouth, and were often recorded in home remedy books. Because of response to the chapter on rural remedies in my earlier book *Country Wisdom*, I am listing more here for their interest value. I must emphasize that they are not necessarily recommended for trial!

Abscess

- Dip a cabbage leaf into hot water and apply to the abscess.
- Cut open a fresh fig. Soak it for 1 minute in warm water. Apply it as a poultice to inflamed abscesses and boils.

Alcoholism

- Have the patient eat an owl's egg without his knowing what kind of egg it is.
- Place a live minnow in his bottle of spirits, and let it die there.

Arthritis

- Massage the areas afflicted by arthritis with the following mixture: 1 pint of whiskey, 3 ounces of chloroform, 2 ounces of wintergreen. Use 4 times a day.
- To cure arthritis eat ½ pound of fresh cherries daily.

Asthma

- Simmer a bit of skunk cabbage root in ½ cup of hen's grease. Take 1 teaspoon 3 times each day to relieve asthma symptoms.
- For relief of asthma a muskrat skin should be worn over the lungs, the fur side against the body.
- Simmer 1 heaping teaspoon of dried, ground okra leaves in 1 quart of hot water until but 1½ pints of liquid remain. Add 1 teaspoon of freshly chopped onion. Cover and let stand until cool. Stir and strain. Drink equal portions during the day as an asthmatic remedy.

- Fasten a live frog on the throat of one suffering from asthma. When the frog dies, the patient will be cured.

Athlete's Foot

- To remedy athlete's foot, anoint the feet with whale oil mixed with a little oil of cloves.

Baldness

- Blend ½ ounce of castor oil and 5 drops of oil of rosemary into ½ ounce of goose fat. Massage the scalp with this preparation 3 times daily to combat baldness.
- Pound peach kernels, and boil them gently in vinegar until a thick paste forms. Apply 3 times a day to bald spots on the scalp to regenerate hair growth.

Bed-wetting

- To cure bed-wetting use 1 spoon of corn silk every day to make a tea or in salad.
- Make a plaster of vinegar and the root of the herb tormentil. Apply it against the kidneys.

Bleeding

- To stop the bleeding from a cut, sprinkle the fungus spore of the puffball on it.
- Black tea in powdered form bandaged over a cut will stop the bleeding.
- To arrest bleeding and relieve the pain and swelling of a cut, pour lamp oil over it.

■ Bleeding due to tooth extraction can be checked if the cavity is packed with cotton soaked in alum water.

Blood

■ To purify the blood take a small glass of the following mixture 3 times daily: 1 quart of hard cider, ½ ounce of horse-radish, 1 ounce of yellow dock.

■ Combine equal amounts of blueberries, sassafras bark, thyme, and water cress. Make a tea of 1 spoonful of the mixture to 1 cup of hot water. Cover and let stand until cool. Stir and strain. Take 1 cupful 4 times daily to purify the blood.

Breath

■ To make the breath pleasing, rub the gums with wool coated with honey.

■ In 1 cup of hot water, steep ⅓ teaspoon each of anise, mint, and rosemary. Cover and allow to stand for 10 minutes. Strain. Rinse the mouth daily with this solution to combat bad breath.

Bronchitis

■ Mix ½ pint of cider vinegar; ½ pint of water; 1 ounce each of elecampane root, licorice extract, and coltsfoot; and ½ ounce of bloodroot. Steep in a covered pot in a warm place for 5 to 6 hours. Strain and sweeten with honey. Take 1 teaspoon-ful 4 times a day for bronchitis.

■ Simmer 1 teaspoonful of each of the following spices in spirits of turpentine for ½ hour: cinnamon, cloves, mustard, pepper. Strain. Stir ¼ teaspoon of pure, powdered camphor into 1 ounce of the liquid. Blend into 4 ounces of goose grease.

Rub on the chest to relieve congestion due to coughs and colds. Cover with flannel.

Bruises

- Apply a paste of butter and chopped parsley to bruises.
- Use the skin of a freshly peeled banana to reduce the pain and discoloration of a bruise. Place the inner side of the peel on the bruise and hold in place with wet cold bandages.
- Make a brew of the roots of bouncing Bet. Use it in poultice form to relieve the discoloration of a bruised eye.
- Treat a bruise by applying brown paper coated with molasses.
- Mix 1 part oatmeal and 2 parts of flaxseed, blending in sufficient water to make a thick poultice for bruises.

Burns

- Mix 4 ounces of lard with 1 ounce of powdered wood soot. Apply the mixture to burns and scalds on a dab of cotton.
- Honey applied to burns will relieve the pain and prevent blisters from forming.
- Thoroughly blend 1 egg yolk with 2 ounces of flaxseed oil. Apply to a burn.
- Soak soft linen in cod-liver oil and leave on a burn for 48 hours. Apply fresh oil as needed.
- Make a poultice of cold water and oatmeal to benefit a burn.
- Mix 2 portions of corn meal with 1 of powdered charcoal. Add milk to make a paste. Use this as a poultice for burns.
- Mix the freshly squeezed juice of pokeberries with a little glycerine as an application for burns.

Canker Sores

▪ Several times a day apply ashes from a burned corn cob to canker sores.

▪ Boil 2 tablespoons of dried pomegranate rind in 3 cups of water until the liquid is reduced to 2 cups. Strain and let cool. Use as a mouthwash for canker sores.

Chapped Skin

▪ Boil flakes of tragacanth, 1 inch in size, with a few quince seeds. Strain when cool. Thin the solution with some glycerine. Use as a soothing lotion for chapped hands.

▪ To benefit chapped hands, wash them in sugar and water.

Chicken Pox

▪ Tie bran in a cheesecloth bag. Steep it in boiling water for 2 minutes before applying it to chicken pox sores.

▪ To treat chicken pox externally, apply witch hazel to the sores.

Chilblains

▪ As a cure for chilblains, mix ¼ ounce of each of the following: ammonia, turpentine, olive oil, oil of peppermint. Apply mornings and evenings.

▪ Boil parsnips until soft, and bandage them on affected areas to treat chilblains.

Childbirth

- When labor is prolonged in childbirth, blow snuff, held on a goose feather, up the mother's nose. This will induce a sneezing fit, resulting in delivery.
- If complications occur during childbirth, give a strong tea of raspberry leaves.

Chills

- Mix 1 teaspoon of grated jack-in-the-pulpit with milk and sugar. It causes sweating and will cure chills or a cold.
- Make a tea of smartweed. Drink it very hot. Go to bed and keep well covered when suffering from chills.

Choking

- Into a cup break an egg. Have the choking patient swallow it whole.
- When something is stuck in the throat causing choking, blow forcefully into the sufferer's ear.

Colds

- As a head-cold remedy, put 2 drops of spirits of camphor on a sugar cube; dissolve it in ½ glass of water. A teaspoonful should be taken every 2 hours. Grease the nostrils with a mixture of lard, mutton suet, and sweet oil.
- Eating a hot roasted onion before retiring can be helpful in curing a cold.
- To overcome a cold with its accompanying miseries of sore throat and fever, drink a tea made from the white flowers of the elderberry shrub.

■ To relieve congestion due to a cold, rub throat and chest with skunk's oil.

Colic

■ Put sliced green walnuts into enough whiskey to cover them. Let them soak for 10 days. Take 1 teaspoonful of the liquid every ½ hour as a remedy for bilious colic.

■ To cure colic in children, give a dose of 1 drop of camphor in 1 teaspoon of water.

Constipation

■ Stir 2 teaspoons of flaxseed into 1 cup of cold water. Allow to stand for ½ hour. Drink both seeds and liquid to relieve constipation.

■ Boil for 15 minutes 2 ounces each of barley, figs, and raisins. Put in ½ ounce of licorice root and let steep. Allow to cool, strain out the water, and mash together. Take a dose of 4 ounces, night and morning, as a laxative.

Convalescence

■ A nourishing drink for those convalescing is barley coffee. Roast barley until brown. Boil 1 tablespoon of it in 2 cups of water for 5 minutes. Strain. If desired, add a bit of sugar.

■ Put 1 tablespoon of grated garlic into ⅔ glass of red wine. Take 1 teaspoonful 5 times daily as a strengthening tonic following illness.

Corns

■ To remove corns easily, bind on bread soaked in vinegar. Renew the application mornings and evenings.

■ Burn willow bark. Mix the ashes with vinegar and apply to the corn.

■ Mix and warm 1 teaspoon of brown sugar, 1 teaspoon of pine tar, and 1 teaspoon of saltpeter. Apply to corns on a plaster.

■ Insert the toe in a lemon. Keep it on during the night. The corn can then be removed with ease. If not, repeat the procedure.

Cough

■ For a cough, chop 2 large turnip roots into small pieces, and boil them in 1 quart of water. Cool and strain the liquid. Add an amount of honey equal to whatever portion is taken.

■ Simmer ⅜ ounce of senna leaf, ⅜ ounce of licorice root, and 1 ounce of anise seed in 2 cups of water until but 1 cup of liquid remains. Strain and cool. Add ½ pint of syrup. Take when necessary to relieve a cough.

■ Beat together 3 egg yolks, 3 tablespoons of honey, and 1 teaspoon of pine tar, adding 2 ounces of wine. Take 1 teaspoonful 3 times daily before meals as a cough remedy.

■ Scoop out a hollow in the middle of a good-sized beet; fill it with honey. Bake. Eat a little when needed to relieve a cough.

■ Chew a piece of ginger root, swallowing the juice to benefit a cough.

■ Mix 1 teaspoon of oil of sesame and 1 teaspoon of honey in 1 cup of warm milk. Slowly sip the beverage to relieve a cough.

Cramps

■ Cramps in neck or legs can be relieved by an application of whiskey and red pepper.

■ To 1 gallon of denatured alcohol add 1 ounce of monarda

oil, 1 ounce of cajaput oil, 1 ounce of oil of thyme, ½ ounce of oil of peppermint, and 1 ounce of camphor gum. Shake thoroughly. Allow to stand for 24 hours. This is a good rub for cramps in the muscles of men or animals.

Croup

▪ Administer 1 teaspoon of goose oil and one teaspoon of molasses to a child suffering from croup.

▪ Boil pig's feet in a vessel of water. Allow to stand overnight. Skim off the fat, put it in a pot, and boil until all moisture has evaporated. To cure croup, give a teaspoonful every ¼ hour and also rub well on throat and chest.

Cuts

▪ Remove the inside skin, or coating, from the shell of an uncooked egg. Place its moist side on a cut to promote healing with no scarring.

▪ Bathe the cut in a weak solution of water and baking soda. Sprinkle it, while still wet, with black pepper.

Dandruff

▪ Dissolve 1 ounce of borax in 1 pint of water. Wash the head with this mixture once a week to prevent dandruff.

▪ To cure dandruff make a mixture of 1 ounce of water, 2 ounces of bay rum, 2 ounces of glycerine, and 2½ ounces of tincture of cantharides. Rub this mixture into the scalp once a day.

▪ Make a tea from dried peach leaves and apply to the scalp as a treatment for dandruff.

Deafness

- To cure deafness, drop a mixture of onion juice and ant eggs into the ear.
- Combine ½ ounce of olive oil, 15 drops of sassafras oil, and 1½ drams of glycerine. Put a few drops into the ear several times a day to reduce excess wax accumulation that is causing deafness.
- Melt hedgehog fat, and drop a little into the ear to dissolve hard earwax that can cause temporary deafness.

Diarrhea

- For mild diarrhea eat burned rhubarb.
- Combine 3 tablespoons of vinegar with the same amount of hardwood ashes. Cover with hot water. Stir and allow to settle. Take 1 teaspoonful of the solution every now and then to check diarrhea.

Earache

- To alleviate the pain of an earache that is not too severe, blow pipe or cigarette smoke into the ear.
- For a very painful earache, drop mutton juice, as hot as can be tolerated, into the ear.
- Place a brass button in the mouth of one suffering from an earache. Surprise him by discharging a gun at his back. This will cure the pain.

Eye Inflammation

- Mix 3 whole eggs with 4 cups of cold rain water. Bring to a boil, stirring frequently. Add ½ ounce of zinc sulphate and boil for 2 minutes more. Remove from heat. Take the curd that forms at the bottom of the vessel and apply it to inflamed eyes, using a bandage. Filter the liquid through cloth and use as an excellent eyewash.

▪ To soothe sore eyes, boil black mesquite gum. Dilute the liquid and apply to afflicted areas.

▪ Steep ⅛ teaspoon of eyebright and ⅛ teaspoon of fennel in 8 ounces of hot boiled water. Stir and strain through cloth. Use as an eyewash every 3 hours or when required.

▪ Chew ground ivy leaves, and apply the pulp to an inflamed eye.

Feet

▪ To combat offensive odor of the feet, soak them in water in which the green bark of oak has been boiled.

▪ For excessive perspiration of the feet, put bran or oatmeal into the socks.

▪ Make a powder of equal amounts of powdered starch, fuller's earth, and powdered zinc. Sprinkle this mixture in the socks as a remedy for perspiring feet.

Fever

▪ Pound horse-radish leaves until they are of the consistency of pulp. Apply them as a poultice to the soles of the feet to draw out fever.

▪ Simmer 4 cups of water containing a handful of cockleburs until 2 cups of liquid remain. Drink a small glassful of the solution every ½ hour until the fever dissipates.

Fits

▪ To arrest fits, throw a teaspoonful of salt as far back into the mouth as possible.

■ Relieve fits by splashing water on the patient's hands and face. Plunging the feet into cold water will prove particularly beneficial.

Flatulence

■ To alleviate wind in the stomach, chew saffron flowers and swallow the juice.

■ Into 2 cups of boiling water put 1 teaspoon of dried orange or lemon peel, 1 teaspoon of coriander, and 1 teaspoon of gentian. Simmer for 10 minutes, strain when cool, and re-serve the liquid. Slowly sip a small glassful 3 to 4 times a day to relieve flatulence.

Hair

■ Check hair from falling by washing the head each day with a strong sage tea. For best results use pure spring water.

■ To make hair thicker, massage the juice of water cress into the scalp.

Hay Fever

■ Use the following mixture as a snuff to cure hay fever: 10 grains of ammonium carbonate, 15 grains of capsicum, 20 grains of sodium borate.

■ Steep several rose petals in a cup of hot water. Filter the liquid. To relieve eye irritation due to hay fever, apply 1 or 2 drops to each eye 5 times a day.

■ Crush fresh milkweed in cheesecloth, and inhale it to combat hay fever.

■ Mix the leaves and flowers of goldenrod and ragweed. Put ½ ounce of the herb mixture in 2 cups of boiling water and allow to steep for 10 minutes. Drink a small glassful 4 times a day to cure hay fever.

Headache

- Moisten a cloth with camphor spirits. Sprinkle black pepper on it and apply to the forehead to relieve a headache.
- Apply the fresh leaves of burdock or the fresh roots of pokeweed to the bottoms of the feet to assuage a headache.
- Mix 3 ounces of Castile soap, 1 ounce of camphor, and 2 ounces of ammonia in 2 quarts of alcohol. Bathe the forehead with this solution to relieve a sick headache.
- To dispel a headache, apply a poultice of grated uncooked potato to the forehead.
- For migraine headache, swallow a tablespoonful of honey.

Hemorrhoids

- Simmer 2 parts of fresh butter with 1 part of tobacco. Strain, and use as a poultice 3 times daily to relieve inflamed hemorrhoids.
- Remove the outer shell of 4 fresh horse chestnuts. Slice the chestnuts fine. Place them in a tin cup and cover with melted lard. Allow to steep for 1 hour in a warm place. Strain and squeeze out the lard. Apply the salve, when cool, twice daily to hemorrhoids.
- Mix equal amounts of horsemint oil, oil of fireweed, and pumpkin-seed oil. Apply twice a day to hemorrhoids.

Hiccups

- Make a mint tea, adding 5 drops of oil of amber. Drink the brew every 10 minutes until the hiccups are arrested.

■ To cure hiccups, eat a sugar cube that has been dunked in vinegar.

■ Work the jaws as though chewing food while pressing the fingers in the ears. This procedure will speedily cure hiccups.

High Blood Pressure

■ With mortar and pestle crush 2 teaspoons of dried watermelon seeds. Steep them for 1 hour in 1 cup of hot water. Stir and strain out the seeds. To relieve high blood pressure, drink 1 cupful 4 times each day.

■ Forsake salty foods and partake of honey.

Hives

■ Cure hives by rubbing them with buckwheat flour.

■ Make a tea of ground ivy, using 1 teaspoon of the herb to 1 cup of boiling water. Take 1 cupful 3 times daily to cure hives.

Hoarseness

■ Dry nettle roots in the oven. Powder, and add them to the same amount of molasses. A dose of 1 teaspoon 3 times a day will cure hoarseness.

■ Drink milk and red pepper every so often, and hoarseness will disappear.

Hunger

■ To allay the feeling of hunger, chew beechnut leaves.

■ Chewing elm leaves will quickly dissipate the sensation of hunger.

Indigestion

■ Stir 1 teaspoon of each of the following into 1 cup of hot water: fennel seeds, peppermint, caraway seeds, spearmint. Cover and allow to stand for 10 minutes. Mix and strain. Take 1 cupful 4 times a day to counteract excess stomach acid and resulting indigestion.

■ Within 10 or 15 minutes after eating, swallow 15 drops of chloroform in a small amount of sweetened water to counteract too much stomach acid.

■ To prevent indigestion, take 1 teaspoon of whole white mustard seeds before meals.

■ Take 1 ounce of Peruvian bark and the same amount of gentian root and ½ ounce each of coriander seed and orange peel. Steep them in 4 cups of brandy. Allow to stand for 5 days. An hour before eating take 1 teaspoonful in a wineglass of water to prevent indigestion.

■ Stir ¼ teaspoon of ground cinnamon into 1 cup of hot water. Cover for 15 minutes and stir again. Strain. Take 1 tablespoonful for chronic indigestion. Repeat if necessary.

Ingrown Toenail

■ Apply mutton tallow to an ingrown toenail for several days. The nail can then be cut without harm.

■ Cut a notch in the center of the toenail's edge. In attempting to grow together, the nail will pull away from the skin on either side, providing relief from the pain and swelling of ingrown toenail.

Insect Bites

■ Dissolve 1 heaping teaspoonful of sodium bicarbonate in 1 cup of cold vinegar. Apply as a compress to insect bites.

■ Apply a poultice of plantain leaves to insect bites.

Insomnia

■ Make a medicinal tea of ¼ teaspoon of celery seed, ¼ teaspoon of valerian, ½ teaspoon of catnip, and ½ teaspoon of skullcap in 4 ounces of hot water. Keep the brew covered for 10 minutes. Mix and strain. Take the tea 1 hour before retiring.

■ To overcome sleeplessness eat a dish of baked onions before retiring.

■ Mix lettuce juice with oil of roses and apply to the forehead and temples to induce sleep.

Irritable Infant

■ Onion tea will cure a baby of fretfulness.

■ To arrest postweaning restlessness, put molasses on the baby's hands. Give him chicken feathers to hold. During repeated attempts to remove them from first one hand and then the other, the babe will tire and fall asleep.

Itching

■ Combat itching by bathing with hot water and soap, scrubbing with a corn cob. Follow this with an application of sulphur and lard.

■ In a small amount of alcohol, dissolve ½ teaspoon of pure camphor. Add this to 4 ounces of calamine lotion and mix. Shake the solution thoroughly before applying to skin afflicted with itching.

■ A blend of lard and the powdered root of pokeweed makes a good salve for itching.

■ Apply mutton tallow to skin affected by itching.

Jaundice

▪ Chop fine a handful of black alder. Boil it in 4 cups of old cider. Allow to cool. Drink it liberally to cure jaundice.

Kidney Disorders

▪ Steep fresh yellow corn silk, cut fine, in 1 cup of hot water. Cover, let stand until cold, and strain. Take 1 cupful 4 times each day for kidney complaints.

▪ Mix artichoke juice with an equal amount of white wine to increase the discharge of urine.

▪ Steep strawberry and mullein leaves with cleavers in water. Drink the solution to assuage kidney ailments.

Lockjaw

▪ Have the patient suffering from lockjaw take a small amount of spirits of turpentine. Warm some, and apply it to the wound.

▪ To treat lockjaw, place moistened tobacco on the patient's stomach. Remove immediately when a cure is effected.

Measles

▪ Steep ⅓ teaspoon each of catnip, marjoram, and yarrow, adding a pinch of marigold or saffron. Give the warm tea each hour to one afflicted with measles to reduce the fever.

▪ Take a tea of elderberry flowers as a remedy for measles.

Mustache

■ For a fine, healthy mustache, apply a mixture of the following: 5 drops of oil of bergamot, 7 drops of tincture of cantharides, ½ ounce of simple cerate.

Nervousness

■ Combine equal portions of the following: wood betony, root of valerian, scullcap herb, and mistletoe. Boil 1 ounce of this mixture in 2 cups of water for 5 minutes. Allow to cool, and strain. Take a small glassful 3 times daily for nervousness.

Nettle Sting

■ Rub the area that has been pricked by nettles with mint, sage leaves, or rosemary.

Neuralgia

■ In 2 cups of boiling water, steep 1 ounce of burdock seeds for 1 hour. Strain. Take 1 tablespoonful before meals and retiring to relieve neuralgia.
■ Bind wilted horse-radish leaves on the area affected by pain of neuralgia.

Nosebleed

■ To stop bleeding from the nose, chew paper.
■ Blood flow from the nose can be stopped by insertion into the nostrils of wool saturated with rose oil.
■ To arrest nosebleed put grated dried beef into the nostrils.

■ In cases of nosebleed, soak cotton in nettle juice and insert it into the nostrils.

Overweight

■ Put 1 teaspoon each of fennel seed and chickweed with ½ teaspoon of sassafras bark, sweet flag root, kelp, and licorice in 1 quart of boiling water. Simmer for 5 minutes. Keep the liquid covered for 15 minutes. Strain. Drink ⅔ cupful, warmed, 3 times daily to reduce excess weight.

Pain

■ Sprinkle brown sugar on a pan of burning coals. To alleviate the pain of a wound, hold the injured part over the smoke.

■ To relieve pain in the back, mix vinegar and beef gall. Apply the solution to the affected area morning and evening.

Phlegm

■ Dry the leaves of coltsfoot. Smoke them as you would tobacco to loosen phlegm in the chest.

■ To remove phlegm from the stomach, make a tea of chicory leaves.

Pleurisy

■ To cure pleurisy, ingest a tea of catnip or pennyroyal, and then apply a poultice of hot boiled nettles.

■ Boil 1 ounce of pleurisy root in 2½ cups of water for 10 minutes. Strain. Take a small glassful 3 times daily to treat pleurisy.

Poison Ivy

- Put 1 tablespoon of carbolic acid and 1 ounce of glycerine in 2 cups of boiling water. Bathe areas affected by poison ivy with this solution.
- Apply milk, heavily salted, to skin affected by poison ivy. Allow to dry.
- For protection all year from the rash of poison ivy, eat a small amount of either the leaves or roots of the plant at the onset of spring.

Poultices

- Boil grape leaves with barley meal to make a soothing poultice for wounds and inflammations.
- Roast pokeweed root in hot ashes. Mash them and use in a poultice for felon.
- Thicken yeast with finely powdered elm bark and charcoal. Apply as a poultice to open sores.

Prickly Heat

- Dust the skin with browned cornstarch to cure prickly heat.
- As a remedy for prickly heat, keep a piece of alum in the pocket.
- Add 1 quart of alcohol, 1 ounce of borax in powdered form, and 2 ounces of cologne to 3 quarts of rain water. Bathe with this mixture 3 times daily as a remedy for heat rash.

Quinsy

- Sprinkle densely with red pepper a rasher of salt pork. Bind it about the throat upon retiring to alleviate quinsy.

- A good remedy for tonsillitis is a dose of rattlesnake oil.
- Boil 1 quart of water containing 1 tablespoon of tincture of benzoin. Inhale the vapors to soothe tonsillitis.
- Use kerosene externally and internally to treat quinsy.
- Rub a combination of turpentine and oil of anise on the throat to relieve the soreness of tonsillitis.

Rheumatism

- Powder the following: bloodroot, blue flag root, sweet flag root, prickly ash. Steep in spirits. Take a dose of from 1 tablespoon to a small glassful 3 times daily for rheumatism.
- Heat a sadiron. Cover the iron with woolen cloth, and moisten it with vinegar. Apply as hot as can be tolerated to parts afflicted with pain of rheumatism.
- Put 4 eggs into 2 cups of cider vinegar, dropping in the shells as well. When the vinegar has eaten up the eggs, add 2 cups of turpentine. Bathe on parts affected by rheumatic pain.
- Combine 2 cups of bear or coon oil, 2 cups of spirits of turpentine, and 2 cups of spirits of camphor. Rub sore areas with this solution for 25 minutes to relieve the pain of rheumatism.
- Simmer 2 ounces of camomile flowers and 3 ounces of celery seed in 2 quarts of water until the liquid is reduced to 3 pints. Strain. Take 1 small glassful before eating to cure rheumatism.
- Steep 1 tablespoon of sulphur and 2 cups of pokeberries in 4 cups of brandy. Let stand for 24 hours. Take 1 tablespoon 3 times daily as a remedy for rheumatism.
- Blend 1 ounce of cream of tartar, 1 ounce of sulphur, ½ ounce of rhubarb, and 1 teaspoon of guaiacum into 2 cups of honey. Stir 1 tablespoon of this into a glass of water and take in the morning and evening.
- The miseries of rheumatism can be eased by a massage with goose oil. Follow this with a drink of calomel mixed with cayenne pepper, gum camphor, and tartarized antimony.

Ringworm

- Dissolve 1 teaspoon of borax in 2 ounces of warm cider vinegar. Apply on the scalp to combat ringworm.
- Mix vinegar and gunpowder. Apply the paste to ringworm.
- Drop a copper coin in vinegar. While it is still wet, place it in the area affected by ringworm.
- Wash the root of yellow dock, and chop it into small sections. Simmer in vinegar. Strain. Apply the solution 3 times daily to cure ringworm.

Scalp

- Steep ¾ ounce of nettles and ¾ ounce of sage in 2 cups of alcohol for 1 week. Strain, and gradually add 2½ ounces of castor oil. Apply to the scalp to heal irritation.

Scarlet Fever

- Steep 1 teaspoon of yarrow, 1 teaspoon of catnip, and ¼ teaspoon of saffron in 1 cup of hot water. Drink 1 cupful each hour to treat scarlet fever.

Scratches

- Crush the leaves of the blackberry bush between your fingers, and rub them on a scratch to immediately check the bleeding.

Scrofula

- Cover areas affected by scrofula with codfish skins.

Seasickness

- To overcome seasickness, drink great quantities of strong green tea as frequently as possible.
- Chew several leaves of sage or mint until they reach the consistency of pulp and no longer have flavor. This is a good remedy for seasickness.

Sinus

- To relieve the congestion and pain of sinus trouble, chew honeycomb.

Snake Bite

- Incise the snake bite, and apply a mixture of tobacco and salt.
- To treat snake bite, cut open a freshly killed chicken and place it on the wound.

Sores

- To heal sores apply a poultice of powdered comfrey root.
- Boil the following in weak lye: blue vervain, smartweed, wormwood herb. Apply with a feather to sores.
- Boil over a low flame for 30 minutes ½ pound of rosin, 1 pound of lard, and 10 ounces of elder bark. Strain and apply to sores.

Sore Breasts

- Roast turnips until soft. Mash them with oil of roses. Apply this mixture to sore breasts twice daily and cover them with flannel.

■ Massage stiff joints 4 times a day with olive oil in which camphor gum has been dissolved.

Stomach Distress

■ Take an infusion of horehound to remedy stomach distress.

■ Dry and powder peach leaves. Mix 1 teaspoon of this powder and the same amount of chalk into a glass of hot water. Take after meals to prevent stomach upset.

Stye

■ Into a small cloth bag, put 1 teaspoon of black tea. Moisten it with boiling water. While the bag is yet warm, place it on the eye during the night. By morning the stye should be gone. Repeat the application if necessary.

■ Make a poultice of milk and linseed meal. Apply it warm to a stye. Renew the poultice every 6 hours.

Sunburn

■ Apply the following ointment for relief of sunburn: Mix 2 tablespoons of almond oil, 2 tablespoons of spermaceti, and ½ teaspoon of honey. Add attar of roses for a pleasant scent.

■ Mix lime juice in Vaseline to make a soothing salve for sunburn.

Tapeworm

■ Drink a tea made from pumpkin seeds to be rid of tapeworm.

■ In 2½ cups of water, boil 1 ounce of fern root until 2 cups of liquid remain. Abstain from eating before going to bed. Upon arising, take a small glassful of the liquor to combat tapeworm.

▪ Make a tea of 2 ounces of pomegranate root in 2 cups of water. Drink this remedy for tapeworm in 3 doses before eating breakfast.

Teeth Coming Loose

▪ Dissolve ¼ ounce of myrrh in 1 pint of port wine; add 1 ounce of oil of almonds. Wash the teeth each morning with this solution to make loose teeth more secure.

Toothache

▪ Mix 1 dram of powdered alum and 3 drams of nitrous spirits of ether. Apply on a dab of cotton to an aching tooth.

▪ Melt 16 parts of beeswax and 4 parts of lard. Cool. Then add 8 parts of oil of cloves and 8 parts of creosote. Thoroughly soak cotton in the mixture. Roll into small sticks and chew slowly when needed to alleviate a toothache.

▪ To relieve a toothache chew the leaves of catnip.

▪ Roast an onion. Cut it in two and place a half, while still hot, over the pulse of the wrist on the side opposite the painful tooth.

Vomiting

▪ Remove the peel from a good-sized onion and slice it in two. Put a half in each armpit to check vomiting.

▪ Brown field corn, but do not burn it. Immerse it in boiling water. Drink the liquid when necessary to arrest vomiting.

▪ Pound green wheat, and pour boiling water over it.

Squeeze out the juice, and sweeten it with sugar. Take 1 table-spoon at 10-minute intervals to stop vomiting.

▪ Skin and clean the gizzard of a freshly dressed chicken. Simmer it in 1 pint of water for 30 minutes. Discard the gizzard. Sipping the broth cures most cases of vomiting.

Warts

▪ To remove warts, rub them with green walnuts or bacon rind.

▪ Collect cobwebs to form a mass big enough to cover a wart but not touch the flesh around it. Place the wad of cobwebs on the wart, and ignite it. When the fire has consumed the cobwebs, the wart will turn white and disappear in several days.

▪ Remove warts by applying freshly crushed marigold leaves and their juice.

▪ Make a paste of vinegar and hickory-wood ashes. Use as an application to destroy warts.

▪ To be rid of warts, apply oil of cinnamon to them 4 times daily.

Whooping Cough

▪ Cook 2 ounces of garlic in 2 ounces of oil. Strain. Mix in 1 ounce of camphor and 2 ounces of honey. A dose of 1 teaspoon taken 4 times a day, or as required, will relieve whooping cough.

▪ Cut into pieces 3 prickly pear leaves, and boil them in 1 quart of water for 30 minutes. Filter the liquid through a cloth to strain out all prickles. Add a bit of sugar to sweeten, and boil for a short time. Take 2 teaspoonfuls to cure whooping cough.

▪ Add sweet oil to brandy and simmer with a slice of onion. To treat whooping cough externally, spread the solution, morning and evening, on the soles of the feet, the spine, and the chest.

▪ Rub the spine with garlic to cure whooping cough.

Wounds

▪ To treat wounds apply a mixture of 1 tablespoon of crushed rosemary and a pinch of salt.

▪ Treat wounds with an application of fresh warm cow dung.

▪ Sprinkle the dried, powdered leaves of wild sunflowers on a wound to arrest blood flow.

▪ To treat the wound from a rusty nail, apply peach leaves that have been pounded into pulp.

16
Country Pastimes

There be delights, there be recreations and jolly pastimes that will fetch the day about from sun to sun, and rock the tedious year as in a delightful dream.

—John Milton
Areopagitica
1644

Chautauqua Circuit

When the faded red of barns and the windows of small-town emporiums were enlivened by brightly colored posters announcing the coming of Chautauqua, the pulse of the countryside quickened. Anticipation of this yearly occurrence was savored as much as the actual event.

Men and boys lingered about the local railroad station, awaiting the arrival of the traveling tent company. Country lads, eager for a summer job providing excitement as well as remuneration, labored to set up the great brown tent, acted as ticket takers, or strove to protect audiences and performers from inclement weather. Armed with long poles, they gingerly elevated sagging canvas, dangerously heavy with collected rain, in an attempt to drain away the water. Failure would oftentimes result in a drenching as rents developed, but the enthusiasm of both troupers and viewers was never diluted.

Circuit Chautauqua arose independently of the Chautauqua Institution which germinated in southwestern New York State, a stationary center providing cultural nourishment for those who came from far and wide to attend. Adopting the name and idea from this source, traveling Chautauquas carried lectures, drama, and music to well over nine thousand towns throughout the country, their sojourn in any one community lasting from five days to a week or more.

When Chautauqua was in its prime, radio had not yet become common. So it was the Chautauqua circuit that satisfied the hankering of rural townsfolk for enlightenment and diversion.

From the darkness of a summer night, one stepped into the blazing interior of the huge brown tent. Golden straw, its satiny polish glinting under the bright illumination from naked bulbs strung between tent poles, softened the continual tread of new arrivals and deliciously scented the atmosphere. Seats were usually folding wooden chairs of questionable comfort. Sometimes benches were improvised from planks supported on nail kegs. Children were generally assigned to these, for their restless wriggling during "cultural features" too often set the folding chairs to creaking. After what seemed an interminable but pleasurably tantalizing wait, the tent was darkened, and coughing, chattering, fanning, and fidgeting magically stopped as if on cue. The hushed audience strained to glimpse the first performer to appear on stage, his rouged cheeks and heavily penciled brows dramatically accentuated by the footlights' glare.

Participants in scheduled programs were a varied lot, ranging from explorers to elecutionists; monologists to magicians; pianists to politicians; singers to scientists; teachers to preachers; xylophonists to yodelers—naming but a few. The diversified offerings included lectures on a wide range of subjects by the prominent and not so prominent, Punch and Judy shows, banjo players in blackface, bell ringers, and the barbershop quartet, said to be an innovation of circuit Chautauqua. As early prejudice against theatrical productions dwindled, plays and operas gradually came to lead in popularity. Shakespearean plays were enacted, Gilbert and Sullivan operettas performed, and operatic arias rendered by renowned singers. As time passed, however, fewer cultural events were presented, and Chautauqua became synonymous simply with entertainment.

Many an old-timer relishes his memories of the magical moments of Chautauqua season—vivid moments that enriched his youth and flavor his latter years with pleasant nostalgia.

Harness Racing

Harness racing became a country pastime after originating in the town. Early in the 1700's, trotting in harness was a customary mode of travel. Roads suitable for wheels were limited to the towns. Occasionally, as four-wheeled vehicles passed each other in the street, impromptu races came about. Street matches of this kind were known as "brushing," and their popularity spread throughout the country. Eventually such racing was permitted on tracks.

In states controlled by puritanical principles, thoroughbred racing was regarded with disfavor. Horse racing was defined as a contest of horses at their fastest speed. Because a horse runs faster than he trots, harness racing was accepted by the morally righteous as a harmless diversion.

At the beginning of the 1800's, the two-wheeled sulky was invented for harness racing. The body of this awkward vehicle hung on springs from enormous wheels, densely spoked with fine rods.

Enthusiasm for trotting became so great in many parts of America that local horses could not satisfy the need. Outstanding thoroughbreds began touring in exhibition matches. Fine trotters were developed by farmers who bred their mares to stallions of prominent lines.

The start of country fairs germinated in the early 1800's when a farmer in Massachusetts tethered some imported Merino sheep to a tree and charged people a small sum to view them. A new custom was established which spread rapidly. All types of animals and produce were exhibited and judged, including harness horses. A fair in Philadelphia was the first to include harness racing in its program. From that time on, such races were the star attraction at country fairs, greatly influencing attendance rates. Soon the smallest, most remote villages had their races, which became part of rural tradition.

In the last quarter of the nineteenth century, the ball bearing and the pneumatic tire were developed. The two were combined in the bicycle. When wheels of this revolutionary design were put on the sulky, the vehicle's appearance was ridiculed by old-timers. But the new sulky was considerably lighter, and the seat lower for less wind resistance. The reinsman was now situated close to his horse. To prevent the tail from whipping its face, it was braided with an extension, which was placed on the sulky's seat.

People enjoyed a day in the country watching the grace of trotters and pacers in action. Trotters with their long-striding, high knee-action trot, heads rhythmically swaying from side to side, were magnificent in their harness. The pacers, too, stepped with precision in synchronized strides, both pairs of side legs moving in unison.

Harness racing was considered a proper event for ladies to witness as well as gentlemen. However, when it became a gambling medium, every sort of criminal was drawn into the sport. Consequently, the social tone deteriorated with the moral tone. After a reform group restored its respectability, ladies could once again attend the affair with impunity.

In recent years, after a period of lagging interest, harness racing has been fast regaining its former popularity.

Hoedown

That typically American rustic diversion known as the square dance is believed to have developed in the 1600's in England. Many of the square-dance tunes were brought to America by English, Scottish, and Irish settlers. From the Eastern Seaboard they spread westward with the pioneers.

The square dance, known also as a barn dance or "hoedown," was regarded with approval or disapproval according to the moral outlook of each community. In some locales it was considered a wholesome social pastime; in others, where dancing and music-making were associated with the Devil, it was frowned upon.

When word of a barn dance got about, people from miles around arrived on horseback. Unfortunately, some brought their own refreshment in the form of hard liquor, and disturbances often resulted. But on the whole, a barn dance meant a night of conviviality and rhythmic movement to the tune of a fiddle.

The chief personage at a barn dance was the caller. To qualify, he had to have a strong, clear voice, a sense of rhythm, and a knack for concocting impromptu rhymes when necessary. His role was to call out directions for the movements of the dancing couples. Four couples composed a set. Besides a good many basic calls, there were songs which indicated action to follow. Some square-dance tunes were without words, and the caller would improvise as he went along.

A hoedown was a simple and satisfying social event, participated in by young and old alike. Those beyond the age of "do-si-doing" could always engage in a little toe-tapping to the tempo of the fiddle's music.

Husking Bee

In times past, a farm chore too big to be managed by one family was turned into a social event. So it was with the husking bee.

Before the onset of winter, farmers gathered in the cornstalks, storing them in the barn. Neighbors from miles around showed up with helping hands and expectations of a high old time.

Seated on stools around the pyramid of stalks, bushel baskets beside them, they spiritedly worked by lantern light. The crisp autumn air was alive with animated chatter, the rustle of cornhusks, and the snap as ears were wrenched from them. The labor was spiced with excitement by the commonly observed custom concerning the red ear of corn. The fellow who unsheathed one was permitted to kiss the woman of his choice. Some young rascals attended husking bees forearmed, concealing red ears in their clothing to reveal when the time was ripe.

With the last of the stalks stripped of corn, short work was made of refreshments: platters of steaming pork and beans, hot pumpkin pie, doughnuts, and cider.

There was always a fiddler in the group to stir up some dancing. If the cider was hard, the evening was topped off with some pretty lively stepping.

Maple-sugaring Time

Maple-sugaring time meant a combination of hard work and fun. In late winter with snow still carpeting the ground, country people set off for the woods equipped with freshly washed buckets, tapping irons, and sap spouts.

Choosing the right time and weather was vital. A bright, sunshiny morning with a west wind blowing, following a night of hard freeze, was best for good sap flow. It was important to tap the trees before their buds swelled; otherwise the syrup had a leathery taste and was fit only for sweetening tobacco.

On the side of the tree where the most limbs grew and at a spot showing new bark growth, the tapping iron was driven in at a convenient height and a metal or wooden spout inserted in the hole. Old-time steel spouts were fashioned by the local blacksmith from discarded scythe blades; wooden spouts were whittled from the young shoots of the staghorn sumac. The pails were hung, and soon the rhythmic drip of sap into buckets sounded through the maple groves.

The sap was usually collected twice a day, in the morning and the late afternoon. A team of horses hauled a low sled bearing a large tank into which the buckets were emptied. The contents of the gathering tank were poured into an evaporator in the boiling house. When it had reached the right consistency for syrup, the liquid was drawn off into cans. If sugar was desired, the sap was boiled longer at a higher temperature. The liquid sugar was poured into wooden tubs, where it hardened.

The foaming evaporator pan was watched through the night in an atmosphere of wood-smoke fragrance, sweet-smelling steam, and great expectation. At last "sugaring off" time arrived. Sometimes young folks would have a party. Snow was brought in and hot syrup poured over it, which quickly cooled and thickened into delicious taffylike strips. Sour pickles or salt were often on hand to counteract the sweetness.

Indians, in the past, collected maple sap in buckets of birch bark. Their evaporator consisted of a hollowed-out segment of tree trunk; they boiled the sap by dropping in heated stones. An easier method employed by the Indians was to let the sap freeze over and over again, the ice being removed each time. Eventually the sap thickened to become syrup.

Along about February, squirrels will bite twigs from the maple tree to lap the oozing sap. The resulting small squirrel-made spigots sometimes drip for days, the sweet liquid attracting warblers and other birds.

Today, sugar maples are piped for sap gathering, and the

maple syrup and sugar are made in modern evaporating apparatus in factories. However, there are still many country folks who have fond memories of the maple-sugaring times of bygone years.

Marble Game

Country boys knuckling down for a brisk game of marbles probably didn't know they were engaging in a pastime popular among the ancient Romans.

Summers were usually filled with farm chores, fishing along a shaded stream bank, or cooling off in the old swimming hole. But come autumn, boys arrived at school with serious pursuit in mind, their pockets bulging with marbles.

Each player selected the marble he judged best for a shooter, whether because of its appeal to the eye or because of the luck it had brought in the past. The shooter was known as a taw, and the fellow who could boast of one made of agate, fondly called an "aggie," was the envy of all. To decide who would shoot first required "lagging" one's taw up to a line. The owner of the taw nearest the line began the game, and so on down the line. Within a small circle drawn in the dirt, each participant placed four or more marbles. The object of the game was to knock as many marbles as possible out of the circle, those marbles becoming the prizes of the shooter, who continued until he missed. When all the marbles had been claimed, the game ended.

In more recent generations, playing for "keeps" became popular, though this was much frowned upon by the school as being in the realm of gambling. However, unhampered by the eye of authority, the game proceeded in earnest, resulting in a good shooter's lugging home a heavy bag of marbles by day's end.

Winter with its frozen ground and occasional blankets of snow temporarily interrupted the sport, which revived with the first hint of spring warmth. By the end of a season, a serious player displayed quite a set of callused knuckles.

Today the game of marbles is less enthusiastically played among schoolboys. Instead it has been organized as an international sport, played by a few adult professionals, who cannot possibly enjoy the game as much as we did years ago.

Mumblety-peg

In the old days, standard equipment in the pocket of every country boy was a good, sharp jackknife. One with a long, stout blade and fancy handle for killing a bear or one on a ring attached to a long chain and concealing a variety of useful tools—bottle opener, can opener, screwdriver, and leather punch—had its place. But the knife commonly carried and cherished by every young lad was a plain, solid one with a good-sized sturdy blade plus a smaller blade, having a strong spring and a well-shaped handle harmonious with the owner's grip. It was a kind of symbol that the boy had reached a responsible age. He employed it in a variety of ways—for whittling useful articles, cutting fishing line, and scraping animal skins. In addition, it was used for sheer amusement.

A popular game in those times was variously known as mumble-the-peg, mumblety-peg, or mumblepeg, depending upon the area from which you hailed. Two players or more could take part, the only prerequisites being their jackknives and soft ground. A starting line was marked, and each player in turn attempted to toss his knife, held in stipulated positions, so that it would stick into the ground. These are the basic holds, often altered or embellished upon at whim, that were required in playing mumblety-peg:

▪ The knife is held flat on the palm with the point out. It is flipped up, makes one revolution, and, if all goes well, lands point first in the ground.

▪ The same procedure as above is followed with the knife balanced on the back of the hand.

▪ This time a fist is made, the knife lying between the fingers and palm. The knife must be tossed three times in succession.

▪ The knife is held by the tip and flipped.

▪ The hand is held palm up in the policeman's Stop position; the knife point is directed downward in the lower palm.

▪ The knife point is held between the left thumb and forefinger; the handle is struck smartly with the fingers of the right hand. This position is known as "spank the baby."

A number of others followed, some rather dangerous, such as tossing the knife over the head or through a circle made by the thumb and forefinger. Any position in which it landed was considered fair, no matter how far it inclined to one side, if another could be passed beneath it.

The person first to complete the required throws was the winner. It was the privilege of the victor to drive a 2-inch peg into the ground with three sound whacks from the handle of his knife. Then, with eyes closed, he was entitled to three more blows. He strove desperately to drive in the peg until it was flush with the ground, because the loser, on hands and knees, had to extract the peg from the dirt using his teeth as pincers. This obligatory penance of the vanquished gave the game its title.

Pitching Horseshoes

The clang of a horseshoe landing bestride its mark is a summer sound that evokes memories of good companionship, good exercise, and possibly a good cold drink of well water. Country folk used to say that the best stakes (or stobs, as they are called) for horseshoe pitching are old railroad spikes driven firmly into the ground 40 feet apart. Favored was a 2½-pound shoe, the claim being made that lighter ones don't carry the distance as well.

Rules vary according to the whims of players, but in pitching horseshoes according to standard rules, a ringer gives you 3 points and a leaner, 1 point; otherwise, the shoe closest to the peg gets a point, provided it is not more than 6 inches away. The first player to chalk up 50 points is proclaimed the winner.

The horseshoe itself has a long history dating back to the second century B.C. Prior to that time, horse owners attempted to protect hoofs from wear and breakage by covering them with socks or sandals. Not until the fifth century of our era was horseshoeing widely known in Europe, but by the Middle Ages it was a common practice. The Japanese attached slippers of straw to the horse's feet, replacing them as they wore out. This archaic custom survived until the 1800's, when rimming the hoof with iron was introduced.

An aura of superstition has surrounded the horseshoe for centuries. Ancient Romans attributed magical properties to anything made of iron, and so equine hardware was regarded as a good-luck symbol. Finding a horseshoe meant good fortune, provided the shoe pointed toward, not away from, the finder. Since the horses of many dignitaries in Roman times were shod in gold or silver, chancing upon such a horseshoe, no matter the direction it faced, was doubtless considered good luck! Sages of the time advised that horseshoes were a dependable defense against witchcraft. In bygone days, owners of race horses were careful to keep a horseshoe in the stable. This practice was supposed to prevent witches from riding the horses all night before a race. Generations ago the belief was widespread that a new moon had the force to counteract the influence of the evil eye. Perhaps because of the horseshoe's resemblance to a new moon, it became associated with supernatural power.

All manners of hanging a horseshoe are advocated for ensuring the very best of fortune. Some say the open end should point downward; others argue that the open end should be uppermost to prevent the luck from running out; and then there are those who believe that tacking it up in a horizontal

no more and no fewer. If he exceeded that score, he lost as surely as if he had failed to meet the required number of points.

Sometimes money was bet on the outcome of the game—considerably adding to the excitement and importance of a well-placed washer in an old tin can!

General Index

[*A Recipe Index will be found on page 319.*]

abscesses, 190, 264
  dental, 183, 191
aching muscles, 20, 63, 168, 183
acid stains, 242
Adams, Blacky, 99
agrimony (sticklewort), 169,
  171
air fresheners, *see* deodorizers
Alaskan Indians, 121
alcoholism, 264
alehoof, 168
Algonquian Indians, 100
alkanet, 175
All Fools' Day, 34
All Saints' Day, 35
aloes, 168
aluminum pots, brightening,
  248
ambergris, 170
anemia, 174, 177, 179, 185, 186
angelica, 168
animals, 83–111
  game, 58–61
  life spans of, 111
  and weather, 31–33
ant, 27, 140, 254–56
  red, 255
antifreeze substitute, 199
antiseptics, 168, 190, 191
ant lion, 134–35
aphids, 140, 255
aphrodisiacs, 190, 197–98
apoplexy, 183
Areopagitica (Milton), 293
armadillo, 83–87
arteries, hardening of, 184
arthritis, 173, 180, 185, 190, 264
  see also rheumatism

ash (tree)
  black, 148
  blue, 148, 166
  white, 73, 147–48, 166
asparagus, 194–95
assassin bug, 140
asthma, 162, 173, 183, 190, 192,
  264–65
athlete's foot, 265
atmospheric pressure, 18–21
Audubon, John James, 113
axle grease, 238

badger, 33–34, 87–90
bait, 68–73, 77
baked-on food, removing, 243
Baker, Roy, 48
baldness, *see* hair loss
balm (melissa), 169, 170, 183
bamboo, 73–74
barberry, 178
Barlow, Mose, 75
barn dance, 297
barometric changes, 38–39
barometric weather signs,
  18–19
barrel, cleaning of, 243
barrel cactus, 74
basil, 169, 187
basket tree, 148
bass, 68, 70, 75, 77
  black, 68
  smallmouth, 70
  striped, 71, 75
bat, 25, 111
bay leaves, 168
  oil of, 257

Recipe Index